Debt Relief for the Poorest Countries

Debt Relief for the Poorest Countries

John E. Serieux
Yiagadeesen Samy
editors

Transaction Publishers
New Brunswick (U.S.A.) and London (U.K.)

This work originated with a research project led by The North-South Institute and was originally published as a thematic special issue by the Canadian Journal of Development Studies, University of Ottawa.

The North-South Institute (NSI) is a charitable, not-for-profit corporation established in 1976 to provide professional, policy-relevant research on relations between industrialized and developing countries. The Institute is independent and cooperates with a wide range of Canadian and international organizations working on related activities. NSI is based in Ottawa, Ontario, Canada.

The Canadian Journal of Development Studies (CJDS) is an international and interdisciplinary forum for the discussion of development issues. While it publishes contributions dealing with all regions or countries of the developing world, CJDS is particularly interested in the policy applications of innovative theory and research, and the role of such countries as Canada toward the promotion of international development and a more equitable world order.

Library of Congress Catalog Number: 2002029107
ISBN: 0-7658-0161-2
Printed in Canada

Library of Congress Cataloging-in-Publication Data

Debt relief for the poorest countries / John E. Serieux and Yiagadeesen Samy, editors.
    p. cm.
    Includes one article in French.
    "This work originated with a research project led by the North-South Institute and was originally published as a thematic special issue by the Canadian journal of development studies [volume XXII, no. 2, 2001], University of Ottawa"--Copyright p.
    Includes bibliographical references.
    ISBN 0-7658-0161-2 (alk. paper)
      1. Debts, External--Developing countries. 2. Debt relief--Developing countries.
    3. Poverty--Developing countries. I. Serieux, John. II. Samy, Yiagadeesen.

HJ8899.D4385 2002
336.3'6--dc21

2002029107

Contents

List of HIPC Countries

Angola	Ethiopia	Malawi*	Sierra Leone
Benin*	Ghana	Mali*	Somalia
Bolivia*	Guinea*	Mauritania*	Sudan
Burkina Faso*	Guinea-Bissau*	Mozambique*	Tanzania*
Burundi	Guyana*	Myanmar	The Gambia*
Cameroon*	Honduras*	Nicaragua*	Togo
Central African Rep.	Kenya	Niger*	Uganda*
Chad*	Lao, People's D. R.	Rwanda*	Vietnam
Congo	Liberia	São Tomé and Principe*	Yemen, Rep. of
Congo, D. R.	Madagascar*	Senegal*	Zambia*
Côte d'Ivoire			

List of abbreviations used in this issue
Abbréviations et sigles utilisés dans ce numéro

AFDB	African Development Bank
APD	Aide publique au développement
BCEAO	Banque Centrale des États de l'Afrique de l'Ouest
BFP	Budget Framework Paper
CABEI	Central American Bank for Economic Integration
CD	Certificates of Deposit
CONPES	National Council for Economic and Social Planning
CSLP	Cadre stratégique de la lutte contre la pauvreté
DAC	Development Assistance Committee of the OECD
DSA	Debt-Sustainability Analysis
EDMO	External Debt Management Office
EPRP	Export-led Poverty Reduction Program
ESAF	Enhanced Structural Adjustment Facility
FDI	Foreign Direct Investment
HIMC	Heavily Indebted Middle-income Country
HIPC	Heavily Indebted Poor Country
IBRD	International Bank for Reconstruction and Development
IDA	International Development Association

---

* countries that have reached the decision point of the HIPC Initiatives as of June 2001.

IDB	Inter-American Development Bank
IED	Investissement étranger direct
ITC	International Trade Center
LSMS	Living Standards Measurement Survey
MBA	Mexico, Brazil and Argentina
MDF	Multilateral Debt Fund
MTCS	Medium-Term Competitiveness Strategy
MTEF	Medium-Term Expenditure Framework
NGO	Non-governmental Organization
NPV	Net Present Value
ODA	Official Development Assistance
OECD	Organization for Economic Cooperation and Development
ONG	Organisation non gouvernementale
ONU	Organisation des Nations-Unies
PAS	Programme d'ajustement structurel
PAF	Poverty Action Fund
PAPSCA	Program to Alleviate Poverty and the Social Costs of Adjustment
PEAP	Poverty Eradication Action Plan/Plan d'action pour l'élimination de la pauvreté
PED	Pays en développement
PFP	Policy Framework Paper
PMA	Pays moins avancés
PPP	Purchasing Power Parity
PPTE	Pays pauvres très endettés
PRGF	Poverty Reduction and Growth Facility
PRSP	Poverty Reduction Strategy Paper
SAF	Structural Adjustment Facility
SAL	Structural Adjustment Lending
SAP	Structural Adjustment Program
SILIC	Severely Indebted Low-income Country
SPA	Special Program of Assistance for Africa
SPRS	Strengthened Poverty Reduction Strategy
SSA	Sub-Saharan Africa
SWAPs	Sector-wide Approaches
TOA	Treasury Office of Accounts
UBN	Unsatisfied Basic Needs
UE	Union européenne
UEMOA	Union économique et monétaire de l'Afrique de l'Ouest
UNDP	United Nations Development Program
UNFPA	UN Population Fund
UPPAP	Uganda Participatory Poverty Assessment Project
VAN	Valeur actualisée nette

Introduction

Debt, Debt Relief and the Poorest: Small Steps in a Long Journey*

In the closing months of the last century, the debt problems of heavily indebted poor countries (HIPCs) enjoyed unprecedented exposure as Jubilee 2000, and related non-governmental organization (NGO) campaigns for debt forgiveness for these countries, shifted into high gear. The governments of creditor countries and international financial institutions responded to that challenge. First, at their annual meeting in Cologne in June 1999, the G7 governments committed to broader, faster, and deeper debt relief for the poorest countries. Then, at the annual general meetings of the International Monetary Fund (IMF) and the World Bank in September 1999, the HIPC Initiative, the instrument for delivering multilateral debt relief to these countries, was upgraded to the Enhanced HIPC Initiative. This new initiative offers more generous interpretations of debt sustainability, the chance for more rapid qualification for debt relief, and the conditioning of debt relief on a commitment by these countries to poverty reduction.

However, despite the unprecedented attention given to these countries' debt burdens, and the related debates about the appropriate level of forgiveness

---

* The project from which these papers are derived would have been impossible without the financial support of the Ford Foundation, the Inter-American Development Bank (IDB), and the Canadian International Development Agency (CIDA). Particular thanks, therefore, go to Manuel Montes at the Ford Foundation, Euric Bobb at IDB and Bill Singleton at CIDA. The original idea for this project came from Roy Culpeper, President of the North-South Institute. He can justifiably take great pride in and credit for the work it has generated. Also, at the North-South Institute, the work of Eugenia Gallegos in all supporting aspects of the research – editing, administration and conference organization – handled so masterfully and good-naturedly, must be acknowledged. In addition, the contribution of the members of the reference group, too numerous to mention here, and Dane Rowlands as a referee, must be justly credited.

and the conditions attached to it, some questions remain relatively unexplored:

- Why was debt relief so long in coming for these countries?
- What has been the cost of a persistent debt overhang for these countries?
- Does the Enhanced HIPC Initiative offer a permanent exit from overindebtedness or merely a short-term respite?

Most importantly though, while both the challenge provided by the international NGO community and the response of creditor governments and institutions have gained and maintained the spotlight over the last few years, the experience and views of the citizens and governments of the HIPCs themselves have remained largely muted. Though the Jubilee 2000 coalition has always included a southern membership, the voices of southern members have never been particularly individuated at the country level. Similarly, the governments of these countries have contributed their voices in such fora as the G77 and G24, but their views have remained largely submerged within the wider developing country groupings.

In executing its *Study of the Debt of the Poorest Countries*, the North-South Institute (NSI) hoped to move toward correcting these deficiencies in the ongoing inquiry and debate on debt and debt relief. This special edition of the *Canadian Journal of Development Studies* presents seven papers resulting from that research endeavour.

The NSI study had essentially two parts. The first part involved in-house research by NSI researchers looking at the broader issues relating to debt and debt relief for the poorest. They include the development cost of the debt crisis, the underlying causes of the delay in resolving the crisis, the efficiency of current approaches to debt relief, and the prospect for long-term poverty reduction and growth beyond debt relief for the poorest. The second part of the study involved case studies of five HIPCs, undertaken by resident researchers in each of these countries. The countries were chosen to ensure diversity in both geographic location and stage of consideration for debt relief. Hence, two of them are in the Americas – Bolivia and Nicaragua, and three are in Africa – Ethiopia, Mali and Uganda. When the study began in May 1999, Bolivia and Uganda had already received assistance under the original HIPC Initiative and would later be in line for early consideration for additional relief under the Enhanced HIPC Initiative. Mali had reached the decision point of the original HIPC Initiative but not the completion point. It would eventually skip directly to another decision point under the Enhanced HIPC Initiative. Nicaragua had not reached its decision point under the original HIPC Initiative but was already under consideration. It too would skip directly to a decision point under the Enhanced HIPC Initiative. Ethiopia was never considered under the original HIPC Initiative, and would not be considered under the Enhanced Initiative until 2001.

The study made an explicit, and we believe, successful attempt at inclusiveness and relevance at all stages. One of the early developments in the research program was the convening of a *Reference Group* for the study. This group included individuals knowledgeable on the issues from academia, the NGO community, the public service, the private sector, and HIPC diplomatic missions in Ottawa. The group met four times during the study to assess the study questions, the terms of reference for the country case studies, the overall impact of the study, and possible ways forward. In addition, there was an insistence that resident (and usually native) researchers undertake the country case studies. These researchers were in turn encouraged to address issues and present the results of their research, as much as possible, from the country perspective.

As lead researcher, John Serieux attempted to tackle the broad issues that he believed, should inform current approaches to debt relief and the post-debt relief agenda. Therefore, in the two papers that begin and end this volume, bookending the country case studies, he examines the nature of the debt crisis, the strengths and limitations of current approaches to debt relief, and the prospects for mitigating future crises. The country case studies reflect particular country concerns, but they are consistent in terms of evaluating the countries' debt situation and their recent economic histories, estimating the expected budgetary savings from debt reduction (the debt dividend), and examining the attitudes of various sectors of the population toward debt relief and conditionality.

In the first paper of this issue, Serieux attempts to put poor-country debt and debt relief into perspective. The paper explains the expected negative effects of heavy debt burdens on poor countries and provides evidence to suggest that these countries did experience those effects, particularly in human development terms. Serieux argues that, though substantial debt relief for these countries did not come until the end of the 1990s (in the form of the Enhanced HIPC Initiative), most of these countries were already heavily indebted by the mid-1980s. By comparison, most of the middle-income countries that faced heavy debt burdens during the 1980s availed themselves of substantial debt reduction by the early 1990s. The delay for poor countries is explained by the twin characteristics of the public ownership of these countries' debts and the relative systemic irrelevance of these countries. These factors allowed the fiction of a temporary (liquidity) crisis to be sustained for poor countries long after it had ceased to be tenable for the middle-income countries. It was thus no accident that the offer of appreciable debt relief came only after a vociferous NGO campaign for debt reduction. The paper also offers some estimates of the size of the debt overhang faced by these countries, and thus potential bases for determining the adequacy of current debt-reduction efforts.

The second paper, and first country case study by Lykke Andersen and Osvaldo Nina, provides an excellent review of Bolivia's experience with debt relief in general and the HIPC Initiative in particular. The authors describe Bolivia's recent debt and adjustment history and provide a detailed review of the process that led to the development of the country's poverty reduction strategy. The paper is most noteworthy for its presentation and analysis of Bolivian views on debt, debt relief, and conditionality. The authors find that despite the impressive bottom-up nature of the consultative process (leading to the preparation of Bolivia's *Poverty Reduction Strategy Paper* [PRSP]), most Bolivians remained unaware or unimpressed by the process. This could be attributed largely to the general haste with which the process was implemented and the pervasive distrust of government. The paper also provides a detailed analysis of the municipal development plans that collectively constitute the national poverty-reduction program. By comparing expected costs and available funding, the authors show that Bolivia can expect a financing gap equal to approximately 17% of desired outlays over the next five years. Given that the net flows from debt relief will decrease quite rapidly thereafter, it would take superlative growth and export performances to keep human development targets within reach. These are precisely the expectations on which current debt-relief amounts are based, and the authors correctly point out that these expectations are perhaps unduly optimistic.

In the third paper, and the second country case study, Befekadu Degefe attempts to put Ethiopia's debt problems and prospects for debt relief into perspective. At the time of authorship, Ethiopia was in a qualitatively different position from the other countries being studied. It had yet to reach active consideration for debt relief, partly because of the war with Eritrea. Thus, the author treats debt relief as hypothetical rather than an immediate possibility. Degefe clearly shows that Ethiopia's debt burden is unsustainable by far – even 100% of export proceeds would be insufficient to service the current debt. Further, as one of the poorest countries in the world, Ethiopia faces a formidable task in terms of poverty reduction. Degefe uses a simple economic model to show that, even if the target of halving the country's poverty rate was extended to 20 years (rather than the 15 years set by the Millennium Summit), even 100% debt forgiveness for Ethiopia would not release sufficient resources to achieve the required rate of growth and poverty reduction.

In the third country case study, Massa Coulibaly, Amadou Diarra and Sikoro Keita argue that Enhanced HIPC debt reduction is an important break-through for Mali, given that two thirds of the population live below the poverty line; however, important challenges remain. Among these is the movement to the completion point; the Bretton Woods Institutions granted Mali its decision point with some reluctance, as a result of weaknesses in the Interim PRSP and the consultative process. Mali still faces the challenge of dealing with its remaining debt. Given Mali's weak economy – it is a Sahel country subject to cyclical droughts but is, nevertheless, dependent on a small range of primary agricultural commodities – even the remaining debt may prove beyond the country's repayment capacity. The authors suggest additional measures to improve the country's ability to manage its remaining debt, including debt-for-equity SWAPs with expatriate Malians, measures to reduce capital flight, and the issuing of domestic public securities.

In the fourth country case study, Ligia María Castro-Monge compares Nicaragua's debt relief under the HIPC Initiative to previous (non-Paris Club) debt-reduction experiences. She also compares the implied flows from debt-service reduction under the HIPC Initiative to the other major flows of external resource – aid and foreign direct investment (FDI). Despite the fact that, of the 22 countries that reached their decision point by the end of 2000, Nicaragua can expect to receive the largest absolute reduction in its debt and the third highest proportional reduction, the author finds that HIPC debt relief is eclipsed by a previous debt-reduction agreement with non-Paris Club countries – in terms of both absolute amount of debt forgiven and discount rate. Likewise, the flow implications of debt relief would be equivalent to only a modest increase in aid over the next 15 years and will be less than recent levels of FDI. In short, despite the long string of conditions attached, HIPC stock and flow quantities will not dominate Nicaragua's external balance sheet.

Given Uganda's special position as the model country for the development of participatory poverty reduction strategies, Peter Mijumbi's paper provides important clues to what went right in that process and what remains to be done. Mijumbi describes the genesis of Uganda's first explicit poverty reduction strategy – an attempt by Ugandan public servants to improve and indig-enize a program to mitigate the social cost of adjustment – and its development from the first Poverty Eradication Action Plan (PEAP) of 1997 to the PEAP of 2000 (which serves as the country's PRSP). Mijumbi also describes the related institutional arrangements, including the Poverty Action Fund (PAF), and attempts to assess the PEAP's strengths and weaknesses. The Ugandan experience is also interesting because of the continued attempts to improve both the approaches to and effectiveness of poverty reduction. The country has also instituted a strict policy on foreign borrowing in the hope of reducing the likelihood of future debt-related crises.

Despite their varying emphases, these papers address some common issues. Notably, they all provide estimates of the expected budgetary savings from debt relief, attempt to assess local attitudes to debt relief and conditionality, and try to imagine a post-debt relief reality. For all these countries, the implied budgetary savings from debt relief, or debt dividend (measured as the difference between recent (average) debt-service amounts and expected future debt-service amounts) are found to be only slightly less than the actual flow of debt relief over the next five years (2001-2005) but significantly less than the actual flow of debt relief when the period of measurement is stretched over 15 years (2001-2015). In fact, for Bolivia, the budgetary savings will evaporate beyond 2005 as expected debt-service amounts surpass recent levels.

Public opinion surveys in these countries show generally limited knowledge of debt issues and debt-relief arrangements, and among those who are aware (or who have been made aware by the research), there appears to be general distrust of the motives of both the government and international financial institutions. Though tying debt relief to poverty reduction, as a general principle, finds resonance among most local groups, expectations for future poverty reduction are quite low. What is perhaps most interesting is the clear understanding among many in these countries that HIPC debt relief, no matter how generous, does not provide a means to sustained growth. They see trade opportunities and more innovative domestic development strategies as holding far more promise for a future exit from poverty.

In the final paper, Serieux moves away from the single-country perspective and attempts to determine for the 22 HIPCs that had reached their decision point by the end of 2000, the degree to which the HIPC debt relief is likely to provide the wherewithal for significant and sustained poverty reduction, and a permanent exit from over-indebtedness. He finds that the broader picture supports the country-level results that suggest that, as a net flow, HIPC debt relief is relatively minor when compared, for instance, with recent aid levels. In fact, if aid levels are significantly reduced over the next few years, as many fear, much of the net flow effect of debt relief will be wiped out.

In examining the expectations on which HIPC debt relief is based, the author finds them to be overly optimistic and argues that more modest and realistic amounts would lead to a much more sobering scenario for these countries. He thus concludes that unless measures are put into place in anticipation of the very real possibility that these countries will need further assistance soon, and resource flows are structured to accommodate the very real structural weaknesses in those economies in the short to medium run and to correct them over the long run, debt crises among poor countries may not be a thing of the past.

John Serieux
& Yiagadeesen Samy

Introduction

L'endettement et l'allégement de la dette des pays les plus pauvres : de petits progrès dans un long cheminement*

Au cours des derniers mois du siècle dernier, les problèmes d'endettement des pays pauvres très endettés (PPTE) ont été mis en évidence plus que jamais dans le cadre de la campagne Jubilé 2000 et des campagnes connexes menées par des ONG pour l'élimination des dettes de ces pays. Les gouvernements des pays créditeurs et les institutions financières internationales ont répondu au défi qui leur était lancé. D'abord, pendant leur réunion annuelle tenue à Cologne en juin 1999, les gouvernements du G7 se sont engagés à accroître et à accélérer l'allégement de la dette des pays les plus pauvres. Ensuite, au cours des assemblées générales annuelles du Fonds monétaire international (FMI) et de la Banque mondiale tenues en septembre 1999, l'initiative multilatérale d'allégement des dettes des PPTE est devenue l'Initiative renforcée en faveur des PPTE. Cette nouvelle initiative offre une interprétation plus généreuse de ce qui constitue une dette insoutenable, rend les pays plus rapidement admissibles à l'allégement de la dette, et rend l'accès à l'allégement conditionnel à un engagement de ces pays à réduire la pauvreté.

* Le projet dont ces documents sont issus n'aurait pas pu être réalisé sans l'aide financière de la Fondation Ford, de la Banque interaméricaine de développement (BID), et de l'Agence canadienne de développement international (ACDI). Il y a donc lieu de remercier particulièrement Manuel Montes, de la Fondation Ford; Euric Bobb, de la BID; et Bill Singleton, de l'ACDI. L'idée de réaliser ce projet est de Roy Culpeper, président de l'Institut Nord-Sud. Il peut à juste titre s'enorgueillir du travail qu'elle a engendré. Il y a aussi lieu de remercier Eugenia Gallegos, également de l'Institut Nord-Sud, de l'excellent travail de préparation de textes, d'administration et d'organisation de conférences qu'elle a généreu-sement accompli pour appuyer toutes les étapes de la recherche. De plus, il faut remercier de leur apport tous les membres du groupe de référence, trop nombreux pour que nous les nommions ici, et Dane Rowlands qui a servi d'arbitre.

Toutefois, en dépit de l'attention sans précédent prêtée aux fardeaux de la dette des pays en question et des débats connexes au sujet du niveau d'allégement approprié et des conditions dont l'allégement doit être assorti, certaines questions demeurent relativement négligées, et particulièrement les suivantes :

- Pourquoi a-t-on mis tant de temps à alléger les dettes des PPTE?
- Quel a été le coût de la persistance de l'endettement de ces pays?
- L'Initiative renforcée en faveur des PPTE leur permet-elle d'échapper en permanence à l'endettement ou ne leur apporte-t-elle qu'un répit à court terme?

Ce qui importe le plus, cependant, c'est que, bien que le défi lancé par la collectivité internationale des ONG et la réponse des gouvernements et institutions créditeurs aient attiré et maintenu l'attention sur la question depuis quelques années, on n'a presque pas entendu parler de l'expérience et des points de vue de la population et des gouvernements des PPTE. La coalition du Jubilé 2000 a toujours compris des membres du Sud, mais leurs voix n'ont jamais été dégagées à l'échelle nationale. Dans le même ordre d'idées, les gouvernements des PPTE se sont exprimés pendant les réunions du G77 et du G24, par exemple, mais leurs points de vue ont été essentiellement éclipsés par ceux des grands groupes de pays en développement.

En réalisant son étude intitulée La dette des pays les plus pauvres, l'Institut Nord-Sud (INS) espérait contribuer à combler ces lacunes de la recherche et du débat sur l'endettement et l'allégement de la dette. La présente édition spéciale de la Revue canadienne d'études du développement présente sept documents issus de cette étude.

L'étude de l'INS comprenait essentiellement deux parties. La première a été constituée de recherches internes effectuées par des chercheurs et chercheuses de l'INS au sujet des principales questions ayant trait à l'endettement et à l'allégement de la dette des pays les plus pauvres. Ces questions comprennent le coût de la crise de l'endettement du point de vue du développement, les causes du retard de règlement de la crise, l'efficacité des mesures actuelles d'allégement de la dette et les perspectives de réduction de la pauvreté et de croissance des pays les plus pauvres au-delà de l'allégement de leur dette. La deuxième partie de l'étude comprenait des études de cas sur cinq PPTE réalisées par des chercheurs et chercheuses habitant ces pays. Les pays ont été choisis de manière à assurer une diversité sous les rapports de leur situation géographique et du stade d'avancement de l'approbation de l'allégement de leur dette. Deux d'entre eux, soit la Bolivie et le Nicaragua, se trouvent dans les Amériques et trois, soit l'Éthiopie, le Mali et l'Ouganda, se trouvent en

Afrique. Quand l'étude a commencé, en mai 1999, la Bolivie et l'Ouganda avaient déjà reçu de l'aide en vertu de l'initiative initiale sur les PPTE. Ils ont compté parmi les premiers pays à l'égard desquels une aide supplémentaire a été envisagée dans le cadre de l'Initiative renforcée en faveur des PPTE. Le Mali en était au point de décision dans le cadre de l'initiative initiale mais n'était pas arrivé au point d'achèvement. Il a fini par passer directement au point de décision dans le cadre de l'Initiative renforcée en faveur des PPTE. Le Nicaragua n'avait pas atteint le point de décision dans le cadre de l'initiative initiale mais faisait déjà l'objet d'un examen. Il est passé, lui aussi, directement au point de décision de l'Initiative renforcée en faveur des PPTE. L'Éthiopie n'avait jamais fait l'objet d'un examen dans le cadre de l'initiative initiale et ne l'a fait dans celui de l'Initiative renforcée qu'en 2001.

Les auteurs de l'étude ont fait un effort explicite et, à notre avis, fructueux pour voir à ce que leurs méthodes soient englobantes et opportunes à toutes les étapes. Vers le début des recherches, un groupe de référence a été constitué. Ce groupe comprenait des personnes connaissant bien les questions qui appartiennent à la collectivité des universitaires, à celle des ONG, à la fonction publique, au secteur public et aux missions diplomatiques des PPTE à Ottawa. Le groupe a tenu quatre réunions pendant l'étude afin d'évaluer les questions d'étude, les mandats des études de cas, les répercussions globales de l'étude et les moyens possibles d'avancer. De plus, il était primordial que les études de cas soient effectuées par des chercheurs et chercheuses habitant le pays (et habituellement originaires de celui-ci). Ces derniers ont été encouragés à traiter des questions et à présenter les résultats de leurs recherches le plus possible dans l'optique du pays.

En tant que chercheur principal, Serieux s'est efforcé d'aborder les grandes questions qui devraient, à son avis, éclairer les lignes de conduite actuelles à l'égard de l'allégement de la dette et le programme ultérieur. C'est pourquoi, dans les deux études qui encadrent les études de cas nationales dans le présent volume, il examine la nature de la crise de l'endettement, les forces et les limites des lignes de conduite actuelles d'allégement de la dette et les perspectives de prévention des crises futures. Les études de cas témoignent des préoccupations propres aux pays mais elles comprennent toutes, à la lumière des évaluations de l'endettement du pays et de son histoire économique récente, des estimations des économies budgétaires prévues par suite de la réduction de la dette (dividende de la dette) et un examen des attitudes de différents secteurs de la population à l'égard de l'allégement de la dette et des conditions dont il s'assortit.

Dans le premier document de ce numéro, Serieux tente de mettre l'endettement des pays pauvres et l'allégement de leur dette dans leur contexte. Il indique les effets négatifs prévus du lourd fardeau de dette des pays pauvres et présente des preuves qui portent à croire que ces pays ont effectivement subi ces effets, particulièrement en matière de développement humain. Serieux soutient que, même si ces pays n'ont bénéficié d'une remise de dette appréciable que vers la fin des années 1990 (dans le cadre de l'Initiative renforcée en faveur des PPTE), il est très évident que la plupart d'entre eux étaient déjà très endettés vers le milieu des années 1980. Par comparaison, la plupart des pays à revenu moyen qui avaient de lourds fardeaux de dette pendant les années 1980 ont pu bénéficier d'une réduction de dette considérable vers le début des années 1990. Le retard de l'allégement de la dette des pays pauvres tient à deux caractéristiques : les dettes de ces pays sont celles de leur secteur public et ils sont d'une importance relativement négligeable dans le système mondial. Ces facteurs ont permis de prétendre qu'il existait une crise temporaire (des liquidités) dans les pays pauvres longtemps après qu'il a cessé d'être possible de le prétendre dans les pays à revenu moyen. Ce n'est donc pas par hasard qu'une remise de dette appréciable n'a été offerte qu'après la bruyante campagne des ONG pour la réduction de la dette. De plus, le document présente des estimations du surendettement des pays en question et, par conséquent, des bases qui ont pu être employées pour déterminer si les efforts actuels de réduction de la dette sont suffisants.

Le deuxième document, qui est la première étude de cas, réalisée par Andersen et Nina, présente un excellent tour d'horizon de l'expérience de l'allégement de la dette, particulièrement dans le cadre de l'initiative sur les PPTE, vécue par la Bolivie. Ses auteurs décrivent l'histoire récente de l'endettement et de l'expérience de la Bolivie face à l'ajustement, et présentent une description détaillée de la procédure d'établissement de la stratégie de réduction de la pauvreté de ce pays. Le document se distingue surtout par sa présentation et son analyse des points de vue des Boliviens et des Boliviennes sur l'endettement, l'allégement de la dette et les conditions dont il s'assortit. Les auteurs ont constaté qu'en dépit de l'impressionnant caractère démocratique de la procédure de consultation (en vue de l'établissement du Cadre Stratégique de Lutte contre la Pauvreté [CSLP] de la Bolivie), la plupart des Boliviens et Boliviennes n'en étaient pas conscients ou elle les laissait indifférents. Cela peut être attribuable dans une grande mesure à la rapidité de la mise en oeuvre de la procédure et à la méfiance répandue à l'égard du gouvernement. Le document présente en outre une analyse approfondie des plans de développement municipaux dont l'ensemble constitue le programme national de réduction de la pauvreté. En comparant les coûts prévus et les fonds disponibles, les auteurs montrent que la Bolivie peut s'attendre à avoir un déficit de financement correspondant à environ 17 % des dépenses souhaitées au cours des cinq prochaines années. Puisque les flux nets de l'allégement de la dette diminueront rapidement par après, il faudrait que la croissance et l'augmentation des exportations soient très fortes pour que les objectifs de développement humain demeurent réalisables. C'est précisément ce sur quoi reposent les montants de la remise de dette actuelle, et les auteurs signalent à juste titre que les prévisions sont peut-être trop optimistes.

Dans le troisième document, qui est la deuxième étude de cas, Degefe tente de mettre les problèmes d'endettement et les perspectives d'allégement de la dette de l'Éthiopie dans leur contexte. Au moment où le document a été rédigé, l'Éthiopie était dans une situation différente qualitativement de celle des autres pays étudiés. Elle ne faisait pas encore l'objet d'un examen en vue d'une remise de dette (partiellement à cause de la guerre avec l'Érythrée). Il s'ensuit que l'auteur traite l'allégement de la dette comme une hypothèse plutôt que comme une possibilité immédiate. Degefe prouve clairement que le fardeau de la dette de l'Éthiopie est nettement insoutenable; même une remise correspondant à 100 % des recettes d'exportation du pays ne suffirait pas à payer le service de la dette actuelle. Qui plus est, en tant que pays comptant parmi les plus pauvres du globe, l'Éthiopie a un travail herculéen de réduction de la pauvreté à accomplir. Degefe emploie un modèle économique simple pour prouver que même si l'objectif de réduire de moitié le taux de pauvreté du pays devait être atteint en vingt ans (plutôt que dans le délai de 15 ans fixé pendant le Sommet du millénaire), une remise de dette de 100 % ne dégagerait pas suffisamment de ressources pour permettre le taux nécessaire de croissance et de réduction de la pauvreté.

Dans la troisième étude de cas, Coulibaly, Diarra et Keita soutiennent que l'Iinitiative renforcée de réduction de la dette des PPTE est un progrès important pour le Mali puisque les deux tiers de la population vivent sous le seuil de la pauvreté. Toutefois, il reste d'importants défis à relever. Ceux-ci comprennent celui d'atteindre le point d'achèvement de l'Initiative car les institutions de Bretton Woods ont permis au Mali de passer au point de décision avec une certaine réticence à cause de la faiblesse de son CSLP provisoire et de son processus de consultation. Un autre défi que doit relever le Mali consiste à rembourser le reste de sa dette. Compte tenu de la faiblesse économique du Mali (il s'agit d'un pays du Sahel qui est sujet à des sécheresses cycliques mais qui dépend quand même d'un éventail restreint de produits agricoles), même le reliquat de sa dette peut dépasser la capacité de remboursement du pays. Les auteurs proposent que des mesures supplémentaires soient prises pour accroître la capacité du Mali de gérer le reste de sa dette, y compris des échanges de créances contre actifs avec des Maliens et Maliennes expatriés, des mesures de réduction de la fuite de capitaux et l'émission d'obligations.

Dans la quatrième étude de cas, Castro-Monge compare l'allégement de la dette du Nicaragua en vertu de l'initiative sur les PPTE aux mesures antérieures de réduction de la dette (visant les pays ne faisant pas partie du Club de Paris). Elle compare également les flux implicites de la réduction du service de la dette en vertu de l'Initiative aux autres principaux flux de ressources extérieures – aide et investissement étranger direct (IED). Même si, des 22 pays qui avaient atteint le point de décision à la fin de 2000, le Nicaragua peut s'attendre à recevoir le montant le plus élevé de réduction de dette et la troisième proportion de réduction en importance, l'auteure conclut que l'allégement de la dette des PPTE est éclipsé par l'accord antérieur de réduction de dette conclu avec les pays ne faisant pas partie du Club de Paris des points de vue du montant de l'allégement et du taux d'escompte. Dans le même ordre d'idées, l'effet de l'allégement de la dette sur les flux n'équivaudrait qu'à une légère augmentation de l'aide au fil des 15 prochaines années et serait inférieur aux niveaux récents d'IED. En somme, malgré les nombreuses conditions dont s'assortit l'allégement, les flux et les stocks de l'Initiative PPTE, ne domineront pas le bilan extérieur du Nicaragua.

Compte tenu de la situation particulière de l'Ouganda en tant que pays illustrant l'établissement participatif de stratégies de réduction de la pauvreté, le document de Mijumbi est important parce qu'il donne des indices au sujet de ce qui a été efficace dans ce processus et des rapports sous lesquels il y a lieu de l'améliorer. Mijumbi décrit la genèse de la première stratégie explicite de réduction de la pauvreté de l'Ouganda – effort fait par les fonctionnaires ougandais pour améliorer et adapter au pays un programme consistant à réduire au minimum le coût social de l'ajustement – et le passage du premier plan d'action pour l'élimination de la pauvreté (PAEP) dressé en 1997 au PAEP de 2000 (qui sert de CSLP du pays). De plus, Mijumbi décrit les arrangements institutionnels comprenant le Fonds d'action contre la pauvreté et tente de déterminer les forces et les lacunes du PAEP. Ce qui est intéressant au sujet de l'expérience ougandaise, ce sont les efforts continuels faits pour améliorer les lignes de conduite et l'efficacité de la réduction de la pauvreté. Le pays a par ailleurs adopté une rigoureuse politique sur les emprunts à l'étranger dans l'espoir de réduire la probabilité des crises d'endettement futures.

Malgré leurs accents différents, ces documents portent sur certaines questions communes. Notamment, ils comprennent tous des estimations des économies budgétaires projetées par suite de l'allégement de la dette, des évaluations des attitudes locales à l'égard de la réduction de la dette et des conditions qui y sont associées, et une description de ce que pourrait être la réalité après l'allégement de la dette. Dans le cas de tous les pays étudiés, l'économie budgétaire découlant de l'allégement de la dette, soit le dividende de la dette (différence entre la moyenne des montants récents des paiements du service de la dette et les montants futurs prévus de ces paiements) ne sera que légèrement inférieur au flux d'allégement de la dette pendant les cinq prochaines années (de 2001 à 2005) mais sera considérablement inférieur à celui-ci si l'on regarde une période de quinze ans (de 2001 à 2015). En fait, l'économie budgétaire de la Bolivie s'évaporera après 2005 car les montants prévus des paiements du service de la dette dépassent les montants récents.

Selon les sondages d'opinion réalisés dans les pays en question, le public a généralement peu de connaissances au sujet des questions relatives à la dette publique et aux dispositions d'allégement de la dette. Cependant, les personnes qui connaissaient ces questions (ou qui y ont été sensibilisées par la recherche) semblent en général se méfier des motifs tant des gouvernements que des institutions financières internationales. La plupart des groupes locaux conviennent qu'il existe un rapport entre l'allégement de la dette et la réduction de la pauvreté mais leurs attentes quant à la réduction future de la pauvreté ne sont pas très élevées. Le point qui est peut-être le plus intéressant est que les gens comprennent bien dans bon nombre des PPTE que l'allégement de la dette, si généreux soit-il, ne donne pas des moyens d'assurer une croissance durable. Ils estiment que les possibilités commerciales et les stratégies innovatrices de développement national sont beaucoup plus prometteuses pour ce qui est de l'élimination de la pauvreté.

Dans le dernier document, Serieux prend du recul par rapport aux points de vue portant essentiellement sur un seul pays afin de tenter de déterminer la mesure dans laquelle l'allégement de la dette peut permettre aux vingt-deux PPTE qui avaient atteint le point de décision à la fin de 2000, de réduire la pauvreté de façon appréciable et durable et d'échapper en permanence au surendettement. Il trouve que l'examen global concorde avec les résultats des études de chaque pays, selon lesquels le flux net de l'allégement de la dette des PPTE est relativement mineur en regard, par exemple, des récents niveaux de l'aide extérieure. En fait, s'il y a une réduction importante des niveaux de l'aide au cours des prochaines années, ce que bon nombre de personnes craignent, cela neutralisera une grande partie de l'effet de l'allégement de la dette. L'examen des attentes sur lesquelles l'allégement de la dette est fondé porte l'auteur à les trouver trop optimistes et à soutenir que des montants plus faibles et réalistes permettraient d'établir des prévisions beaucoup moins reluisantes pour les pays en question.

En conclusion, Serieux avance que ces pays auront encore besoin d'aide. Les grandes lacunes structurelles de l'économie nécessitent à court, moyen et long termes, une réallocation des flux de ressources pour éviter de nouvelles crises d'endettement.

John Serieux
& Yiagadeesen Samy

Debt of the Poorest Countries: Anatomy of a Crisis Kept on Hold

John E. Serieux

ABSTRACT

This paper argues that the twin attributes of public ownership of the heavily indebted poor country (HIPC) debt, and the relative systemic irrelevance of these countries' economic performance led to an almost decade-long delay in the provision of substantial debt relief for these countries. While private creditors were forced to come to terms with the middle-income country debt, public creditors could afford to sustain the fiction of a liquidity crisis much longer (implying little need for debt reduction). This delay was costly for these countries as they fell behind other countries of comparable income levels in both human and economic development terms. The paper also offers some estimates of the size of the debt overhang facing these countries, and hence potential bases for determining the adequacy of current debt-reduction efforts.

RÉSUMÉ

Cet article maintient que deux attributs, notamment le caractère public de la dette des pays pauvres très endettés (PPTE) ainsi que le faible impact de leurs performances économiques dans le système mondial, ont retardé de presque dix années l'allégement de la dette pour ces pays. Les faits exposés ici démontrent que la plupart de ces pays, de même que plusieurs pays à revenus moyens, étaient déjà excessivement endettés vers le milieu des années 80. Alors que les créanciers privés étaient obligés de faire face à l'endettement des pays à revenus moyens, les créanciers publics ont appuyé le mythe d'une crise de liquidité pendant longtemps (ce qui suggère qu'il n'était pas nécessaire de réduire la dette). Ce délai fut coûteux pour ces pays car ils furent devancés, en termes de développement humain et économique, par des pays ayant des revenus comparables. L'article offre aussi des estimations de l'ampleur du surendettement de ces pays, et propose ainsi des critères potentiels pour déterminer si les efforts actuels pour diminuer la dette sont suffisants.

INTRODUCTION

The typical heavily indebted poor country (HIPC) has a low per capita income, a low level of human development, an extremely high debt stock and scheduled debt-repayment levels, and a long history of adjustment attempts. Even among low-income countries, these countries do not compare favourably. This profile is not a recent development; it applied to these countries as early as the mid-1980s. At that time, they shared the attributes of a heavy and unsustainable debt burden, and impaired growth and human development, with several middle-income countries. However, while the middle-income countries (such as Mexico, Brazil, Argentina and Costa Rica) had obtained significant debt-stock reductions by the early 1990s, the HIPCs were only offered substantial debt relief since 1999 and, even then, it came with many strings attached. Why did it take a decade longer to reach real debt reduction for the poorest countries?

This paper argues that the public ownership of most of the HIPC's debts, and their relative systemic irrelevance, are the main factors behind the long delay in the offer of significant debt forgiveness to these countries. Despite the substantial and obvious cost of the heavy debt burden for the HIPCs, these countries had to wait much longer than middle-income countries for debt reduction because, in spite of ample evidence to the contrary, public creditors sustained the fiction of a liquidity crisis (rather than a debt overhang) for nearly two decades. These creditor countries and international financial institutions could afford the delay because the systemic cost – the cost to the world economy – was minimal and, until recently, no signal was sufficiently emphatic to overcome denial and the very real burden-sharing problem that stood in the way of substantial debt relief. By comparison, the private institutions that held the debt of the middle-income countries, when faced with the discounted prices of these countries' debts on the secondary market in the mid-1980s, could no longer sustain the fiction of a liquidity crisis. Further, the systemic importance of these countries obliged the international community to provide the necessary framework for addressing the debt problems of these countries in an orderly fashion, through the Brady Plan under the auspices of the International Monetary Fund (IMF). It took another decade for the international campaign for debt forgiveness by Jubilee 2000 (and other Northern civil-society organizations) to induce anything close to a similar response from public creditors.

The next section describes the HIPCs relative to other country groups, explains the means through which a heavy debt burden is expected to affect a country's development, and provides evidence to suggest that it has done so in those countries. The third section describes the chronology of debt relief, demonstrating the glacial pace of movement on the publicly owned versus privately owned debt of heavily indebted countries, and presents some of the underlying reasons for this difference. The paper concludes with a summary of the issues raised and a discussion of areas for further research.

I. THE DEVELOPMENT COSTS OF HEAVY DEBT BURDENS

A.   A PROFILE OF HIPCs

"Heavily indebted" and "poor" clearly spell out the combined attributes that set HIPCs apart from other developing countries and make them a focus of concern for Northern governments, international public agencies, and international civil-society organizations. As one might suspect, these two attributes are closely related. In fact, given the relative systemic irrelevance of these countries, the strong possibility (if not certainty) of an ongoing negative feedback loop between those attributes lends a sense of urgency to current attempts at debt relief. Although these are neither the only poor countries nor the only heavily indebted ones, the evidence suggests that in terms of both poverty and indebtedness, they do not compare favourably with other developing countries.

The HIPCs are, generally, the poorest of the poor. As table 1 indicates, they have a lower average per capita income level than the rest of the low-income country group (regardless of whether income is denominated in purchasing power parity [PPP] equivalents or US dollar equivalents).[1] Despite receiving much higher levels of aid and managing a higher savings rate in 1998, these countries' average investment rate was more than five percentage points (of GDP) lower than that of the other low-income countries.[2] In effect, the other low-income countries were able to sustain larger savings-investment gaps by attracting higher levels of FDI and managing larger net flows on debt.

In human development terms, the HIPC group ranks below average even among the poorest countries. The unweighted average life expectancy in the

---

1. Alhough China and India are classified as low-income countries, they are not included in the group because their size gives them many of the characteristics of middle-income countries despite their low average income.
2. That difference would have been even higher if China and India had been included in the low-income group.

Table 1.   Comparison of HIPC and other low-income countries, 1998

Economic and social indicators (average per country)	HIPC countries	Other low-income countries*
GDP per capita (PPP$)	1,239.0	1,653.0
GDP per capita (US$)	360.0	425.0
Gross domestic investment (% of GDP)	19.4	24.9
Gross domestic saving (% of GDP)	8.9	6.5
Foreign direct investment (% of GDP)	1.9	5.5
Aid (as % of GDP)	13.6	8.4
Debt service (as % of GDP)	4.1	3.4
Net flows on debt (% of GDP)	1.8	2.9
Life expectancy	51.2	61.1
Literacy rate	56.3	64.2
Net primary school enrollment levels (% of eligible pupils)	62.6	75.3
Public health expenditure (% of GDP)	1.9	1.8

* These countries are: Afghanistan, Armenia, Azerbaijan, Bangladesh, Bhutan, Cambodia, Comoros, Eritrea, Haiti, Indonesia, North Korea, Kyrgyz Republic, Lesotho, Moldavia, Mongolia, Nepal, Nigeria, Pakistan, Solomon Islands, Tajikistan, Turkmenistan, Zimbabwe.

Source: World Bank, *World Development Indicators 2000*.

HIPCs is 10 years lower than it is in the other low-income countries, and primary school enrolment is nine percentage points lower. Of the attributes compared, public spending on health is the only area in which the HIPC group compares favourably with the other low-income countries.

The HIPCs are not the only group of countries to face a debt crisis in recent years. During the mid-1980s, several middle-income countries also faced high and unsustainable debt burdens — resulting in what has been called the "MBA debt crisis" of that period.[3] However, the debt profile of these countries at that time was quite different from that of the current HIPCs.[4] As table 2 indicates, the stock of debt held by HIPCs (relative to GNP) is more than twice that held by the heavily indebted middle-income countries (HIMCs) of the mid-1980s. This is, however, largely compensated for by the lower interest rates faced by the HIPCs because most of their debt was incurred on concessional terms. Also, while in both groups the public sector was responsible for

---

3. "MBA" refers ostensibly to Mexico, Brazil and Argentina – three of the countries at the centre of the crisis. The term is also a backdoor stab at commercial bank executives in the North and company executives in middle-income countries (most of whom are presumed to have MBA degrees) whose poor decision-making was felt to lie at the heart of the problem.

4. The 13 countries that make up that sample of middle-income countries are Argentina, Brazil, Chile, Costa Rica, Gabon, Malaysia, Mauritius, Mexico, Peru, the Philippines, Turkey, Uruguay and Venezuela.

Table 2.   **The HIPCs of the 1990s and the heavily indebted middle-income countries in the 1980s**

Debt related indicators (average per country)	HIPCs in 1998	Heavily indebted middle-income countries in 1986
Debt stock ratios		
Total debt (% of GNP)	165.6	74.4
Long-term debt (% of GNP)	144.0	61.4
Public sector debt (% of long-term debt)	97.9	89.2
Private sector debt (% of long-term debt)	2.1	10.8
Public and public guaranteed debt (% of GNP)		
Bilateral	43.5	16.2
Multilateral	50.2	16.6
Private	6.3	67.2
Arrears (as % of total debt)	19.2	3.5
Flow related ratios		
Debt service (% of GNP)	5.9	8.9
Net resource flow (% of GNP)	12.4	3.3
Official (% of GNP)	10.6	1.4
Private (% of GNP)	1.8	1.9
Net debt flow (% of GNP)	1.8	1.9
Average interest on public sector borrowing		
1970-85		8.6
1980-95	3.1	

Sources: World Bank, *World Development Indicators 2000*;
World Bank, *Global Development Finance 2000*.

most of the debt, this is much more so for the HIPCs (97.9% versus 89.2% for the HIMCs). But what perhaps differentiates them most, in terms of the stock of debt profiles, is that while most of the HIPC group's debt is owed to public (bilateral and multilateral) lending institutions, the HIMCs of the 1980s owed most of their debt to private institutions.

The HIMCs of the mid-1980s achieved a higher average level of debt-service payments (relative to their GNP) in 1986 than the HIPCs achieved in 1998. The differing economic situation of the countries currently in crisis is such that, despite much higher net resource inflows, with few exceptions, they have never been able to achieve the punishing debt-repayment levels that the HIMCs achieved in the mid-1980s. For the poorer countries, the ratios at which debt-service payments become simply unsustainable is much lower. Arrears have accumulated as a result (table 2).

Thus, several characteristics distinguish the HIPCs from the rest of the developing world:

- In general, the HIPCs are poorer than even the average low-income countries.

Table 3.   Some five-year economic aggregates

Economic Aggregates	HIPCs*					Selected non-HIPCs**				
	1975-79	1980-84	1985-89	1990-94	1995-98	1975-79	1980-84	1985-89	1990-94	1995-98
Total external debt (in $US billions)	32.7	74.1	134.8	201.9	215.4	42.0	85.6	149.3	190.8	203.8
(% of GNP)	42.2	71.2	127.3	181.4	169.8	27.0	40.3	58.3	51.1	47.3
Debt service payments										
(% of GNP)	3.2	5.5	6.6	6.9	6.1	1.9	3.5	5.0	4.5	4.1
(% of exports)	11.8	21.5	27.5	22.3	19.4	8.8	12.8	16.1	14.1	12.0
(% of government revenue)	12.1	19.9	22.5	30.4	26.0	6.7	11.6	17.2	17.9	17.0
Arrears (% of total external debt)	4.5	5.2	10.5	17.3	19.5	0.9	0.7	2.9	3.4	3.5
Government revenue (% of GDP)	16.5	17.8	16.3	17.3	16.7	21.0	23.7	24.3	25.5	25.7
Government expenditure (% of GDP)	20.7	26.3	25.1	27.5	22.0	27.2	29.0	29.3	29.2	29.3
in education (% of govt. expenditure)	18.8	16.1	16.3	15.3	15.6	17.4	16.1	14.6	15.1	17.5
in health (% of govt. expenditure)	6.4	5.6	5.6	5.7	5.3	5.6	6.0	6.2	6.8	6.5
Capital expenditure (% of govt. expenditure)	22.6	25.5	21.4	24.7	25.3	28.5	23.4	24.0	22.9	20.2
(% of GDP)	4.4	4.8	3.6	4.5	4.9	7.0	6.0	5.7	6.1	5.2
Terms of trade multiplied by the export ratio	29.7	26.0	24.9	24.4	25.3	24.5	25.4	26.6	26.8	27.3
Total exports (% of GDP)	25.5	23.2	22.0	23.9	27.5	25.4	28.7	29.6	30.1	31.9
Foreign direct investment (% of GDP)	0.7	0.4	0.3	1.1	1.9	1.6	0.9	1.8	1.6	3.3
Aid (% of GDP)	9.8	11.6	15.6	22.0	16.6	9.8	9.4	9.3	7.6	4.8
Gross domestic investment	19.6	19.0	16.9	18.3	19.2	24.5	22.5	23.6	26.7	25.6
Gross domestic saving	11.5	9.0	8.4	7.7	9.2	14.9	12.2	15.6	15.6	14.8

Notes: * Because of incomplete coverage, the HIPC aggregate measures do not generally include Angola, Guinea,
          Liberia, Laos, Somalia, Vietnam and Yemen. In a few cases Sao Tome and Principe, and Tanzania are also
          missing.
       ** The group of countries defined as "selected non-HIPCs" were those countries (for which data was generally
          available) that were defined in the World Bank's *Global Development Finance 2000* as moderately or less
          indebted; whose per capita GNP was less than $US1,000 in 1975 (and are thus comparable to the HIPCs
          whose maximum per capita GNP in 1975 was $US1,010) and were not included in the Jubilee 2000 choice
          of 52 heavily indebted countries. The countries in that group are Belize, Botswana, Comoros, Dominican
          Republic, Egypt, El Salvador, India, Lesotho, Morocco, Nepal, Pakistan, Solomon Islands, Sri Lanka, Swaziland
          and Zimbabwe.
Sources: World Bank, *World Development Indicators 2000*; *Global Development Finance*;
          IMF, *International Financial Statistics*; *Government Financial Statistics*; UNESCO, *Education Statistics*;
          Ebel, B. (1991), *Patterns of Government Expenditure in Developing Countries During the 1980s.*

- HIPCs tend to have lower levels of human development.
- Several of the HIPCs carry a much higher stock of debt (relative to GDP) than any ratios observed during the debt crisis of the mid-1980s.
- They have generally been unable to meet debt-service payments, even after recourse to traditional debt-relief mechanisms and adjustment programs.
- Unlike the middle-income countries of the mid-1980s, the HIPCs owe most of their debt to public agencies.

B.   THE ORIGINS OF THE CRISIS

As will be made clear later in this section, the heavy debt burdens of some of the world's poorest countries have significant growth and human develop-

Table 4.   Performance comparison of HIPC and selected non-HIPCs*

	HIPCs					Non-HIPCs				
	1975-79	1980-84	1985-89	1990-94	1995-98	1975-79	1980-84	1985-89	1990-94	1995-98
Average annual growth of GDP (%)	3.2	1.7	2.2	0.9	4.0	5.4	4.1	5.6	4.1	3.0
Percentage annual growth of GDP per capita	0.5	-1.0	-0.5	-1.6	1.3	2.7	1.5	2.9	1.6	1.3
Average ratio of per capita incomes ($PPP) to incomes in high-income OECD countries (%)	9.0	7.7	6.5	5.5	5.2	12.7	12.5	12.2	12.8	12.7
Average life expectancy (years)	46.6	48.2	50.4	50.3	51.6	55.8	58.2	61.5	63.3	65.2
Primary school enrollment (% of eligible age group)	-	58.3	59.5	59.1	61.9	-	77.8	80.1	83.2	83.7
Secondary school enrollment (% of eligible age group)	-	36.0	36.1	36.6	37.7	-	47.0	53.9	57.6	62.5

* Data coverage was incomplete for the variables estimated here but was above 50% in all cases. To avoid the bias created by situations of internal conflict, war-torn countries such as Angola, Liberia, Somalia, and Sudan were excluded from the data set.
** To prevent distortion, the data on life expectancy excludes countries with a high incidence of HIV/AIDS (HIPCs: Malawi, Uganda and Zambia; non-HIPCs: Botswana and Zimbabwe).
Sources: World Bank, *World Development Indicators 1999*; *Global Development Finance 1999*; IMF, *International Financial Statistics*.

Table 5.   Distribution of public and public-guaranteed debt among creditors for 38 HIPC countries*

Year	Public and public-guaranteed long-term debt/GNP	Multilateral (% of total PPG)	Bilateral (% of total PPG)	Private (% of total PPG)
1980	37.3	19.9	47.7	32.5
1985	58.6	23.3	53.0	23.7
1990	94.6	25.5	58.6	15.9
1995	125.1	31.4	55.9	12.7
1998	98.0	51.7	35.6	12.6

* Excludes Liberia, Myanmar and Somalia because of incomplete GNP data.
Source: World Bank, *Global Development Finance 2000*.

ment costs. However, before turning to this issue, the question of how we came to the point where most of the world's poorest people, outside of China and India, carry an additional burden of unrepayable debt must be addressed. This crisis does not share the same genesis as the MBA debt crisis of the mid-1980s. Because of their limited ability to borrow on international capital markets, these countries did not receive significant amounts of the large flows of private credit that poured into several developing countries in the late 1970s. They were only minor players in that theatre of excess. In fact, during that period, most of these countries' debt was accumulated through the provision of credit by bilateral credit agencies (table 5). More recently, most of their debt has been accumulated through multilateral credit, provided by international financial institutions as counterparts to stringent adjustment programs. For answers, we must look beyond the mere accumulation of debt itself, to the ability of these countries to fulfil even the most basic assumptions that underpin large-scale sovereign borrowing.

Foreign borrowing – and the resultant accumulation of foreign debt – has been a key element of the development process for well over a century and has been used effectively by the most successful economies. Sound economic and accounting logic favours public sector foreign borrowing in developing and developed countries, but that logic is not impervious to the sobering reality of economic underdevelopment.

In countries with less-than-spectacular savings rates, foreign borrowing by the public sector simultaneously provides needed resources for public investment, avoids the crowding out of private investment that results from domestic borrowing, and provides scarce foreign exchange. Such borrowing should have a net positive effect on the economy if:

- the additional investment results in increased output (and a commensurate increase in government revenues) that provides the additional revenues needed to cover debt-servicing obligations or, in the absence of requisite growth, there is sufficient room for revenue expansion without deleterious growth and income-distribution effects;
- new foreign exchange earnings from exports and FDI (or substantial foreign reserves) can readily accommodate the requisite foreign exchange demand for debt servicing (in addition to normal import demand).

However, if these conditions are not met, the country may quickly find itself unable to meet its foreign debt-repayment obligations. If a significant economic upturn can be predicted with some certainty (i.e. if the situation is temporary), the country faces a liquidity crisis. However, if such a turnaround is not forthcoming (or is unlikely in the near future), the country faces the situation of a debt overhang – full repayment of existing debt without severe economic consequences is, at best, improbable and, more likely, out of the question.[5]

For most low-income countries, because of their dependence on a narrow primary export base and their limited ability to attract FDI, non-debt-related foreign resource inflows are both limited and irregular. As a result, their debt-

5. As Krugman (1998) pointed out, the description of a country as "insolvent" misses the point that it is the uncertainty of repayment that often lies at the heart of the problem rather than any knowledge that the country is absolutely incapable of meeting its payment commitments (though that is also possible).

Figure 1.　Average indices of export capacity to import: HIPCs and Non-HIPCS

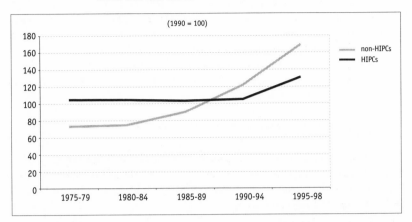

carrying capacity (the level of indebtedness at which they can readily sustain the relevant debt-service requirements) is quite low. Thus, even at modest levels of indebtedness, a decline in the foreign exchange value of these countries' exports (whether through a terms of trade decline or volume contraction) can lead to debt-servicing difficulties. A terms of trade decline that results from structural shifts in the global economy is unlikely to be quickly reversed. Thus, for a weak economy with a substantial debt load, a return to an external balance that allows for the full resumption of debt-service payments (including the servicing of debts incurred during the interim) is an unlikely scenario, and the country faces a debt overhang.

Such a situation occurred in the early 1980s. Most developing countries had already accumulated modest debt loads by the late 1970s (table 3). In 1979 and the years immediately following, the combined effect of the second oil shock (and the ensuing global recession) and a shift from expansionist to restrictive monetary policies in developed countries led to a general decline in world trade, higher interest rates, and lower prices for most primary products. For HIPCs, this meant a decline or stagnation in their foreign exchange earning capacity just as both the need for, and the cost of, credit increased (figure 1). This structural shift also meant that a terms of trade recovery was not imminent and, as these countries continued to accumulate debt (mostly from bilateral credit agencies), they slipped beyond the point where full repayment was a real possibility to a debt overhang situation. By contrast, the current non-

HIPCs faced more favourable terms of trade conditions and were able to sustain debt-service payments even as they continued to increase their debt burdens into the late 1980s (figure 1 and table 3). Thus, the current debt crisis facing the poorest countries has little to do with the large transfers of private credit that precipitated the MBA debt crisis of the 1980s. Rather it is the result of changes in the global economy that placed new, long-term limits on these countries' debt-carrying capacities – a reality the rest of the world was slow to recognize.

C. DEBT, HUMAN DEVELOPMENT AND GROWTH

When most of a country's foreign debt is public and public-guaranteed (consisting mostly of central government debt and the debt of loss-making state-owned corporations), its social and economic conditions can be negatively affected through three main avenues:
- the budgetary process;
- the external accounts;
- the disincentive effects of "debt overhang."

The first two avenues relate directly to the size of (current) debt-service requirements; the third relates to the size of the stock of debt (relative to expected output) and the future debt-service burden it portends.

1. *The budgetary process*

There is a simple arithmetical relationship between public debt-service obligations and other areas of government spending. The interest payments and principal repayments that make up debt-service requirements (for public debt) must come from the government budget. Therefore, if revenues do not increase to match the increase in debt-service requirements, meeting those requirements implies a contraction in other areas of government spending. Even in the presence of a revenue increase, unless the growth in revenues exceeds the new debt-related expenditure demands, the debt-service burden may still pre-empt growth in other areas of expenditure.

Increasing government revenue to generate the resources for debt-repayment appears to be the natural response to a mounting debt-repayment burden. As mentioned above, if previous borrowing had provided an impetus to economic growth in the first place, the resultant increase in incomes would likely have provided room for revenue expansion, and thus the budgetary space for debt repayment. If that growth is not forthcoming, the revenues-to-income ratio will need to be raised. However, most developing countries have a narrow tax base, dominated by indirect (particularly trade) taxes, and limited institutional infrastructure (Bird 1990; Manuelli 1994; Carciofi and Cetrángolo 1994). In the absence of significant tax reform, large across-the-board tax increases are likely to be both institutionally and politically unfeasible, particularly in the face of falling terms of trade and economic stagnation.

Without significant revenue increases, debt-service obligations can be met only by reducing expenditure in other areas or by increasing the government deficit. Deficit financing generally consists of some combination of inflationary finance (borrowing from the central bank), the accumulation of domestic debt, or the further accumulation of foreign debt. The latter two options essentially amount to exchanging one form of debt for another and, at best, simply delay the problem or put it in another guise. Inflationary finance brings with it the disruptive effect of high inflation rates on economic activity. In addition, the resulting "inflation tax" falls disproportionately on the lowest income groups. Tax incidence studies for Mexico and Argentina, for example, indicated that the inflation tax incidence was U-shaped for Mexico and definitely regressive for Argentina (Carciofi and Cetrángolo 1994).[6] Beyond this, the resources that can be mobilized through inflationary finance are definitely limited: attempts to sustain that maximum will inevitably lead to hyperinflation.

This leaves government spending contraction as the third, and most probable, means of accommodating debt-service obligations. Two areas of government spending likely to suffer the consequences of this "decrease in budgetary space" are social spending (health, education, housing, welfare, social insurance, etc.) and public investment. Social spending cuts imply a contraction in the resources available for addressing human development goals (including poverty reduction). Reduced public investment will probably result in lower overall investment (both, because public investment is a significant proportion of total domestic investment in most developing countries and because it may complement private investment). Lower overall investment means reduced potential for medium- and long-term growth.

The Latin American experience during the debt crisis of the 1980s suggests the likely effects of high debt-repayment burdens on budgetary choices, particularly with respect to health and education spending. Reimers (1990, p. 545) showed that in the 1970s the unweighted average per capita expenditure on education in Latin America grew at 3.4% annually, but in the 1980-

---

6. A U-shaped pattern indicates that the tax falls heavily on the lowest-income groups, less so on the middle-income groups, and heavily on the highest-income groups.

1988 period fell by 2.4% annually. In fact, per capita expenditure on education fell in only 1 of 19 countries during the 1970s but fell in 15 of the same 19 countries between 1980 and 1988. Even more distressing, the evidence suggests that in some countries the decline in education spending was most acute at the lower levels of the system – the education most consumed by the poor. In Costa Rica, expenditure on basic (largely primary) education declined in real terms at 4.8% per annum in the 1980-1987 period, but expenditure on higher education fell by only 0.25% during the same period (Reimers 1990, p. 546).

The story of health care is similar. Cornia (1994:44) showed that combined spending on health and education in Latin America fell from 24.4% of the budget in 1980-1981 to 18.4% in 1985-1987. In Mexico, for example, health care expenditure fell by 53% between 1981 and 1987 (Rivero, Ascencio and Vinagre 1991). Though the country continued to expand the coverage of health services, the quality of health services declined. That effect was apparent in the dramatic slowdown in the rate of decline of child mortality to only 4% in the 1978-1982 period. Rivero et al. (1991) also noted that others had observed similar effects in Brazil.

The figures in table 3 tell a similar story for the HIPCs. In the late 1970s, the HIPCs spent a larger proportion of their total expenditure on health and education than did the non-HIPCs; however, because expenditure was a smaller proportion of total income, the proportion of total income spent on health was smaller.[7] In the succeeding years, expenditures on both education and health, as a proportion of total expenditure, not only declined but were already at or below the average level for the non-HIPCs as early as the early 1980s, and they have remained so. This is particularly true of health expenditure, which has been declining in relation to total expenditure since the 1970s, whereas the opposite was true for the non-HIPCs. When one considers that total government expenditure in non-HIPCs has been close to or more than two percentage points (of GDP) higher than in HIPCs, it is clear that expenditure in these areas relative to GDP was diverging even more rapidly between the two groups of countries.

---

7. Because of data limitations, the figures on health and education expenditure provided in the tables come from a limited sample of the two groups of countries. The respective samples included a larger proportion of non-HIPCs than HIPCs . Although this limits the credibility of the data, it also lends a strong upward bias to the HIPC data (because the worse-off countries were more likely to be excluded because of the poor data). Thus, although the results cannot be treated as conclusive, the picture they paint is likely to be better, rather than worse than reality.

Capital expenditure, as a percentage of total expenditure, was lower among HIPCs since the 1970s, remained lower as it declined through the 1980s and showed signs of recovery in the 1990s. Capital expenditure for non-HIPCs showed no clear pattern, falling in the late 1980s and late 1990s. However, total investment was another matter altogether. Not only has investment been higher among non-HIPCs since the 1970s, it has increased steadily, after a small decline in the early 1980s, with higher levels in the 1990s than those achieved in the late 1970s. HIPCs, however, experienced a decline in average investment during the 1980s and have not since recovered the investment levels of the late 1970s. Given that the public expenditure performance of non-HIPCs was not particularly noteworthy (and public expenditure is a good proxy for public investment) it appears that the biggest difference in investment performance for the two groups of countries was in private investment. If this is so, it suggests that private investment, even in relatively underdeveloped economies such as these, may be much more sensitive to the countries' debt burdens than has generally been presumed.

As table 4 indicates, their material fortunes reflect the difference in social and economic investment in the two groups of countries. The period of heavy and increasing debt for the HIPCs coincided with a slowdown in the rate of both economic and human development (even when the war-torn countries of Angola, Liberia, Somalia and Sudan are excepted). The unweighted average per capita growth rate slipped below zero in the early 1980s and did not become positive again until the late 1990s. By comparison, since the mid-1970s, the non-HIPCs have maintained average per capita growth rates substantially higher than 1%. More telling though, is the difference in the performance of these countries relative to that of the developed countries. Average per capita income (unweighted) in the HIPCs, translated at PPP rates, was 9% of that of the high-income OECD countries in the late 1970s but had slipped to 5.2% by the late 1990s – clear evidence of divergence between the two groups of economies (table 4). Non-HIPCs, however, though they did not improve their lot against the developed countries, kept pace with them, averaging 12.7% of high-income OECD-country incomes in both the late 1970s and the late 1990s, with very little variation in the years between.

Though the HIPCs continued to record improvements in the basic human development indicators, the rate of increase slowed perceptibly and was much lower than the corresponding figure for the non-HIPCs. For the HIPCs, life expectancy (at birth) increased by 5 years from an average of 46.6 years in the 1975-1979 period to 51.6 years in the 1995-1998 period. Although the non-HIPCs had already achieved higher average life expectancy levels by the late

1970s (55.8 years), they had improved that average by over 9 years by the late 1990s (to 65.2 years).[8] Achievements in school attendance (an indicator of the rate of increase in human and social capital) tell a similar story. The HIPCs just barely increased primary and secondary school enrolment levels from the early 1980s to the late 1990s. The average (per country) increase in primary school enrolment was only 3.6 percentage points of the eligible population and that for secondary school was an even more lethargic 1.7%. The non-HIPCs, however, achieved greater improvements on already higher levels of attendance. Average primary school enrolment increased by 5.9%, and secondary school enrollment, by an impressive 15.5%.

The relationship between investment (in physical assets) and growth is a well-established empirical and theoretical relationship in economics. Thus, the lower investment rates in HIPCs account, in part, for the lethargic performance of that group of countries in the 1980s and early 1990s. However, the empirical results derived from the application of new endogenous growth theory have highlighted the importance of human capital in that process (Barro 1991; Romer 1989; Grossman and Helpman 1991; Mankiw, Romer and Weil 1992). Hence, the long-term effects of per capita decreases in social spending on economic growth should not be underestimated. Micro studies continue to bring that relationship into sharper focus. Schultz (1998) and Shultz and Tansel (1993) showed that health status was a strong determinant of adult wage-earning capacity (and, by implication, productivity) in Ghana and Côte d'Ivoire. Husbands et al. (1996) showed that primary schooling had a significant and positive effect on the productivity of resources in agriculture in Kenya.

While at least part of the slowdown in human development in HIPCs can be attributed to negative per capita growth in the 1980s and early 1990s, the effect of reduced social spending should not be underestimated. Using a series of micro studies, Schultz (1998) showed that, whereas a 10.5% increase in per capita income was concomitant with a reduction in infant mortality of 1.5 per thousand and increased male and female life expectancy of less than one year, increasing women's schooling by one year was associated with a decrease in infant mortality of 7.4 per thousand, a 1.5-year increase in average female life expectancy, and a 1.1-year increase in average male life expectancy. Clearly,

---

8. For both HIPCs and non-HIPCs, the measurement of average life expectancy (per country) excludes countries affected by a high incidence of HIV/AIDS in both samples (Botswana, Malawi, Uganda, Zambia and Zimbabwe). However, the inclusion of these countries would have exaggerated the difference between the two groups.

certain forms of social investment (such as changes in female enrollment in school) achievable through relatively modest increases in social expenditure, can have a far greater effect on human development indicators than an increase in incomes.

In effect, the constraints imposed on budgetary allocation by debt burdens (as well as the disincentive effects) appear to have compromised growth in the HIPCs by causing lower rates of investment in both human and physical capital. In turn, the lower levels of growth, in addition to the reduced social spending, compromised human development. In short, a negative circle of causation appears to have been in effect in those countries. These effects are even more alarming when it is recognized that throughout most of this period most of these countries were meeting only a fraction of scheduled debt-service payments, resulting in a continuous buildup of arrears throughout the 1980s and the 1990s (table 3).

2.   External account effects

For foreign debt obligations, the allocation of budgetary resources is only the first requirement in debt repayment. Since debt repayments are made in foreign currency, provision for debt-service payments must also be made in the country's external account. For countries blessed with a traded currency or substantial foreign reserves – and no such country exists among the HIPCs – this transaction would probably have no measurable economic impact. However, for countries with limited reserves (most developing countries), in the absence of debt refinancing, the required foreign currency must be com-mandeered out of current foreign exchange earnings from exports, FDI, untied official development assistance (ODA),[9] or private debt inflows. For the typical HIPC, FDI and private debt inflows have been insignificant (tables 1 and 3), and though aid levels were substantial, until the mid-1990s, 50% or more of aid to developing countries was generally tied. The foreign currency counterpart of debt-service obligations must come largely from export earn-ings. In the face of decreasing or static export earnings, the net result will be import compression, regardless of the exchange rate regime in effect.

Whether the foreign exchange demand imposed by debt-service require-ments is passed on through the price mechanism (exchange rate depreciation)

---

9.   Tied ODA, to the extent that it generates new imports equal to net financial flows, adds little to the net supply of foreign exchange. (In the case of aid in kind, there is no supply at all). If it does not generate new demand, but instead displaces normal import demand, it can reduce the foreign exchange crunch, however, that effect is likely to be partial at best.

or through non-price rationing (import restrictions), the effect is similar. If the country has a flexible exchange rate, the currency will depreciate as the demand for foreign exchange exceeds the supply. Alternatively, a country with a fixed exchange rate might choose to devalue the currency; this has the same effect. Depreciation or devaluation of the currency can ease the foreign exchange constraint somewhat by reducing import demand and inducing an increase in exports (since depreciation/devaluation increases the domestic price of both imports and exports). However, as the experience of the last two decades has shown, for countries that export only a limited number of primary products, the export response is neither quick nor substantial, and is often wiped out by negative terms of trade movements. In any case, currency depreciation exacerbates the budgetary choices discussed above by increasing the domestic cost of debt-service obligations. The net result will often be an increase in the price of imported intermediate inputs and capital goods, without a commensurate increase in the capacity to import, and a consequent contraction in aggregate supply and investment.

Countries that attempt to maintain a fixed exchange rate in these circumstances are forced to accommodate the increased demand for foreign exchange through restrictions on imports. The likely outcome is also a reduction in the supply of imported intermediate inputs and capital goods, with similar consequences for aggregate supply and investment. In addition, the non-price restrictions create an incentive for rent-seeking activity, which in turn has an additional negative effect on output and investment (not to mention the possible disruption of constructive institutional development).

3.   The debt-overhang disincentive effect

The disincentive effect of the debt ratio, sometimes referred to as the "debt-overhang effect," is the negative savings and investment effect that a heavy debt burden can generate. Domestic savers and investors may see a high stock of debt as an indicator of the high future tax rates that will be needed to meet debt-service requirements. This acts to lower the expected (after-tax) return on savings and investment. Domestic economic agents may therefore choose to invest their savings elsewhere – capital flight. Foreign investors, in addition to being similarly discouraged by the prospect of future taxes, may be discouraged by the prospect of future currency depreciations that will lower the foreign currency value of their investment. Alternatively, they may be concerned about their ability to repatriate profits in the event of non-price rationing of foreign currency.

The extent of this debt-overhang effect, however, remains uncertain. Fry (1989) observed a strong negative relationship between the stock of debt and the level of domestic savings for a sample of 28 developing countries. Deshpande (1995) found a similar negative relationship between debt stock and investment for a sample of 13 countries over the period 1971-1991. Cohen (1993) could find no such effect for a sample of 80 countries. However, he did find a strong negative relationship between current investment and debt-repayment outflows – the external account effect mentioned above.

In the context of developing countries, the difference between those two effects may be more artificial than real. Given the limited reach of the tax system in most of these countries, it is unlikely that potential investors are primarily concerned about legislated taxes. Their more immediate concern probably relates to the uncertainties created by ongoing pressure on the external account (with respect to the future availability and/or price of capital goods and imported intermediate inputs).

The data in table 3 clearly suggest that investment has been lower and mostly falling in HIPCs since the 1970s. The lower investment level probably indicates more fundamental structural problems in these economies. However, the decline in HIPC investment during the 1980s and its lethargic recovery in the 1990s cannot be explained by structure alone. Although the slow rate of economic growth and deteriorating terms of trade were probably contributing factors, it is hard to argue that the size of the debt and the ever-increasing repayment burden were not perhaps equally, if not more, important.

A related "disincentive effect" of the debt overhang is that on policy makers. Given a debt overhang, policy makers may anticipate that the benefits from any increase in growth (increased revenues, foreign exchange, etc.) due to improvement in the policy framework will accrue solely to creditors (through increases in the proportion of debt-repayment obligations met). Debtor-country governments may thus have limited incentive to make hard choices that improve the potential for economic growth.[10]

---

10. This, together with some of the issues mentioned above, forms the basis for the debt Laffer curve.

II. THE INTERNATIONAL RESPONSE TO THE POOR-COUNTRY DEBT CRISIS: FROM DENIAL TO CONDITIONALITY

A. STRUCTURAL ADJUSTMENT AND DEBT – MISSING THE TARGET

As described above, countries with a heavy debt burden face some hard choices. When that situation is exacerbated by a fall in the country's terms of trade and by economic stagnation domestically, the country may slip into a debt-overhang situation – where the debt stock exceeds the country's expected capacity to repay – and hard choices become impossible choices. Short-term deficit financing (of the budget) quickly becomes unsustainable; further cuts in expenditure become unfeasible; and foreign reserves evaporate as export proceeds and limited foreign inflows fail to meet even compressed imports and debt-repayment needs. The ensuing internal disequilibrium (high inflation, non-sustainable government deficits) and the non-viability of the external sector (razor-thin reserve coverage and export earnings that do not cover essential imports in addition to debt-service payments) make exceptional financing and other forms of crisis mitigation an imperative.

As early as 1980, several of the current HIPCs (as well as several middle-income countries) were already showing signs of full-blown or impending, debt-related crises. At least sixteen of these countries had to meet debt-service payments larger than 20% of total exports.[11] In most cases, this was concomitant with large balance of payment deficits (on the current account) and, for several of these countries, large budget deficits as well. Guyana, for example, faced debt-service payments of 21.6% of exports, a current account deficit of 21.3% of GDP, and a budget deficit of 29.2% of GDP. Similarly, Malawi had to meet debt-service payments worth 27.8% of exports, a current account deficit of 21% of GDP, and a budget deficit of 15.9% of GDP. The World Bank responded to these countries' difficulties by initiating Structural Adjustment Lending (SAL):

> to provide maximum support, within the staff and financial levels available to the Bank and within its mandate, to those governments that had requested such support and that had recognized the need to formulate and introduce, as a matter of urgency, a set of comprehensive measures designed to adjust the structure of productive activities of their economies to the markedly deteriorated external condition. (World Bank 1982, p. 39)

---

11. These include Bolivia, the Democratic Republic of the Congo, Côte d'Ivoire, Guyana, Honduras, Kenya, Madagascar, Malawi, Mauritania, Myanmar, Nicaragua, Niger, Senegal, Sierra Leone, Sudan, Tanzania and Zambia. Others, such as Guinea, may also have met similar debt-service payment levels, but this cannot be ascertained from the available data.

Not surprisingly, the current group of HIPCs have been the predominant users of this facility, as well as the IMF's Structural Adjustment and Enhanced Structural Adjustment Facilities (SAF/ESAF), which came on stream in 1986 and 1987, respectively. In fact, between 1980 and the end of 1991, these countries agreed to an average of about six IMF stabilization or IMF/World Bank structural adjustment programs each, covering an overall period of 6.4 years.[12] Similarly, they account for 54 of the 68 SAF/ESAF arrangements approved by the IMF up to December 1994. By contrast, the sample of selected non-HIPCs only agreed to 2.4 programs per country, covering a total of 2.4 years between 1980 and 1991, and only 10 SAF/ESAF programs among the 9 eligible countries in that group.

However, the policies and actions promoted by stabilization and adjustment programs (notably fiscal austerity, export promotion, debt restructuring and new financing) clearly presumed that these countries faced a liquidity crisis rather than a debt overhang. That presumption, which was maintained even in the face of mounting evidence to the contrary, meant that the desired new internal and external equilibria that these programs hoped to re-establish were, in most cases, out of reach. That inherent flaw in program design (the absence of debt reduction as an option in or adjunct to these programs) also meant that debtor governments and other economic agents who stood to gain little from these programs had little incentive to cooperate. With an unsustainable debt-service burden, fiscal austerity simply exaggerated the negative budgetary effects mentioned above. Gains from export promotion stood to be absorbed by impossibly high debt-service obligations, and debt restructuring and new financing would only have made the future even less attractive than the present.

Even if one is unwilling to concede that fundamental shortcoming in the design of adjustment programs at first glance, the failure of these programs to induce the desired turnaround in those economies provides ample evidence to that effect. While the two-decade long slide in the terms of trade is a ready target for blame, two peculiarities of that experience need to be highlighted. The first is the nearly unanimous finding of empirical studies that stabilization and adjustment programs have generally elicited a negative investment response (see, for example, Khan 1990; Corbo and Rojas 1992; Elbadawi 1992; Bird 1995; and Killick 1995). While that association has sometimes been attributed to a reduction in wasteful investment (increased efficiency), that

---

12. Programs were often concurrent, which explains the near equality between the number of programs and the number of years under adjustment.

Figure 2.   Evolution of debt, arrears, and debt reduction for HIPC countries, 1980-1998

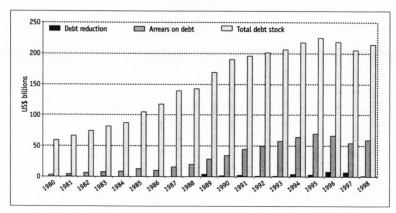

argument is at odds with the fact that the funding for most investment in developing countries comes from retained earnings, and the marginal return on investment in most of these countries was, and remains, high. The second peculiarity is the fact that the debt profiles of these countries did not improve with successive programs. In fact, as figure 2 indicates, the debt profile of these countries, as a group, has worsened over time. These programs may therefore have brought a temporary respite from the resource crunch these countries faced, but they did so at the cost of a worsening, rather than improving, debt profile. In fact, some countries that began the 1980s with modest debt loads, notably Ghana, ended the century as an HIPC.

The non-responsiveness of investment (particularly private investment) to adjustment programs clearly lends support to the view that private agents were unwilling to amend their investment behaviour because the fundamental source of present and future instability – an unsustainable debt burden – was not being adequately addressed. The problems of incompetence and corruption aside, debtor governments too, had little incentive to implement program-related policies, particularly if they involved political costs, because the net benefit, in terms of new revenues and foreign exchange earnings, was likely to be quickly absorbed by debt-service obligations.[13]

---

13. See Krugman (1998) for a theoretical exposition of this disincentive effect.

Figure 3. Market-based debt conversions, 1985-1994

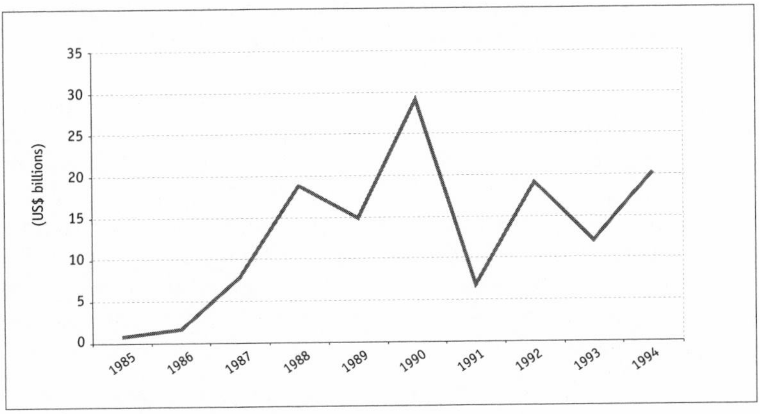

Source: World Bank, *World Debt Tables, 1996.*

With the Mexican threat of default in 1982, the systemic threat posed by the heavy debt loads of several large middle-income countries (such as Mexico, Brazil and Argentina) became obvious – the MBA debt crisis was official. This lent new urgency to the problem of indebtedness, but that sense of urgency, unfortunately, was extended almost exclusively to the problems of middle-income countries. Nevertheless, the presumption that developing countries merely faced liquidity crises, rather than debt-overhang problems, remained. The middle-income countries too were presented only with the adjustment option.

However, two fundamental attributes of the debts of middle-income countries led to a speedier attempt at a long-term solution to their problem:

- Most of these countries' debts were owed to private commercial banks.
- The size of these countries' debts, and the number of financial institutions affected, meant that mass default would have undermined several large financial institutions and compromised the financial and economic health of most developed economies.

The ownership of the debt by private institutions allowed for the development of a secondary market in the privately owned debt of developing countries. This factor played a crucial role in ending the fiction of a liquidity crisis. When the secondary market prices of the heavily indebted countries (middle-income and poor) fell well below their face value, it signalled irrevocably that economic agents did not expect full repayment of these countries' debts. For example, the secondary market prices for Argentinean debt reached 29 cents on the dollar in 1988 and for Brazilian debt was 46.5 cents in 1987 (UN 1990). In effect, the market emphatically established that it viewed these countries' debt problem as one of a debt overhang.

The systemic importance of middle-income countries lent some urgency to the resolution of the problem (in the context of privately owned debt) because the very existence of an unresolved debt problem put the health of the world economy at risk. Thus, by the beginning of the 1990s, most of the middle-income countries were able to exit from the crushing debt burdens that threatened to curtail growth and human development, though not necessarily from heavy debt burdens altogether (figure 3). Conversely, the HIPCs ended the 1980s quite a bit worse off than they had began the decade, as debt relief came in dribs and drabs.

B.   THE EVOLUTION OF DEBT-RELIEF MECHANISMS: FROM THE TORONTO TERMS TO THE ENHANCED HIPC

As already suggested, the creditor community was slow to acknowledge the debt overhang situation in the poorest countries.[14] Certainly, structural adjustment, as it evolved through the SAL, SAF and ESAF arrangements, offered more generous terms on new lending (longer grace and repayment periods and lower interest rates) but no net reduction in debt. The Special Program of Assistance for Africa (SPA) attempted quicker, more generous, and more coordinated action from donors, for African countries in crisis, but although it later incorporated debt reduction (Paris Club) as an option, debt reduction was not originally seen as an immediate need. Bilateral lending also evolved, as OECD countries increased the degree of concessionality of their

---

14. Countries that face temporary problems in servicing their debt and countries that have little hope, given expected states of the world, of repaying their debts differ significantly. The former face a liquidity crisis; the latter, a debt-overhang problem. Taking Krugman's (1998) critique of the concept into consideration, a country can be considered to be suffering from a liquidity crisis when a strong probability remains that the country, given some economic policy reform, temporary assistance, and debt restructuring, will be able to generate future outflows sufficient to pay its debts. (The degree to which debtors are willing to provide new money in this circumstance will depend on several factors including their degree of risk aversion). However, when a country faces a debt-overhang problem, no amount of that medicine will (by itself) make the debt repayable. In fact, failure to reduce the debt to manageable levels will probably make matters worse by creating a net disincentive effect for concerted action on the part of the debtor. In this case, some combination of debt reduction, new financing and restructuring is likely to imply a smaller loss on outlays than any alternative approach.

ODA (several OECD countries, including Canada, had moved to 100% grant aid by the mid-1980s), but the stock of debt continued to grow, and arrears climbed with it (figure 2). However, the continued failure of adjustment could not be ignored forever.

The first major initiative to provide a formal framework for significant debt reduction came from the Paris Club of creditors. In 1988, after some lobbying by Britain (Evans 1999), the Paris Club introduced the "Toronto terms" as a framework for dealing with the debt problems of low-income countries. This new initiative offered three options for creditors in dealing with appeals for debt relief:

Option A: Partial debt write-off. Cancel one third of debt service falling due during the consolidation period and reschedule the remaining two thirds at market interest rates over 14 years with an 8-year grace period.

Option B: Pure rescheduling. Reschedule debt service falling due during the consolidation period at market interest rates over 25 years with a 14-year grace period.

Option C: Implicit debt write-down. Reschedule debt service falling due during the consolidation period at reduced interest rates (3.5% or one-half market rates, whichever was lower) over 14 years with an 8-year grace period (Sevigny 1990).

In its acceptance of the debt-reduction option – and thus, implicitly, the possibility of a debt-overhang in some of these countries – this initiative broke new ground. The actual amount of debt relief offered, however, was marginal relative to the total debt of these countries. Paris Club debt relief (rescheduling and/or reduction) was provided only on debt service falling due within a particular "consolidation period," usually covering no more than 18 months. Further, that debt relief was provided on debt incurred before a particular cut-off date, which was usually set one year before the country's first rescheduling agreement with the Paris Club. In effect, debt relief was provided on *part* of debt service falling due during a *limited* period of time. This rather narrow framework for debt relief appears to presuppose debt relief aimed at alleviating a temporary financing gap (i.e. a liquidity crisis) rather than the long-term debt-servicing problem implied by a debt overhang. Within such a restricted framework, 33% debt reduction could translate into a less than 1% decrease in the stock of outstanding debt, depending on the structure of the country's debt.

The inadequacy of this level of debt reduction soon became quite obvious as the HIPCs' debt burdens continued to increase, arrears continued to accumulate, and per capita growth remained negative on average (tables 3 and 4, and figure 1). In the succeeding years, the Paris Club increased the generosity of the provisions on offer to heavily indebted countries with the "London terms" of 1991, and the "Naples terms" of 1994. By then, the debt relief on offer had risen to a maximum of 67% reduction on eligible debt (Boote and Thugge 1999), but these enhancements did not solve the debt-overhang problem. In fact, besides the continued build-up of arrears, several countries became repeat visitors to the Paris Club, expending inordinate amounts of resources in the related negotiations without any sign of a permanent resolution to their ongoing debt-related difficulties. Bolivia, for example, had four Paris Club agreements between 1988 and 1995, but its ratio of scheduled debt service to exports was still 23% and its ratio of debt stock to exports, 387% in 1996.

The Paris Club's rather grudging approach to debt relief can be attributed to four factors. The first is the burden-sharing problem. Although the existence of the organization itself was meant to overcome that problem, its reliance on consensus meant that the degree to which it could adjust its position on debt relief was determined by the degree to which it could obtain agreement from all members. As Evans (1999) points out, its most powerful member, the United States, was slow to be convinced of the merits of debt reduction; hence, progress depended on the degree to which its leadership could be convinced to set its objections aside. The second factor relates to the fact that debt relief had direct budgetary implications at a time when most countries were attempting to reduce budgetary expenditures. This problem can be viewed as the political parallel to the commercial bank's need to make provisions for the expected losses on sovereign debt in the 1980s. Creditor governments felt a need to put their financial houses in order before they could justify large outlays for erasing the debt of other countries. The issue is not so much the necessity of that prerequisite as the degree to which it was felt to be important for ensuring the support of political shareholders. The third factor relates to the varying debt-reduction procedures in different countries. While some export credit agencies had long begun to make provisions against bad debts, and expected to be compensated at less than the face value of debt owed, others had either not done so or still expected full compensation.[15]

---

15. Making provisions for impaired loans (or loans that are not properly serviced) is an established accounting procedure that involves the institutions setting aside balances that bridge the gap between the face value of the loan and its (now lower) anticipated repayment (or market) value. Debt forgiveness, therefore, means a direct accounting loss only on the anticipated repayment value of the loan rather than on the face value.

Thus, for the creditor governments, the perceived budgetary cost of debt reduction (per dollar of debt forgiven) varied significantly. This difference in financial practices, together with the budgetary implications mentioned previously, tended to make those creditor governments who saw debt relief as a one-to-one budgetary cost more cautious about substantial debt reduction and others less so (Evans 1999). The fourth factor was the attractiveness of the leverage provided by chronic indebtedness. While repeated adjustment and regular visits to the Paris Club may have been vexing for HIPCs, it provided creditor countries with a ready opportunity (directly and through international financial institutions) to influence policy choices in HIPCs whose policy records were seen as indicators of misguided or incompetent management (Evans 1999). In this context, debt reduction was erroneously perceived as implying an end to this leverage.[16] Given this context, the economic logic of debt reduction was secondary to the political considerations and diplomatic niceties necessary in achieving a consensus.

The second major initiative to propose debt reduction was the "Brady Plan," announced in March 1989 by US treasury secretary, Nicholas Brady.[17] The Brady Plan enjoined commercial banks to work with developing countries and make use of a "menu of options" that included debt swaps, debt-for-equity conversions, and refinancing to reduce the total debt of these countries. Further, IMF and World Bank resources could be used to facilitate these transactions. The IMF also no longer had to make its adjustment programs contingent on a country's prior agreement with its creditors – effectively reducing the bargaining power of the commercial banks and increasing the potential for significant debt-reduction operations.

This debt-relief plan had major implications for middle-income countries such as Mexico, Brazil, Argentina, Costa Rica and Chile, whose debts were owed predominantly to private commercial banks. One fundamental difference between the Brady Plan approach and the Paris Club approach was that the Brady plan presupposed a debt overhang, and thus, the options on offer allowed for substantial reduction of the debt stock (the amount to be dictated largely by the market perceptions of the countries' capacity to repay). However, as table 5 suggests, it had limited potential for providing a dramatic

---

16. That perception was erroneous because these countries are so heavily dependent on concessional (aid) flows that they will be vulnerable to a significant degree of external influence on their development policies for a very long time.

17. Though the Baker Plan, by endorsing the "menu of options" approach in 1987, included the potential for debt reduction, that potential was not emphasized and was more of an afterthought than an area of explicit focus.

Table 6. Some Brady-Plan related transactions, 1990-1994

Country	Year	Eligible debt (US$ billions)	Reduction equivalent (US$ billions)	Percentage reduction
Mexico	1990	47.17	14.15	30.0
Costa Rica	1990	6.60	2.38	36.1
Philippines	1990	1.61	0.98	60.9
Venezuela	1990	19.01	3.76	19.8
Bulgaria	1993	6.80	3.40	50.0
Argentina	1993	29.34	8.43	28.7
Brazil	1994	50.00	14.00	28.0

Source: Bowe and Dean (1997, table 2, p. 13); World Bank, *Global Development Finance 2000*.

Figure 4. Evolution of debt stock/GNP ratios for HIPCs and some middle-income countries

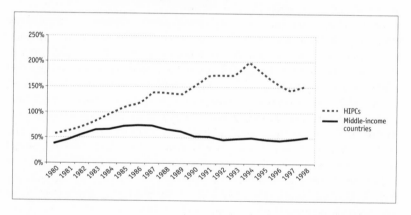

exit from the debt overhang for low-income countries because these countries' debts to private institutions had never been substantial. Nevertheless, poor countries have taken advantage of that initiative through the International Development Association's (IDA's) Debt-Reduction Facility, established in 1989. That facility provides grants to IDA-eligible countries for debt buyback operations on the privately held, public or public-guaranteed debt of lower-income countries. By 1999, 17 countries, 16 of them HIPCs, were able to take advantage of that facility to reduce their privately held debt to relatively insignificant amounts (IDA 1999).

While it cannot be said with certainty that the Brady Plan debt reductions were sufficient to remove the debt overhang of middle-income countries (it can be argued, for example, that Ecuador's failure to meet its Brady bond obligations in 1999 provided evidence that they were overpriced), it certainly was instrumental in accelerating a fairly rapid decline in the average debt-to-GNP ratios of these countries from the late 1980s to the late 1990s (figure 4), as well as a general improvement in their economic performance (Berry and Serieux 2001). However, for the HIPCs, the combined offerings of the Paris Club initiatives and the Brady Plan were insufficient to halt the increase in debt-burden indicators. The debt-related fortunes of these two groups of countries sharply diverged after 1988 (table 6 and figure 4).

The third major debt-reduction initiative, the HIPC Initiative, jointly launched by the World Bank and the IMF in 1996, sought to extend debt reduction to multilateral debt, which had previously been covered under neither Paris Club debt relief nor the Brady Plan but which had been steadily rising as a proportion of the total debt of these countries because of the financing of unsuccessful attempts at adjustment (table 5). At first, that initiative offered debt-relief consideration to poor countries (IDA-eligible) whose debt was considered to be unsustainable even after Paris Club debt-relief terms (or better) were applied to all debt other than multilateral debt.[18] Sustainable debt in that context meant a net present value (NPV) of debt-to-export ratio below or in the 200-250% range, and a debt-service-to-exports ratio not above the 20-25% range (the choice of an exact amount within those ranges was determined on a case-by-case basis).[19] Alternatively, open economies with a strong fiscal stance (countries with an export-to-GDP ratio of at least 40% and fiscal revenue-to-GDP of at least 20%) could be judged according to the "fiscal criteria," which defined sustainability as an NPV of debt-to-fiscal revenue of 280% or less (IMF 1999).

A country became eligible for the level of debt forgiveness necessary to attain debt sustainability (i.e. it arrived at the decision point) when it had gone

---

18. "IDA-eligible" means that the country is a member of the IDA of the World Bank Group and borrows mostly from that institution rather than the International Bank for Reconstruction and Development (IBRD). Its low per capita income level (usually below US$895), and generally limited level of economic development, means that it is not sufficiently credit-worthy to borrow on international capital markets.

19. NPV is determined by discounting the future stream of debt payments at a market interest rate.

through three years of structural adjustment and could not attain a sustainable debt level using traditional debt-relief mechanisms.[20] Debt relief, if required, was provided after a further three years of adjustment (the completion point). Debt forgiveness beyond Paris Club terms was to be distributed proportionally across all creditors. However, debts owed to the IMF and the World Bank would not be written off directly. Instead, these were to be paid off on behalf of the relevant country out of the ESAF facility and the HIPC trust fund, respectively (IMF 1999).[21]

While the HIPC Initiative of 1996 substantially increased the debt reduction potentially available to HIPCs, the structure of the debt-relief process – its insistence on three years of adjustment before debt relief could be considered, its insistence on traditional debt relief ahead of HIPC Initiative consideration, and three more years of adjustment before debt relief would become available — seemed to suggest that the creditor countries continued to give greater importance to the leverage provided by HIPCs' circumstances, than the essential impossibility of meaningful economic restructuring and long-term improvements in performance in the face of continuing debt-overhang conditions. Debt relief under this initiative would be considered only after it was clear, after the country's best efforts at adjustment and traditional debt relief, that it indeed faced a debt overhang and not a liquidity crisis. In short, the program retained the general tone of the Paris Club process – the presumption of the best-case scenario unless otherwise demonstrated beyond dispute, and an awful laxity about time. Given the profile of these countries (high debt ratios, negative per capita growth, slowed levels of human development, etc.) after a full 15 years of structural adjustment and 8 years of Paris Club efforts at incremental debt relief, the persistence of this approach was astonishing.

The incredibility of that perspective was not lost on civil-society and religious organizations in the North, who organized campaigns through the Jubilee 2000, Eurodad, and others, to push for more significant and more immediate debt relief for the poorest countries. The campaign succeeded in breaking the deadlock that had delayed substantial debt reduction for the

---

20. Traditional debt-relief mechanisms involve Paris Club terms or better on all bilateral and commercial debt (facilitated by IDA debt-reduction operations on commercial debt), some forgiveness of ODA debt, and new financing on appropriate concessional terms.

21. Although the regional development banks also avail themselves of the trust fund facility, the arrangement is not as formalized.

poorest countries through the Cologne Initiative of 1999 that offered more generous Paris Club debt relief and called for a revision of the HIPC Initiative.

At the World Bank and IMF annual meetings in September 1999, the Enhanced HIPC Initiative replaced the HIPC Initiative. This new initiative, flowing from the recommendations of the Cologne summit of the G8, offered a more generous interpretation of debt sustainability and formally linked debt reduction with poverty reduction. A sustainable debt level was now defined as an NPV of debt-to-export ratio of 150% or less. Eligibility for the fiscal criteria would require an export-to-GDP ratio of 30% or more, and a government revenue-to-GDP ratio of at least 15%. Under those criteria, sustainability was defined as an NPV of debt-to-revenue ratio of no more than 250%. In addition, the time between the decision point (when eligibility for additional debt relief, beyond traditional debt relief, was determined) and the completion point (when debt relief would be guaranteed) was to have no fixed time frame. Interim debt relief would be delivered between the decision and completion points. Countries that had gone through the original HIPC Initiative debt-reduction procedures retained eligibility for the Enhanced HIPC debt-reduction procedures. Also, debt relief under the Enhanced HIPC Initiative was to be conditional on the development of a poverty reduction strategy by the debtor country.

The Enhanced HIPC Initiative proved far more successful in bringing countries on stream than the previous HIPC Initiative. Despite its three-year existence before being replaced by the Enhanced HIPC Initiative, the original HIPC Initiative managed to provide debt relief to only 4 out of 41 potentially eligible countries. By comparison, after only 15 months of operation, 22 countries had reached the decision point under the new initiative with average expected debt-reduction rates of 50% of the NPV.

As will be shown in the next section, the adequacy of the Enhanced HIPC Initiative in terms of its ability to fully eliminate the debt overhang is not assured. Nevertheless, together with Paris Club debt relief (under Cologne terms), it offers a substantial reduction in outstanding debt. But this debt reduction will come more than a decade after the middle-income countries obtained similar levels of debt reduction under the Brady Plan, although, as the data clearly shows, these countries were, even then, just as heavily indebted as the middle-income countries. Why the decade-long delay? As has already been suggested, the answer can be attributed to two fundamental differences between the two sets of countries:

- The relative systemic irrelevance of the HIPC countries (i.e. the state of their economies and financial systems had very little effect on the world economy).
- The predominant public ownership of HIPC debt.

Both private and public creditors denied the existence of a debt overhang (and not merely a liquidity crisis) when the first sign of debt difficulties in the 1980s became evident. However, private creditors quickly made provisions for the increasing numbers of impaired loans on their portfolios. With a few exceptions, public creditors did not (Evans 1999). Thus, when the secondary market for debt signalled uncontrovertibly that (at least in the view of third parties) the countries faced a debt overhang, these institutions were ready and able to contemplate debt reduction. All that was needed was the structure provided by the Brady Plan and the institutional oversight of the IMF to overcome the burden-sharing problem that generally inhibits such action.[22]

Public creditors generally did not make provisions for impaired loans (or, as in the case of Canada's Export Development Corporation, did, but were happy to receive 100% restitution on forgiven debt from their government). Thus, to most creditor governments, forgiving even unserviced debt was associated with a higher direct cost than it was for private institutions, hence the greater reluctance to contemplate debt reduction.

The absence of a secondary market for the debt owned by public institutions meant that there was no emphatic signal from third parties in the late 1980s (as there was from private institutions) that forced abandonment of the liquidity constraint argument. While the high debt ratios, negative per capita growth, low investment, and poor human development records may seem to have been more than adequate signals that these countries faced a debt overhang, superficially credible arguments could be made that explained each one of these indicators individually outside the context of the heavy debt burden (as was indeed done). In any case, it was always credible to blame these countries' performances on the poor policy choices, corruption, and economic

---

22. The burden-sharing problem refers to the fact that in a situation where it is known (or at least highly likely) that the debtor will be unable to repay all of its debts, there is a strong incentive for a single institution to "free ride" by allowing others to forgive all or part of their claim first. This is because, with some of its debt forgiven, the debtor will be able to pay a larger proportion of the remaining debt owed to those institutions that have not reduced their claims (i.e. the first mover gets the worst deal). In such a situation, the burden can only be fairly distributed if all creditors move together, usually under the auspices of a third party. In the national economy, this role is generally played by a bankruptcy court for non-financial institutions and by the central bank for financial institutions.

mismanagement of the debtor governments even though this misses the point altogether.[23]

It is no accident that debt reduction for poor countries only made substantial progress after civil-society organizations, through the Jubilee 2000 and other campaigns, lobbied creditor governments for substantial (if not complete) debt forgiveness for poor countries. These campaigns served the same purpose for public creditors as the secondary market did for private creditors. They provided an unambiguous signal, from a third but economically interested party, that these countries were not expected to fully repay their debts. It effectively put an end to the denial that had led to the niggling approach to debt relief practised by the Paris Club and the international financial institutions.

It is also no accident that these governments were open to those arguments at the time (the late 1990s). They had succeeded in "putting their fiscal houses in order" and had therefore made the necessary political provisions for extending large outlays for debt relief.

While the NGO campaigns succeeded in eliciting action on the part of creditor governments, and the reappearance of fiscal surpluses muted objection to new spending on debt reduction, the burden-sharing problem faced by these governments has not been entirely eliminated. Even at its inception, the funding for the Enhanced HIPC Initiative was incomplete and uncertain, and it has remained so throughout its implementation because governments have failed to agree on precisely how to share the burden of debt relief. The IMF and World Bank, although they have played a crucial role in managing the program and in providing the basis for revisions, lack both the distance and authority they had when faced with private creditors. The creditor governments after all, govern them (de facto if not de jure). If, as is distinctly possible, debt relief as provided under the Enhanced HIPC Initiative, is still insufficient to eliminate the debt overhang, the burden-sharing problem will be the most obvious explanation for that failure.

C.   THE SIZE OF THE DEBT OVERHANG

Just as no simple economic technique exists to determine when a country faces a debt overhang (on this the market has proved far more persuasive than economic models), no simple way exists to determine the size of the debt

---

23. In the same way that what leads a firm to bankruptcy is not a factor in determining whether it is bankrupt or not, whether a country is facing a debt overhang or not cannot be determined by how it got there. That may be a factor in what should be done after debt reduction but not whether debt reduction should occur.

overhang (i.e. that portion of the debt for which there should be no reasonable expectation of repayment). This is further complicated by the fact that what constitutes "unrepayable" debt is related to how the "cost" of debt repayment is defined . In strict economic terms, any part of a country's debt that its government has the desire and ability to pay is not part of the debt overhang. Thus, if the debt can be repaid before any implicit developmental costs can have any effect on the country's repayment capacity, and if the government is willing to do so, then a debt overhang does not exist.

However, if the creditor also takes some responsibility for the growth and other developmental costs of debt repayment, debt-repayment levels beyond the point at which a developmental cost is incurred would have to be considered unacceptable. In this situation, a debt overhang can be said to exist once the country has exceeded its capacity to repay its debts without a net developmental cost.[24] The creditor governments, by embracing the DAC's commitments in "Shaping the 21st Century" (OECD 1996), and reasserting them in the OECD's Progress Towards the International Development Goals (OECD 2000) and the Millennium Declaration of 2000 (UN 2000) have essentially embraced the latter definition of a debt overhang. In this context, debt relief must go beyond mere considerations of repayment capacity, it must address the need for resources to ensure growth and human development comparable to that of less-indebted countries.

Therefore, taking poverty reduction (with growth) as the relevant framework, one can readily think of two benchmarks that can help determine a minimum level of debt relief:
- the level of repayment sustained under the debt overhang;
- the discount rate on private debt;

These benchmarks are considered below.

1.   *The level of debt repayment sustained under the debt overhang.*

As table 7 indicates, the HIPCs as a group met (on average) only slightly more than 40% of their scheduled debt-service payments from 1990 to 1994. This occurred even as these countries received significant amounts of concessional resource flows and underwent various degrees of "adjustment." A clear argument can be made that this represents (at the very least) the upper limit of the

---

24. Of course, that issue is complicated by the quality of governance factor – less efficient governments induce a developmental cost earlier than more efficient ones – but the principle applies nonetheless.

Table 7.   Debt servicing ratios

Year	Average ratio of scheduled debt service to GNP	Average ratio of actual debt service to GNP	Average proportion of debt paid*
	(unweighted average)	(unweighted average)	(unweighted average)
1990	17.6	4.1	47.7
1991	15.6	5.0	47.4
1992	19.2	4.9	40.8
1993	16.2	4.6	42.8
1994	17.6	6.2	43.6

* The apparent mismatch between this ratio and the implied ratio from the two previous columns stems from the fact that those countries, whose scheduled service was low relative to GNP, tended to have high repayment rates while those with high ratios relative to GNP had low repayment rates. This is therefore an average of two extremes.
Sources: IMF, "Debt relief for low-income countries: the HIPC Initiative," *IMF Pamphlet Series No. 51*, 1997.

net debt outflows that these countries could bear, given the economic situation.[25] A lower-bound interpretation of the debt overhang can, therefore, be "that part of the debt that requires debt-service payments above the average levels achieved by these countries." Roughly, taking past levels to be 40% of scheduled payments and assuming a one-to-one relationship between debt-service levels and the debt stock (and ignoring the time line of the debt), the overhang would constitute approximately 60% of the debt stock at that time.

However, if the size of the debt overhang is related to the development cost of the debt then, since, as demonstrated above, most countries were incurring a development cost even at these levels of debt servicing, the debt overhang would have to be estimated at significantly more than 60% of the total debt.

2.   The discount rate on private debt

Although the proportion of HIPCs' total debt owed to private commercial banks has always been relatively small, many of these countries carried some commercial bank debts at relatively high interest rates. The IDA Debt Reduction Facility has been used to help these countries deal with that portion of their debt stock by providing funds for the buyback of much of that debt on the secondary market, Brady Plan style. One can argue that the price of these countries' debt on the secondary market is the market's "rational" assessment

---

25. While it is true that some countries, having concluded that debt relief was inevitable, would have made less than a total effort to meet debt-service payments, it is equally (if not more) likely that several countries were making higher debt-service payments than were fiscally prudent for fear of alienating future creditors.

of the proportion of the debt the country would have reasonably been expected to repay."[26] In other words, the implied discount on the secondary market indicates the part of the debt that the private market, unhindered by humanitarian considerations, treats as a debt overhang and is willing to forgive.[27]

The average value of the private debt of the HIPCs that have used the IDA Debt Reduction Facility on the secondary market was 15 cents on the dollar.[28] This represents a discount, or level of debt forgiveness, of 85%, implying a debt overhang of 85% of total debt. Thus, if public entities were subject to the discipline of the secondary markets as commercial banks are, they would likely have had to contemplate a similar level of forgiveness. However, even this level of debt relief does not take into account the development costs of the debt overhang. It is therefore possible that, given that consideration, an even higher proportion of the debt would have been considered excessive.

In reality, the Enhanced HIPC Initiative, when added to traditional debt relief mechanisms and other debt relief, expects a reduction in the 1999-net present value of the total debt of the 22 HIPCs that reached their decision point, before 2001, from US$53 billion to US$20 billion. This implies an average forgiveness rate of 62.2%. This level of debt reduction would meet the first criteria mentioned above but only if the development cost of the debt burden is not considered. In other words, it would just exceed past average debt-service efforts. However, this level of debt relief is well below the levels offered by private creditors. Further, if these countries are faced with another downturn in the prices of their exports or a large change in import prices (particularly oil prices), even the lower proposed post debt forgiveness levels of debt relief may prove deleterious to present and future development.

CONCLUSION

The Enhanced HIPC Initiative of 1999 represents a breakthrough in debt relief for the poorest countries not simply because it offers more debt relief more

---

26. The word "rational" is used here in the spirit of rational expectations, which argues that the unhindered private economic agents will on average use available information optimally in making judgements about the likely movements of economic variables.

27. It should of course be noted that the private market's position is colored by the fact that this debt is de facto (and in the case of the IMF, de jure) junior to the multilateral debt. This reduces its value further because it is anticipated that this debt would be paid only after the multilateral institutions' debt had been paid.

28. Calculated from data provided by the World Bank's Global Development Finance 1999.

quickly than any other initiative before it, but also because it is the first debt-reduction initiative that, at least implicitly, acknowledges that the debt over-hang problem faced by HIPCs is substantial and needs to be addressed with alacrity. But that description would have applied just as well to these countries 15 years ago. Why was this acknowledgement so long in coming? This paper contends that despite the fact that economic indicators clearly suggested that most of these countries, as well as several middle-income countries, were grossly over-indebted since the mid-1980s, these poor countries have had to wait a decade longer than the middle-income countries for substantial debt relief. That delay can be attributed to two factors: the public ownership of these countries' debts, and the relative systemic insignificance of these coun-tries. The public ownership of their debts meant that creditors were not subject to the discipline of secondary markets and could therefore maintain the fiction of a liquidity crisis for much longer than private creditors could. The second factor meant that, despite the heavy price in terms of human and economic development paid by these countries' populations over time, credi-tors could continue to attempt an incremental approach to debt relief because the cost to the world economy (of the time lost) was negligible. It is no acci-dent that the Enhanced HIPC Initiative came into being only after the spirited campaigns for debt relief by international (and national) civil-society organi-zations and the success of deficit-fighting in creditor countries. Indeed, civil-society campaigners played a role similar to that played by buyers on the secondary market for the sovereign debt held by commercial banks in the 1980s – as a third, but economically and politically relevant party, they sig-nalled emphatically that they did not consider most of these countries' debt to be repayable. In short, they forced an end to a decade-and-a-half long stale-mate over debt relief for the poorest countries. At that time governments were also more amenable to these calls than they would have been earlier because they had effectively made political provisions for the implied losses on their balance sheets by removing or reducing fiscal deficits.

The delay in the provision of substantial debt reduction has been costly for HIPCs. Comparison with a group of less-indebted countries at comparable income levels in 1975 (referred to as the non-HIPCs) clearly indicates that these countries spent less on social expenditure (at least on education and health) and capital expenditure, saved less, and invested less. The result was negative per capita growth (on average) through the 1980s and into the early part of the 1990s, compared to positive growth for the non-HIPCs. Though human development indicators have generally not regressed for the HIPCs, they have improved much more slowly than those of countries at similar levels in the 1970s. In short, these countries have lagged behind other developing countries on almost all measures of human and economic development. They have also regressed economically relative to the developed countries, with average per capita incomes relative to those of the high-income OECD countries falling from just below 10% in the late 1970s to just over 5% in the later 1990s. By comparison, the non-HIPCs have kept pace with the developed countries.

Despite the generous debt-reduction terms offered, the Enhanced HIPC Initiative may still prove inadequate. By several explicit gestures, including their insistence that the dividend for debt reduction be used exclusively for poverty reduction, public creditors have made the restoration of human and economic development in those countries the objective of debt relief. However, substantial progress on that front would need more than simply bringing debt levels down to reasonable service-payment levels. It would require sufficient net resource transfers to generate a substantial increase in social spending and investment in those countries. While the expected average reductions in the stock of debt suggests that scheduled debt-service levels will decline substantially in most countries, it does not suggest that the net reduction in resource transfers (the debt-relief dividend) will be substantial. It is likely to take a substantial increase in other resource flows, or more debt relief, to provide that added boost to poverty-reduction spending.

The Enhanced HIPC Initiative, like past debt-reduction initiatives, abstracts from the wider systemic issues related to the flow of credit to poor countries. It should not go unnoticed that the 41 HIPCs represent most least-developed countries and a majority of low-income countries. Most of these countries, even at their best, were never able to match the high debt-service ratios that their middle-income counterparts achieved in the mid-1980s, meaning that a debt overhang arrived much earlier for them. The evidence also suggests that a decline in these countries' terms of trade was the single most important factor in inducing a debt overhang situation. These factors clearly suggest that these countries have very limited debt-carrying capacities and are more vulnerable to external conditions. Thus, issues regarding the nature and extent of the debt these countries can carry, and methods of addressing their vulnerability, are vital but have yet to be substantially addressed by any program to date and still need to be more thoroughly researched. Yet, unless these issues are addressed in short order, the odds in favour of future debt crises will remain quite high.

REFERENCES

Barro, R. J., "Economic Growth in a Cross-Section of Countries," *Quarterly Journal of Economics*, 106, 2, 1991.

Berry, A. and J. Serieux, "Convergence, Divergence or Novergence? Recent Trends in World Income Distribution, 1980-1996," unpublished, 2001.

Bird, G., *IMF Lending to Developing Countries: Issues and Evidence*, London and New York, Routledge, 1995.

Bird, R., *Taxation and Economic Development*, Baltimore and London, John Hopkins University Press, 1990.

Boote, A. R. and K. Thugge, *Debt Relief for Low-Income Countries: The HIPC Initiative*, Washington, D.C., IMF Pamphlet Series, 51, 1999.

Bowe, M. and J. Dean, "Has the Market Solved the Sovereign-Debt Crisis?" *Princeton Studies in International Finance*, 83, August 1997.

Carciofi, R. and O. Cetrángolo, "Tax Reforms and Equity in Latin America: A Review of the 1980s and Proposals for the 1990s," Innocenti Occasional Papers, Economic Policy Series, 39, UNICEF, 1994.

Cohen, D., "Low Investment and Large LDC Debt in the 1980s," *American Economic Review*, 83, 1993, p. 437-449.

Cornia, G. A., "Macroeconomic Policy, Poverty Alleviation and Long-Term Development: Latin America in the 1990s," Innocenti Occasional Papers, Economic Policy Series, 40, UNICEF, 1994.

Deshpande, A., "The Debt Overhang and the Disincentive to Invest," *Journal of Development Economics*, 52, 1995, p. 169-187.

DAC/OECD, *Shaping the 21st Century: The Contribution of Development Cooperation*, Paris, DAC/OECD, 1996.

Ebel, B., "Patterns of Government Expenditure in Developing Countries During the 1980s: The Impact on Social Services," Innocenti Occasional Papers, Economic Policy Series, 18, UNICEF, 1991.

Elbadawi, I., "Have World Bank-Supported Adjustment Programs Improved Economic Performance in Sub-Saharan Africa?" World Bank Working Paper Series, 1001, World Bank, 1992.

Evans, H., "Debt Relief for the Poorest Countries: Why Did it Take so Long?" *Development Policy Review*, 17, 1999, p. 267-279.

Fry, M. J., "Foreign Debt Instability: An Analysis of National Saving and Domestic Investment Responses to Foreign Debt Accumulation in 28 Countries," *Journal of International Money and Finance*, 8, 1989, p. 315-344.

Grossman, G. M., and E. Helpman, *Innovation and Growth in the Global Economy*, Cambridge, MIT Press, 1991.

IMF, *The ESAF at Ten Years: Economic Adjustment and Reform in Low Income Countries*, Washington, D.C., IMF, 1997.

____, "Debt Relief for Low-Income Countries: The HIPC Initiative," IMF Pamphlet Series, 51, Washington, D.C., IMF, 1999.

Khan, M. S., "The Macroeconomic Effects of Fund-Supported Adjustment Programs," IMF Staff papers, 37, 2, June 1990.

Killick, T., *IMF Programmes in Developing Countries: Design and Impact*, London and New York, Routledge, 1995.

Krugman, P. R., *Currencies and Crises*, Cambridge, Massachusetts, MIT Press, 1998.

Manuelli, A., "Tax Reform and Equity in Asia: The Experience of the 1980s," Innocenti Occasional Papers, Economic Policy Series, 42, UNICEF, 1994.

Mankiw, N. G., D. Romer and D. N. Weil, "A Contribution to the Empirics of Economic Growth," *Quarterly Journal of Economics*, 107, 2, May 1992.

OECD, *Progress Towards the International Development Goals*, Paris, OECD, 2000.

Reimers, F., "The Impact of the Debt Crisis on Education in Latin America: Implications for Education Planning," *Prospects*, 20, 4, 1990, p. 539-554.

Rivero, C. C., R. L. Ascencio, J. Q. Vinagre, "The Impact of Economic Crisis and Adjustment on Health Care in Mexico," Innocenti Occasional Papers, 13, Fiscal Policy and the Poor, UNICEF, 1991.

Romer, P. M., "Human Capital and Growth: Theory and Evidence," NBER Working Paper, 3173, Cambridge, National Bureau of Economic Research, 1989.

Schultz, T. P., "The Formation of Human Capital and the Economic Development of Africa: Returns to Health and Schooling Investments," Economic Research Papers, 37, African Development Bank, 1998.

Schultz, T. P. and A. Tansel, "Measurement of Returns to Adult Health: Morbidity Effects on Wage Rates in Cote D'Ivoire and Ghana," LSMS Working Paper 95, Washington, D.C., The World Bank, 1993.

Sevigny, D., *The Paris Club: An Inside View*, Ottawa, The North-South Institute, 1990.

World Bank, *Annual Report*, Washington, D.C., World Bank, 1992.

____, "Heavily Indebted Poor Countries (HIPC) Initiative – Strengthening the Link between Debt Relief and Poverty Reduction," Washington, D.C., World Bank, 1999.

____, *The IDA Debt Reduction Facility*, Washington, D.C., World Bank, 1999.

United Nations, *Debt Equity Conversions: A Guide to Decision-Makers*, New York, United Nations, 1990.

____, *Draft Resolution Referred by the General Assembly at its Fifty-Fourth Session*, New York, United Nations, 2000.

The HIPC Initiative in Bolivia*

Lykke E. Andersen
& Osvaldo Nina

ABSTRACT

This paper examines the Bolivian experience with regard to debt relief through the HIPC Initiative. It has been agreed in principle that the debt-relief funds will be channelled to municipal governments in order to strengthen the decentralization process and to secure maximum poverty reduction. If everything goes according to the plan, the HIPC Initiative could have a substantial effect on poverty in Bolivia. However, the entire project builds on some very optimistic assumptions regarding the performance of the Bolivian economy during the next 18 years. If these assumptions do not hold, Bolivia will not reach the target debt/export ratio of 150. Worse, if the country's economic performance does not live up to expectations, investment projects (roads, schools, hospitals, etc.) may remain half-finished, and unable to be maintained, because the central government cannot deliver the funds that donors have obliged them to commit to the municipalities as a condition of debt relief.

RÉSUMÉ

Cet article examine l'expérience de la Bolivie par rapport à l'allégement de la dette à travers l'initiative pour les pays pauvres très endettées (PPTE). En principe, les fonds pour l'allégement de la dette devraient être acheminés aux gouvernements municipaux afin de renforcer la décentralisation et d'assurer une réduction maximale de la pauvreté. Si tout se passe comme prévu, l'initiative PPTE pourrait avoir un impact considérable sur le

* This paper is the result of a joint research endeavour between the Institute for Socio-Economic Research at Universidad Católica Boliviana and the North-South Institute (NSI) in Canada. It is funded by the NSI with the help of grants from the Ford Foundation, the Inter-American Development Bank, and the Canadian International Development Agency (CIDA). The authors would like to thank Jaime Garrón, Fernando Montaño and Marisol Pérez for their excellent research assistance. We are also grateful for the helpful comments and information from Eduardo Antelo, Alice Brooks, José Luis Evia, John Serieux and participants at HIPC workshops at the World Bank in Washington and the North-South Institute in Ottawa in September 2000.

problème de la pauvreté en Bolivie. Cependant, cette initiative concernant la Bolivie est basée sur des suppositions très optimistes en ce qui a trait à l'économie de ce pays pour les dix-huit prochaines années. Si ces suppositions ne se matérialisent pas, la Bolivie n'atteindra pas son objectif d'un quotient dette/exportation de 150. Pire encore, si la performance de l'économie ne répond pas aux attentes, les projets d'investissements (construction de routes, écoles, hôpitaux, etc.) pourraient ne pas être accomplis et maintenus, parce que le gouvernement central ne sera pas en mesure de livrer les fonds aux municipalités tel qu'imposé par les bailleurs, comme condition de l'allégement de la dette.

INTRODUCTION

Recognizing that the external debt situation of a number of low-income countries, mostly in Africa, had become extremely difficult or outright impossible, the IMF and the World Bank designed a framework for the delivery of additional debt relief for HIPCs that pursued supported adjustment and reform programs. The initial version of the HIPC Initiative, as it is called, was first unveiled in 1996. It has since been replaced by the more generous Enhanced HIPC Initiative.[1] Bolivia qualifies for this program based on all three criteria. First, Bolivia's debt/export ratio in 1997 was about twice as high as the target ratio of 150%. Second, about 63% of the population are considered poor, and 38% extremely poor. Third, Bolivia has been pursuing structural reforms guided by the IMF and the World Bank for the last 15 years.

The main target of the HIPC Initiative is Bolivia's debt/export ratio, which is to be reduced from around 300% to a sustainable level (as defined by the Initiative) of 150%. The ultimate goal is to provide additional resources to pay for structural reforms that reduce poverty.

This paper examines the Bolivian experience of the HIPC Initiative – its relationship to other debt-reduction efforts, public responses to the initiative, the potential for poverty reduction through the Initiative, and the expected long-term effects of the Initiative. It seeks to assess whether the objective of poverty reduction through debt relief is realistic and to identify the potential pitfalls in attempts to achieve that objective. The paper is organized as follows. Section I discusses the three issues – structural reforms, debt, and poverty – that make Bolivia eligible for debt relief. Section II discusses the HIPC Initiatives in Bolivia, including the experience from the initial HIPC Initiative, and the magnitude of relief. Section III addresses the conditions for debt

---

1. Since the Enhanced HIPC Initiative superseded the Initial HIPC Initiative, the generic term "HIPC Initiative" (without qualification) in the rest of this paper refers to the Enhanced HIPC Initiative.

relief, and how they are perceived in Bolivia. Section IV analyses the potential impacts of debt relief. This includes a municipality-level analysis of the expected costs of poverty reduction.

I. BOLIVIA'S QUALIFICATION FOR DEBT RELIEF
UNDER THE HIPC INITIATIVES

Of the 41 countries that are considered HIPCs (and are, therefore, eligible for debt-relief consideration under the Initial or Enhanced HIPC Initiatives), Bolivia is clearly among the richest. Its per capita GDP of US$1,010 in 1998 was nearly three times the average of the other 48 countries. This section will discuss why Bolivia, nevertheless, qualified for debt relief under that mechanism.

A.   STRUCTURAL REFORMS

In 1985, Bolivia started IMF-style structural reforms, the main elements of which were the elimination of barriers to trade, economic stabilization through fiscal austerity, and the development of efficient financial markets. These reforms successfully reduced inflation (from 8,171% in 1985 to 66% in 1986 and 11% in 1987) and fiscal deficits (from more than 20% of GDP in previous years to less than 3% of GDP in 1985).

However, these reforms had a high welfare cost. Open unemployment increased from 6% in 1985 to 10.4% in 1989, partly due to a dramatic contraction of the public sector (whose share of total employment decreased from 26% in 1985 to 17.6% in 1989). This, despite the fact that the informal sector absorbed much of the labour surplus (Jemio 2000).

The policy of eliminating direct and indirect subsidies also implied large changes in relative prices. Most importantly, gasoline prices increased by 833% immediately, creating large transfers from households to the public petroleum company (Antelo 2000). Due to tight fiscal policies, no resources were available to help the people who got hurt by the reforms as public social expenditure reached an all-time low in 1986 (figure 1).

The second generation of reforms targeted human development and increased efficiency. The main elements were privatization of state enterprises, investment in human capital, decentralization, and pension reform. Figure 2 shows clearly the changing priorities given to social investments. In the late 1980s, social investment only amounted to about 10% of total public investment, while it reached almost 50% by the late 1990s.

Figure 1. Public social expenditure, 1980-1998

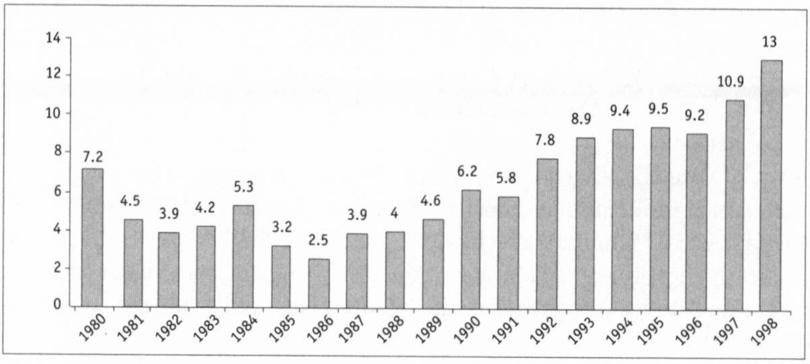

Source: UDAPE (1998).

Table 1. Poverty indicators by area

Indicators	Overall	Urban		Rural	
	1997	1989	1997	1989	1997
Poor population (%)	63.2	57.0	50.7	n.d.	77.3
Extremely poor population (%)	37.8	29.6	21.6	n.d.	58.2
Poverty gap	33.4	27.8	24.4	n.d.	48.7

Source: National Employment Survey 1997.
Note: The poverty gap measures the average distance to the poverty line.

The data generally show reductions in poverty and improvements in living standards during the 1990s. Open unemployment fell from 10.4% in 1989 to 3.5% in 1996 (Jemio 2000), and several studies show that urban poverty fell during the same period (Jiménez and Yáñez 1997; Gray-Molina et al. 1999; Hernani 1999; table 1). Given the substantial migration from smaller towns and rural areas to the cities, the decrease in poverty in the main cities probably indicates a nationwide decrease in poverty.

These second-generation reforms are expected to cost about 5% of GDP annually (IMF 1998). The government has raised about half the necessary funds through fiscal measures. The remaining funds are expected to arrive in the form of external assistance (including the HIPC Initiative).

B.   POVERTY

According to the *Human Development Report 2000* (UNDP 2000), Bolivia ranks 114th of the 174 countries analysed. Poverty in Bolivia is among the highest in Latin America, with 63% of the population unable to satisfy their basic education, health, and housing needs. In 1997, 77.3% of the rural population was considered poor, and 58.2% extremely poor (table 1).

Since poverty measures depend strongly on the chosen national poverty line, it is difficult to compare poverty across countries. Poverty in Bolivia is not as severe as it is in most other HIPCs. The country ranked only 27th out of 85 developing countries given poverty ranking in the *Human Development Report 2000* (UNDP 2000). To illustrate what the aggregate poverty numbers reflect, we give more detailed statistics on living standards in the Bolivian municipalities in table 2. We have divided the 311 municipalities in Bolivia in 1997 into three groups. The first group contains the 9 department capitals and El Alto (a satellite city of La Paz and clearly a major city). The second group contains the 150 least poor municipalities (as measured by the Unsatisfied Basic Needs [UBN] index). And the third group contains the 151 poorest municipalities in Bolivia. For each of the three groups we have calculated averages for a range of basic services indicators.

Table 2.   Basic services indicators by municipality group, 1992

Municipality group	Population with unsatisfied basic needs (%)	Population with piped water (%)	Population with electricity (%)	Population with sanitation (%)	Population with trash collection (%)
Ten major cities	53.7	83.8	95.2	51.4	58.7
Richest 150 municipalities	84.9	52.4	52.5	14.9	15.1
Poorest 151 municipalities	98.1	31.3	17.5	3.3	0.7
Average (all municipalities)	**90.3**	**43.2**	**36.9**	**10.5**	**9.6**

Source: based on data from the *Ministerio de Desarrollo Sostenible y Planificación* (MDSP), 2000.

Table 2 indicates that poverty (in the sense of UBN) is almost universal in the poorest 151 municipalities. Less than a third of the population in these municipalities has running water, and less than a fifth has electricity. Sewage and trash collection is extremely rare. In the 10 largest cities, however, almost everyone has electricity, more than 80% have running water, and more than half have sanitary installations and trash collection. Considering the rapid rate of rural-urban migration in Bolivia, this is an impressive accomplishment. Nevertheless, more than half the population in the major cities still has unsatisfied basic needs.

Table 3. Population densities and urbanization rates by municipality group, 1992

Municipality group	Population per municipality	Density (person/km²)	Urbanization rates
10 major cities	289,841	276	0.93
Richest 150 municipalities	14,586	28	0.27
Poorest 151 municipalities	8,823	9	0.01
Average	**20,659**	**32**	**0.16**

Source: Authors' calculations based on data from MDSP (2000).
Note: Population density is not available at municipality level (municipality borders are simply not clear, and municipalities do not always know how much area they cover), so population density was assumed to be the same for each municipality within the same province.

Table 3 shows that geographical conditions affect the level of poverty significantly. All the poorest municipalities are almost completely rural and have an average population density of only 19 people per square kilometre. With an average of less than 9,000 people per municipality, they have not reached the critical mass needed to generate sufficient opportunities and income for the provision of basic infrastructure. Indeed, the fact that the Bolivian population is thinly spread across a national territory spanning more than one million square kilometres of mountainous or forested terrain is one of the main reasons why poverty remains so high. It is also one of the main obstacles to development.

Since it is substantially cheaper to satisfy people's basic needs when they are concentrated in urban centres, rural-urban migration can provide an advantage in the fight against poverty. Because Bolivia has three urban magnets of approximately equal attraction (El Alto, Cochabamba, and Santa Cruz), it does not have the mega-city slum problems of the degree experienced in many other Latin American countries.

The inequality across municipalities is important to bear in mind. Recent decentralization efforts in Bolivia mean that the local municipal governments will have to raise much of their tax revenue locally. That is obviously difficult for the poor, rural municipalities. In 1997, the three departments on the Central Axis (La Paz, Cochabamba and Santa Cruz) collected 83.2% of all municipal taxes, leaving only 16.8% to the remaining six departments. Within the three rich departments about three quarters of tax income was raised in the four municipalities containing the major cities (MDSP 2000). Thus, four municipalities collected about 63% of all municipal taxes, while the remaining 307 municipalities together collected only 37%. To compensate for the lack of a local tax base, the debt-relief funds from the HIPC Initiatives are

Figure 2. Public social investment, 1987-1998

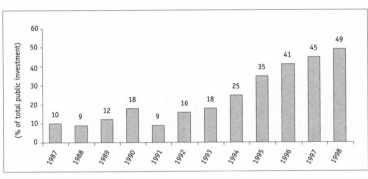

Source: UDAPE (1998).

expected to be directed especially to the poorest and least-developed munici-palities to help them catch up with the wealthier municipalities.

C.   EXTERNAL DEBT

Bolivia's external public debt (excluding short-term) amounted to US$4.4 billion in 1998. This was equivalent to 319% of exports or 51.4% of GDP that year. Figure 3 shows the evolution of Bolivia's debt from 1981 to 1998, just before the initial flow of debt relief from the first HIPC Initiative. External debt grew by an average of 3% annually. At the same time the composition of debt changed dramatically. In the early 1980s, bank loans were more impor-tant than multilateral loans, but in the late 1980s, using international dona-tions, Bolivia bought back most of its private debt at 11 cents on the dollar (Delgadillo Cortéz 1992). At the same time, successful negotiations with Paris Club creditors resulted in the rescheduling and reduction of a large part of the bilateral debt. This temporarily reduced the debt burden by almost 20%; however, it increased again because of expensive second-generation structural reforms in the education, health and pension systems.

The increase in the stock of debt shown in figure 1 actually hides a steady decrease in debt as a percentage of GDP; in 1985 public external debt amounted to 106% of GDP, in 1998 it was only 51% (Antelo 2000).

This is obviously a benefit of the structural reforms that Bolivia has expe-rienced. Bolivia's public external debt is held mostly by the central govern-ment. Public enterprises held less than 9% of the total debt in 1999 (*Banco*

Figure 3. Bolivia's public external debt, 1981-1998

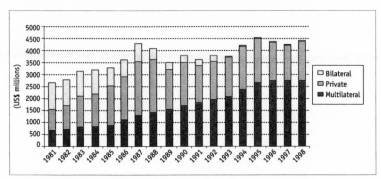

Source: *Banco Central de Bolivia.*
Note: Short-term debt is not included.

Figure 4. Total debt service, 1981-1998

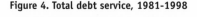

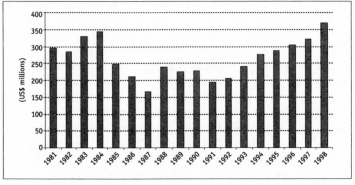

Source: *Banco Central de Bolivia.*

Central de Bolivia). This is partly because few public enterprises remain in Bolivia after the privatization processes of the 1990s, but even in 1990, public enterprises held only 11% of total public external debt. The fact that the central government holds most of the debt is important, because the sources of repayment are much harder to identify for investments carried out by the central government than for projects carried out by companies.

With interest rates typically ranging between 4% and 6%, the service of the total debt averaged US$265 million per year over the 1981-1998 period (figure 4). This corresponds to an average of 28% of exports or 4.4% of GDP.

**Figure 5. Unpaid scheduled debt service on bilateral and private
debt, 1987-1997**

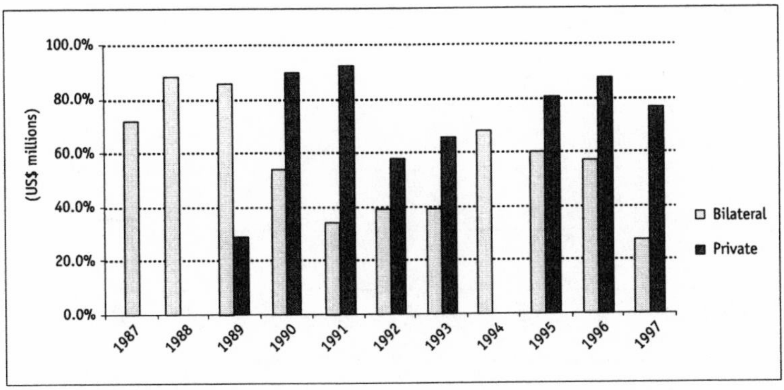

Source: Banco Central de Bolivia.

In order to maintain a good credit rating at the World Bank and the IMF,
Bolivia was servicing virtually all its multilateral debt on schedule (see appendix, table A1). However, the bilateral creditors and the private banks did not
receive the same treatment. In the late 1980s, Bolivia only paid about 20% of
the scheduled payments on bilateral loans. This situation improved in the
1990s, when the economy in general improved. During the 1990-1997 period,
Bolivia paid around half the scheduled payments on bilateral loans (figure 5).
Payment rates for loans with private banks varied greatly from year to year,
but were frequently at or below 20% during the last decade. The amount of
debt to private banks was, however, relatively small.

We do not have data on debt service after 1997 because Bolivia is holding
back service payments until the exact conditions for debt relief have been fully
negotiated. Some of the registered non-payments during the 1990s may be
explained by the fact that Bolivia was involved in many rounds of Paris Club
negotiations during the period (table 5) and was withholding service payments in the expectation of upcoming debt cancellation.

The sustainability of Bolivia's public external debt is related to the structure
of the economy. Metals and natural gas, whose prices fluctuate a great deal,
dominate Bolivia's exports, making the country highly vulnerable to external
shocks. Thus, unfavourable developments in international prices of these
products can easily push Bolivia into a worrisome position with regard to debt
repayment. In addition, it is important to bear in mind that most of Bolivia's
public-sector export companies have been privatized and are now controlled

Figure 6.   Public sector participation in exports, 1981-1999

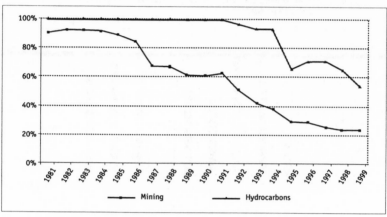

Source: Banco Central de Bolivia.

by foreign companies. This means that public sector participation in exports has been dramatically reduced. Less than 20% of the revenue from mineral exports now goes to the public sector, as opposed to more than 80% 20 years ago. Only half of hydrocarbon revenues go to the public sector as opposed to 100% just 10 years ago (figure 6).

Instead of relying on direct export revenues from public enterprises, the Bolivian government has to increase its tax revenues in order to obtain funds for debt servicing. With very high poverty levels and a large informal sector, income taxes are not a very promising option. Instead there will probably be a heavy reliance on the hydrocarbon sector, which contributed an average of 40% of fiscal revenues in the period 1996-1998 (Ayala 2000). But this reliance on the hydrocarbon sector also makes government revenues vulnerable to external shocks, leading to highly volatile fiscal deficits.

This vulnerability, due to the strong reliance on a few primary exports, is one of the main reasons Bolivia needs debt relief despite the fact that debt, as a percentage of GDP, had been going steadily in the right direction even before the HIPC Initiatives. In short, despite its lower-middle-income status, the country's economic structure and export profile severely compromises its debt-carrying capacity.

II. THE HIPC INITIATIVES IN BOLIVIA

A. THE INITIAL HIPC INITIATIVE

The goal of the Initial HIPC Initiative was to bring the debt/export ratios down to the 215-235 range. Creditors determined that a target of 225 would be acceptable for Bolivia, and the IMF projected that debt relief of US$448 million (in NPV terms) would be needed to reach that target.

In September 1997, the IMF decided that Bolivia was eligible for relief under the Initial HIPC Initiative if it could prove that it could use the relief wisely (through further reform). By September 1998, in view of Bolivia's strong policy record, the IMF decided that the country had reached its completion point, and Bolivia received debt relief worth US$448 million in NPV terms. This corresponded to a 13% reduction in outstanding debt (IMF 1999).

The continuation of second-generation reforms was one of the conditions of Initial HIPC debt relief. It required the government to continue social reforms in key areas, including education and health and the development of rural areas. Overall, Bolivia met almost all the targets set by the Initial HIPC Initiative, and in the few areas where it failed to reach the target, substantial progress was made. For example, the percentage of births attended by professionals within the Maternal and Child Insurance Program called for an increase of 26 percentage points in just two years. Bolivia experienced an increase of 19 percentage points, which was below target, but higher than in any of the other 18 countries for which data was available (IMF 2000). The reform targets and Bolivia's performance, are summarized in appendix A3.

B. THE ENHANCED HIPC INITIATIVE

In the face of worsening terms of trade for most developing countries, creditor countries recognized that a debt/export ratio around 225 would not be sustainable for most HIPC countries. The Enhanced HIPC Initiative therefore calls for a uniform reduction in debt/export ratios to a target of 150%. It also seeks to strengthen the link between debt relief and poverty reduction by requiring eligible countries to develop a locally owned PRSP.

The IMF projected that to reach this target, Bolivia would need further debt relief of US$854 million in NPV terms. The key assumptions used for calculating debt relief for Bolivia are as follows (IMF 2000):

- Bolivia is expected to continue its structural reforms and strong macroeconomic policies;
- the GDP growth rate is expected to increase to 5-6%;
- inflation is expected to remain at around 4%;

- gross domestic investment is expected to increase from 19.7% of GDP to 21% of GDP;
- FDI is expected to fall from 9% of GDP in 2000 to 4% by 2018;
- national savings are expected to rise from 13% of GDP to 16.5% of GDP;
- export volumes are expected to grow at 10% per year in the beginning (mainly due to natural gas) and to slow to 5% from 2007 onwards;
- imports are expected to grow faster than real GDP until 2006, and a little slower thereafter;
- the terms of trade are expected to improve slightly through 2006;
- the combined public sector deficit is expected to move in line with net external financing, which is projected to decline from 2.4% of GDP in 2000 to 1.3% on average during 2008-2018.

These are clearly optimistic assumptions. While GDP projections look simply optimistic, terms of trade projections and fiscal deficit projections appear totally unrealistic. Annual GDP growth rates of 5% to 6% are high by historical standards. The average over the last 50 years is only 2.3%. However, during the 15-year period from 1962 to 1977, Bolivia experienced an average annual GDP growth rate of 5.7%, thus periods of high growth are not unprecedented. After 15 years of structural reforms, with sweeping liberalization and privatization, Bolivia is hoping desperately for such growth again.

Figure 7 shows that the terms of trade for Bolivia have shown a clear and dramatic downward trend over the last 20 years. This is due both to falling mineral prices and falling natural gas prices. These two components make up the majority of Bolivian exports, and there are no signs that prices are going to improve. The price of natural gas is contractually linked to crude oil, and with the current high oil prices, it is reasonable to expect that the price will not fall in the future. Table A2 in the Appendix provides further details on price indices.

Since the government's fiscal revenues are highly dependent on the hydrocarbon sector and thus on oil prices, it also seems overly optimistic to expect the public sector fiscal deficit to decline from 2.4% of GDP in 2000 to 1.3% during most of the forecast period. In fact, the fiscal deficit for 2000 is now likely to reach 4.0% of GDP (*La Prensa*, 15 August 2000). These very optimistic assumptions of course led to a lower debt-reduction amount than more realistic assumptions would have implied. The Bolivian authorities have, nevertheless, agreed with these assumptions. This may be because they were unable to negotiate more favourable terms, but it could also reflect the view that it is more important to present a positive outlook in order to attract

Figure 7. Terms of trade index for Bolivia, 1980-1999

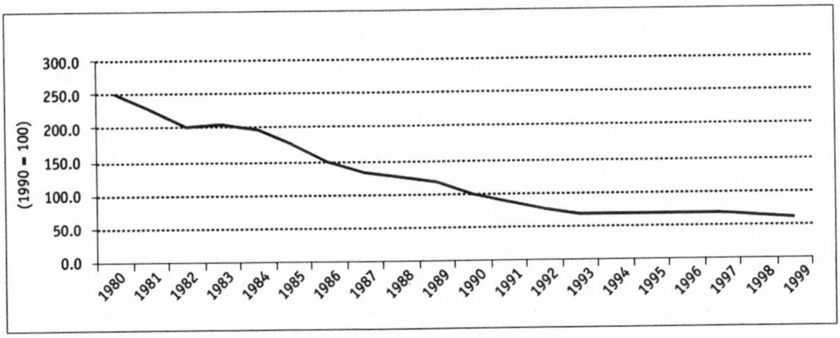

Source: Author's calculations based on UDAPE data.

foreign direct investment than to present a pessimistic scenario for increased debt relief.

C. THE FLOW OF DEBT RELIEF UNDER THE HIPC INITIATIVES

Having accepted the IMF calculations of necessary debt relief, Bolivia expects to be granted enhanced debt relief with a net present value of US$854 million in the first half of 2001. The scheduling details have not yet been negotiated, but the IMF has developed a likely scenario, which is given in table 4, together with the time profile of the relief agreed under the Initial HIPC Initiative.

Bolivia's GDP was US$8.63 billion by the end of 1999 (UDAPE), and the government and the IMF expect it to grow by approximately 5% per year during the next 20 years. The evolution of GDP under this assumption is shown in column 5 of table 4. We use the relief information and the projected GDP to calculate the flow of debt relief relative to GDP over time. The result is given in column 6 of table 4 and presented in figure 8. Based on these calculations, the flow equivalent of debt relief could reach almost 2% of GDP in 2001. Because of growing GDP and the front-loaded nature of the relief, the importance of the relief will fall to just under 1% of GDP in 2006 and a relatively insignificant 0.2% by 2016.

The last column of table 4 shows total debt relief each year as a percentage of scheduled debt service that year. That proportion reaches a maximum of 47.5% in 2001, but by 2008 it will have fallen below 20%, implying that by then, Bolivia will have to pay more than 80% of scheduled debt service before relief.

Table 4.   Scheduled debt relief from Initial HIPC and Enhanced HIPC

Year	Scheduled relief (US$ million)			GDP (US$ million)	Scheduled debt service (US$ million)	Debt relief (% of GDP)	Debt relief (% of scheduled debt service)
	Initial HIPC	Enhanced HIPC	Total				
1999	77	0	77	8,631	363	0.89	21.2
2000	85	0	85	9,062	372	0.94	22.8
2001	70	112	182	9,515	383	1.91	47.5
2002	55	119	174	9,991	394	1.74	44.2
2003	41	119	160	10,491	407	1.53	39.3
2004	36	109	145	11,015	437	1.32	33.2
2005	33	100	133	11,566	460	1.15	28.9
2006	23	92	115	12,144	487	0.95	23.6
2007	21	85	106	12,751	512	0.83	20.7
2008	20	80	100	13,389	558	0.75	17.9
2009	19	77	96	14,058	595	0.68	16.1
2010	19	76	95	14,761	634	0.64	15.0
2011	18	71	89	15,499	665	0.57	13.4
2012	18	66	84	16,274	705	0.52	11.9
2013	18	62	80	17,088	749	0.47	10.7
2014	16	60	76	17,942	802	0.42	9.5
2015	16	58	74	18,839	861	0.39	8.6
2016	17	22	39	19,781	920	0.20	4.2
2017	17	0	17	20,771	981	0.08	1.7
2018	18	0	18	21,809	-	0.08	-
2019	0	0	0	22,900	-	0.00	-

Source: Authors' calculations based on data from IMF (2000), UDAPE, and assumptions in text.

Figure 8. The flow of debt relief, 1999-2019

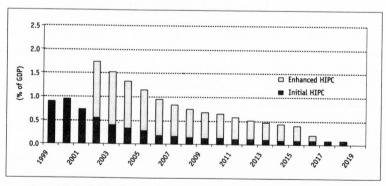

Source: Author's calculations based on information in IMF (2000).

Table 5. Summary of Paris Club negotiations (US$ millions)

	Paris Club Round	Debt rescheduled	Debt reduction
1	(July 1986)	510	-
2	(November 1988)	261	-
3	(March 1990)	127	76
4	(January 1992)	49	121
5	(March 1995)	32	130
6	(December 1995)	-	576
7	(October 1998)	-	451
	Total	**979**	**1354**

Source: Banco Central de Bolivia.

Total debt relief through the Initial and Enhance HIPC Initiatives is less than the relief Bolivia has negotiated over seven rounds of talks with its Paris Club creditors from 1986 to 1998. During the first two rounds, Bolivia obtained temporary relief through rescheduling of debt service with grace periods of 4 to 5 years. During the third round, in 1990, Bolivia received real debt reduction under the Toronto terms (one third of service debt on older than 1985 forgiven) and was the first country outside sub-Saharan Africa to receive this treatment. In later rounds, this reduction was topped up so that by 1998 Bolivia had had US$1,354 million of bilateral debt forgiven. Table 5 shows the results of Paris Club negotiations in summary form.

D.   THE NATIONAL DIALOGUE

The Enhanced HIPC is conditioned on the elaboration of a PRSP with the participation of government, private sector and civil society. The Bolivian government decided to do this through a "national dialogue" (figure 9). This dialogue is a step-by-step process that starts at the municipal level, continues to the department level, and ends at the national level. The output from the national round table will be an integrated development agenda, the proposed use of resources from the HIPC, and a political agenda (e.g. changes in the constitution).

Municipal-level round tables and state-level round tables were carried out between June 6 and July 19, 2000 with the participation of more than 3,000 citizens. First, problems in various areas were ranked according to severity. The top economic development concerns were weak support to micro-enterprises and lack of access to credit, and insufficient productive infrastructure (roads, irrigation, energy). In education the concerns were insufficient infrastructure, equipment, and materials; insufficient training and teachers training; and the high incidence of illiteracy. In health, the main concerns were insufficient infrastructure, equipment, and medicinal supplies.

The main obstacles to fighting poverty were believed to be bureaucratic inertia at the national and state levels and lack of funds at the municipal levels. The most urgently needed actions were considered to be the improvement of infrastructure (especially roads, but some also promoted air transportation of high-value cargo, since it requires less initial investment and would be faster to implement).

The national-level round table took place on 28-29 August 2000. The results of these meetings are still being processed. The government initially thought that the PRSP would be completed by October 2000 but, due to

Figure 9.   Schematic representation of the National Dialogue

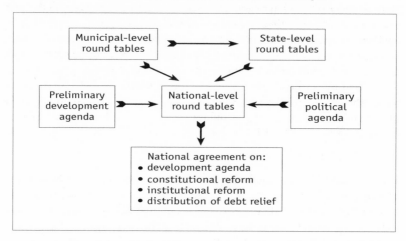

extensive civil unrest in September and October 2000, it postponed the deadline until next year in order to secure stronger civil support.

When completed, the PRSP will outline a proposal for distributing debt relief to the municipalities, and methods for monitoring the distribution of debt relief and evaluating the effect of debt relief. Furthermore, it will provide the basic components of the development agenda. The National Statistical Institute (INE) will coordinate, revise, and disseminate information. The Economic Policy Analysis Unit (UDAPE) of the government, the ministries of the social sector and the INE will analyse and evaluate the PRSP.

III. CONDITIONALITY

While the preparation of the PRSP is considered a very mild and widely accepted condition relating to debt relief, some concerns were raised about the validity and efficiency of the national dialogue. The opposition claims it is unconstitutional because Bolivia has a congress with 162 elected representatives who are supposed to make this kind of decisions. They fear that the dialogue will create a parallel forum for decision making and lead to social instability. Others say it creates unrealistic expectations in the municipalities, with the government implicitly promising to meet any and all demands.

To thoroughly assess the local views on the HIPC Initiatives and the national dialogue, this paper uses the results of two local opinion polls. The first poll was carried out by *Datos, Estadísticas e Información Srl.* (DEI) on 1-2 July 2000 (i.e. during the department-level round tables) in the cities of La Paz and El Alto. The poll included 400 persons representative of the populations in La Paz and El Alto. The second poll was carried out by IISEC on August 21, 2000. It covered 46 government officials, 25 persons from the private sector and 34 persons from civil society.[2] Since there are marked differences between the opinions of government, the private sector, and civil society, we will treat them separately below.

A. PUBLIC SECTOR VIEWS ON HIPC CONDITIONALITY

Almost all government officials polled believe that Bolivia's external debt is a large problem, and 75% of them think it is a good idea to link debt relief with poverty reduction. When asked whether the government would maintain the same high level of public social investment if it was not a condition for debt relief, 42% answered "no" and only 29% "yes". Thus, government officials appear to be happy to have funds ear-marked for social investment because they would not otherwise be able to make these investments despite their high desirability.

---

2. The following institutions were visited: CIDES, MpD, *Cuerpo de Paz-Bolivia*, INECIP, *Conferencia Episcopal Boliviana*, CEPAS, *Periódico Presencia, Asamblea Permanente de Derechos Humanos, Cámara Nacional de Industria, Alcaldía de la Ciudad de La Paz, Estudios Jurídicos Privados, Cámara Nacional de Comercio*, PNUD, ILDIS, *Ministerio de Desarrollo Económico, Directorio Único de Fondos, Ministerio de Hacienda, Viceministerio de Presupuesto y Contaduría, Viceministerio de Política Tributaria*, UDAPE, *Banco Central de Bolivia*, CEDLA, GTZ, International Mining, *Confederación de Empresas Privadas de Bolivia, Superintendencia de Telecomunicaciones, Cámara Nacional de Exportadores*, ENTEL, UPF, *Banco Mercantil-Bolsa*, Price Waterhouse & Coopers, *Viceministerio de Industria y Comercio, Corporación Minera de Bolivia, and Superintendencia de Electricidad.*

Fifty-seven percent of government officials believe that debt relief may or will have a negative effect on other aid flows. This is an important concern, since Bolivia relies on foreign aid, which amounts to 7-8% of GDP (OECD database). At the Ministry of Economic Development and at the *Directorio Único de Fondos*, they thought that the HIPC funds should be used not only for social investment, but also for investment in the productive sector to generate economic growth. In addition, the former group commented that the opening of North American textile markets is very important. A Bolivian government task force has estimated that the lifting of US duties on textiles (currently at 18-24%) would bring in US$400 million annually to the Bolivian economy and create at least 30,000 jobs (*Bolivian Times*, 24 August 2000).

At the Ministry of Finance, several respondents found it unfortunate and embarrassing to have a label of poor, highly indebted, and bad payer put on Bolivia when the country is desperately trying to attract and provide good conditions for foreign direct investment.

B.   PRIVATE SECTOR VIEWS ON THE HIPC INITIATIVE

The private sector generally shares the views of the government, except that the private sector is not as content with the link between debt relief and poverty reduction.[3] Fourty-two percent of respondents from the private sector did not think it is a good idea to link debt relief with poverty reduction. Only 18% of government officials answered "no" to the same question. This is not surprising. Formal businesses will get very little direct benefit from debt relief if it is all spent on social investment.

Some business people at the national dialogue also expressed the view that the opening of North American markets to textile exports was much more important for development and said that they would be happy to return all debt relief if export barriers were removed instead (STDN 2000, p. 63).

C.   CIVIL SOCIETY VIEWS ON THE HIPC INITIATIVE AND THE NATIONAL DIALOGUE

Here we will distinguish between civil organizations and private persons because they were interviewed in different polls. The first group (people from the church, academia and NGOs) also think that external debt is a major

---

3. The private-sector poll only includes persons from large or organized business – none from micro-enterprises.

Figure 10. Private persons' ranking of Bolivia's problems

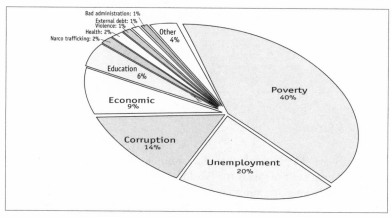

Source: DEI (2000).

problem. However, as many as 45% do not agree that debt relief should be linked to poverty reduction and think that Bolivia deserves unconditional debt relief. Meanwhile, 56% of them are sure that the government would not be able to spend as much on social investment if it were not linked with debt reduction.

Private persons are generally less concerned about external debt than the other groups. When asked to rank Bolivia's problems, they rank external debt far down the list, after poverty, unemployment, corruption, education, drug trafficking, health and violence (figure 10).

Most private persons were not aware of the whole process of debt relief and the National Dialogue. Only 12% of the persons interviewed knew about the National Dialogue, and these were mostly individuals with high income (figure 11). The remainder had either not heard about the dialogue at all or had only a vague idea about it.

Figure 11. Knowledge of the National Dialogue

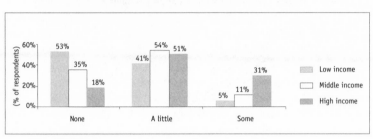

Source: DEI (2000).

Most private people think that the National Dialogue is just a political manoeuvre organized to satisfy the World Bank and other donors (figure 12).[4] High-income people are more likely to believe that the Dialogue is sincere, and middle-income people are the least trusting. Indeed, roughly 86% of low and middle-income respondents wrote the whole thing off as a political manoeuvre.

Figure 12.   Opinions about the National Dialogue

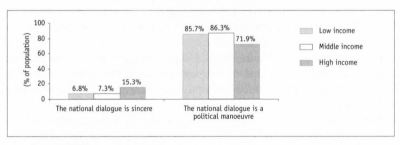

Source: DEI (2000).

Opinions were even less charitable when it comes to the representativeness of the National Dialogue. More than 90% of the interviewed people did not feel that they were represented at the Dialogue. Some of them had not even heard about the Dialogue.

---

4. The questions in this poll are independent, which implies that people who had not heard about the National Dialogue can still have an opinion about it.

People are also obviously worried that the money obtained through debt relief may not be used properly due to corruption and bad government: 76% of those interviewed clearly agree that the church should monitor the use of funds obtained through debt relief. This was also one of the official views coming from the municipal and departmental round tables of the National Dialogue. Almost all agree that there should be a monitoring mechanism at both department and municipal level, and most suggested that this be the Catholic Church (STDN 2000). However, the Church has indicated that it does not have the institutional capacity to carry out such a task, but that it would support and participate in the formation of a group of monitoring institutions. In any case, the responses indicate the need for the creation of some institution to help guarantee that the funds are used appropriately, because the government is not sufficiently trusted. Interestingly, only 29% of government officials thought that it was a good idea to have the Church monitor them.

Overall, the poll of private persons shows little local confidence in the National Dialogue. People do not feel represented, and a large majority sees it as a political manoeuvre that is tolerated because it will bring about more than a billion dollars of debt relief. It is not surprising, therefore, that just weeks after the official National Dialogue ended, widespread strikes and blockades broke out across the country. For three weeks, almost all productive activity in Bolivia ceased. Disgruntled farmers, coca growers, teachers and others who did not feel sufficiently represented, or taken into account, in the National Dialogue, were the main instigators. The Finance Minister at the time, Ronald MacLean, referred to these three weeks of chaos as "part two of the National Dialogue." If the official National Dialogue was somewhat superficial and less than perfectly participatory due to the haste with which Bolivia wanted to qualify for relief, some large overlooked groups violently made sure that they were heard in the unofficial part of the Dialogue. Further, the postponement of the deadline for the PRSP, caused by the civil unrest, is likely to imply that the final PRSP will be of a higher quality and will reflect a higher degree of civil participation.

IV. ANALYSIS OF THE POTENTIAL EFFECTS OF DEBT RELIEF ON POVERTY IN BOLIVIA

This section attempts to determine how far the debt-relief dividend may go toward reducing poverty in Bolivia. We do that by using municipality-level data because Bolivia has decided to fight poverty through a decentralized program.

A. POVERTY REDUCTION STRATEGIES AND COST AT THE MUNICIPAL LEVEL

The current 314 municipal governments of Bolivia are in the process of preparing Municipal Development Plans with the help of the *Viceministerio de Planificación Estratégica y Participación Popular* and various NGOs. So far, we only have cost estimates for 107 municipalities; we will therefore focus on these and use them to extrapolate, where necessary, to the national level. These 107 municipalities represent only 20% of the population, but they are reasonably representative of the poor, rural municipalities that debt-relief funds are expected to target. The average share of people with unsatisfied basic needs in these 107 municipalities is 93.7% (compared to the average of 90.3% across all municipalities).

Table 6 shows the aggregate investment demand for these 107 municipalities. They have a total of 15,728 investment projects that would require US$716 million to carry out. The data does not include information about the time frame envisioned for these projects, but we can fairly assume that they

Table 6. Total investment demand from 107 municipalities

Department	Number of municipalities	Number of investment projects	Demand (US$)
Beni	9	652	47,017,553
Chuquisaca	14	1,755	88,670,819
Cochabamba	12	1,744	81,514,888
La Paz	16	3,696	83,800,355
Oruro	10	1,094	71,753,189
Pando	8	673	27,118,880
Potosí	12	1,588	59,933,094
Santa Cruz	21	2,910	152,927,151
Tarija	5	1,616	103,114,485
Total	**107**	**15,728**	**715,850,414**

Source: MDSP (2000).

are for the five-year period from 2001 to 2005. This implies average annual investment demand of US$143 million from these 107 municipalities.

The ambitiousness of the Municipal Development Plans vary significantly from municipality to municipality. On average, their plans require annual

Table 7. Social investment demand by sector

Sector	Demand (%)
Production	**61.9**
Agriculture	15.0
Communications	0.3
Energy	4.1
Industry and tourism	2.5
Water and irrigation	13.8
Transportation	26.2
Social	**28.8**
Education and culture	13.8
Health and social security	5.5
Sanitation	8.8
Urbanization and housing	**6.5**
Natural Resources	**1.0**
Multisectoral	**2.4**
Others	**0.1**
Total (107 municipalities)	**100**

Source: MDSP (2000).

public municipal investments to increase by a factor of 11 (compared to 1997 levels), but one ambitious municipality in Chuquisaca has developed 223 projects that would require annual investments to increase by a factor of 144. Five municipalities have set forth investments in their Municipal Development Plans that are actually smaller than what they invested in 1997. The vast majority of plans, however, require reasonably realistic investment increases of 100% to 1,000%, compared to 1997 levels.

Table 7 shows a sectoral decomposition of investment demand. Transportation is the single most important component, which corresponds well to the concerns expressed at the National Dialogue. Agricultural projects and irrigation are also considered very important in these mainly rural municipalities. Education and sanitation projects follow. The allocation of investment therefore suggests that the municipalities give a higher priority to investment in productive infrastructure than investment in the social sector. This perspective contradicts the priorities of the central government and the second-generation structural reforms recommended by the World Bank. These anticipate a much higher percentage of investments directed at the social sector. It may well be that social investments were given too low priority in the first-generation reforms but too high priority in the second-generation reforms. People seem to want a compromise of about 30% of total public investments directed towards the social sector.

Figure 13.   Distribution of US$95 million debt relief based on different criteria

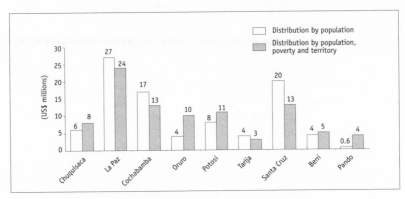

Source: Author's calculations and *Secretaría Técnica del Diálogo*.

A.   THE DISTRIBUTION OF DEBT-RELIEF FUNDS

The preliminary results of the National Dialogue show overwhelming agreement that municipal governments, rather than the central government, should manage the resources to fight poverty. No consensus exists, however, on how these funds should be distributed across municipalities. The three rich departments (La Paz, Cochabamba and Santa Cruz) want a distribution scheme based on population weights, while the poor departments want a scheme based on poverty weights. As a compromise, it has been proposed that the funds from debt relief be distributed among municipalities according to a combination of three criteria: population, poverty and territory. This is in contrast to Popular Participation funds, which are distributed according to population only. The latter distribution is considered highly unfair by the thinly populated, poor, rural municipalities. The new proposal attempts to reach a compromise that all municipalities can accept. Figure 13 shows the distribution, by department, of US$95 million under the two approaches.

The proposed distribution would result in large redistributions from La Paz, Santa Cruz and Cochabamba (the three departments on the central axis of Bolivia) toward Oruro, Potosí, Chuquisaca and Pando, which are all among the poorer departments. Santa Cruz would lose 35% compared to the population-based distribution, but it is the richest department, enjoys the most rapid growth rates, and has the second largest natural gas reserves. The funds for Pando would increase by a factor of 7, but it is also the least developed and most sparsely populated of the nine Bolivian departments (INE 1999), and it would certainly need extra funds to catch up. The proposed distribution has yet to be agreed upon.

If the US$95 million is distributed to the municipalities (using simple population weights) and the additional resources are compared with their public investment, on average, the debt-relief funds would allow an increase in public investment of 136% over 1997 investment levels. This shows that most of the municipal development plans are realistic.

B.   THE POVERTY REDUCTION DEFICIT

Since the Municipal Development Plans were developed before the exact amount of funds (dividend) from debt relief was known, nothing guarantees that desired and available funding will match. The poverty reduction deficit (or surplus) can be defined as the difference between total investment and social spending the local municipalities would need, based on their Municipal Development Plans, and the funds available from debt relief and other known sources.

Since we only have detailed development plans for 107 municipalities, some extrapolation is needed in order to arrive at the national poverty reduction deficit. The average demand from the 107 municipalities was US$6.7 million per municipality. If we extrapolate that number to all 314 municipalities, we get a total investment demand of US$2,101 million, or US$420 million per year, over the five year period considered.

In 1997, the total public municipal investment amounted to US$162 million (MDSP 2000). The desired annual investments during the next five years are therefore 2.6 times higher. Higher investments are likely to lead to higher recurrent expenditures (two schools are likely to cost about twice as much to run as one school). Municipal governments' current expenditures (not including interest payments) amounted to US$83 million in 1997. Assuming that recurrent expenditure increases by a factor of 2.6 as well, it will amount to US$216 million per year over the next five years. Jointly, therefore, municipal governments would thus need US$636 million per year to finance their Municipal Development Plans over the next five years.

HIPC debt relief is expected to give them about US$159 million per year during the period 2001-2005 (see table 4). The municipalities can also generate their own income through taxation (mainly property and vehicle taxes) and user fees (for trash collection, entrance fees to parks, etc). Table 8 shows that, historically, they have been able to collect an average of US$94 million per year in local income. In addition, the municipal governments can receive transfers from the central government. On 28 July 1995, a Law of Administrative Decentralization was passed that dictates the level and distribution of these transfers. We will therefore assume that the levels observed in 1996 and 1997 represents the "normal" level of regular transfers from the central government (about US$246 million per year). After the decentralization law was passed, total municipal income stabilized at approximately US$350 million per year.

However, it would be overly optimistic to assume that transfers will remain at the 1996-1997 level during the period 2001-2005. It is more likely that regular transfers will be reduced, because the central government will be more cash constrained after debt relief. Before debt relief, the highest amount of debt service that the government managed to pay was US$370 million in 1998. In the first five years after debt relief (2001-2005) the government will have to make debt-service payments of approximately US$253 million annually (IMF 2000). When that is added to the debt-relief transfers of US$159 million that has been promised to the municipalities, it implies a commitment of US$412

Table 8. Income to municipal governments, 1994-1997 (US$)

Year	Own income	Transfers	Total income
1994	65,122,210	111,655,119	176,777,329
1995	106,308,251	163,158,052	269,466,303
1996	95,906,016	253,709,309	349,615,325
1997	108,422,257	238,720,059	347,142,316

Source: MDSP (2000).

million (or 11% more than maximum service payment before debt relief). The central government is likely to reduce general transfers to compensate. We can assume (optimistically) that the reduction will be US$42 million per year – bringing debt-related outlays to the 1998 level. This implies (non-debt-relief) transfers from the central government to municipal governments of US$204 million annually, (incidentally, this means that the net increase in transfers engendered by debt relief – the actual debt dividend – would be US$117 million rather than the US$159 million gross transfer).

The recent large discoveries of natural gas in Bolivia and the scheduled sales of natural gas to Brazil, implies that royalties amounting to about US$70 million per year will become available over the next 20 years (VEH 1999). The royalties will be very unevenly distributed, however, because the department of Tarija holds the vast majority of natural gas reserves and consequently will

Table 9. Aggregate budget for the municipal development plans, 2001-2005

	US$ million	% of costs
Annual costs of MDPs (2001-2005)	636	100
Total funding for MDPs	527	83
Debt relief	159	25
Municipalities' own income	94	15
Regular transfers (not including debt relief)	204	32
Natural gas royalties	70	11
Poverty reduction deficit	109	17

Note: Numbers are extrapolated to cover all municipalities.

receive the vast majority of royalties. The central government will therefore have to develop some strategy for redistributing this windfall.

These funding possibilities (debt-relief transfers, tax income, regular transfers and natural gas royalties) are presented in table 9. These funding sources can only cover 83% of the expected annual cost of the Municipal Development Plans. Thus, the annual poverty reduction deficit – the average annual unfunded portion of the municipal development plans – amounts to US$109 million, or 17% of expected costs.

These plans carry no explicit commitment to reduce poverty by half by the year 2015 as the Millennium Declaration (UN 2000), to which Bolivia was a signatory, pledges. However, these are the projects that the local governments believe will help their local populations the most. If corruption is lower in the municipal governments than it is at the central government level, each dollar spent is likely to have a relatively high impact on poverty.

C.   DEBT RELIEF VERSUS TRADITIONAL FOREIGN AID

During the structural reform period, Bolivia has been highly dependent on foreign aid. Net inflows of ODA averaged 9.1% of GDP during the period 1986-1998 (figure 14). Grant aid averaged 6.5% during that period. Though greatly appreciated, such large amounts of aid have a distorting effect on the economy. Food aid tends to displace the supply from local farmers (Prudencio and Franqueville 1995), financial aid tends to crowd out national savings (Orellana 1995), technical assistance drives up the salaries of local professionals (making it expensive for the domestic government and universities to attract the best staff), and all inflows are a magnet for corruption.

Aid in the form of debt relief appears to have fewer negative side effects and more positive side effects than traditional foreign aid. First, since there is no

Figure 14.   Official Development Assistance to Bolivia, 1970-1998

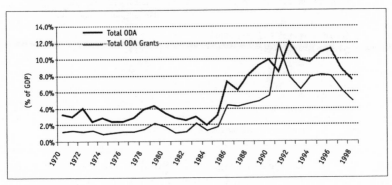

Source: OECD.

inflow of cash, the probability of that aid being diverted away from its intended destination is smaller. Second, debt relief will strengthen the decentralization process in Bolivia and bring the funds out to the municipalities, where it is likely to be more efficiently directed to the most pressing needs. Third, the debt relief is likely to improve rural productivity by eliminating local bottlenecks through better targeting of public investment.

Debt relief is expected to substitute, to some degree, for traditional aid flows, perhaps accelerating the recent downward trend in ODA flows. This may make Bolivia less dependent on traditional aid, but it will also make it more difficult to finance the poverty reduction deficit. The poverty reduction deficit will likely have to be funded through aid flows. More importantly, because the flow equivalent of debt relief, even over the next five years, is small relative to recent ODA flows (less than 2% vs. nearly 10%), a mere 12% contraction in ODA flows over the next five years would imply a resource flow contraction equal to more than half the flow equivalent of debt relief. Despite the potential superiority of debt relief (in terms of poverty reduction), the net effect on poverty and growth in Bolivia would undoubtedly be negative.

CONCLUSION

This paper has shown that the Initial HIPC and the Enhanced HIPC Initiatives together will provide debt relief amounting to an average of slightly less than 1% of Bolivia's GDP over the next 15 years. The funds are to be distributed to municipal governments to help reduce poverty locally through investments in infrastructure, education and health. If all goes well, the HIPC Initiatives will provide funds to cover about 25% of the costs of the Municipal Development Plans during the next five years. It is estimated that tax income, regular transfers from the central government, and natural gas royalties can cover an additional 58%, leaving 17% without any obvious sources of funding.

The HIPC Initiative will strengthen the decentralization process in Bolivia and, given adequate monitoring of the use of funds, the resulting improvements in living standards could be substantial. If the optimistic projections for the Bolivian economy hold, most municipalities will have funds to carry out a majority of the investment projects they have identified as critical for improving local productive capacity and local living standards.

The authors of this paper hold relatively positive views with regard to the HIPC Initiative and the way it is being implemented in Bolivia, but not everyone in Bolivia share those views. A substantial majority of the population is sceptical about the National Dialogue, considering it a show put on for the benefit of the donors. They worry that the funds will not reach the poor, even though that was clearly the agreement reached through the National Dialogue. Indeed, if the positive projections for the Bolivian economy do not hold, the central government will probably have too little funds to make the promised transfers to the municipalities. It may cut both regular transfers and debt-relief funds, making the municipalities severely cash constrained, perhaps placing them in a situation where they do not have funds to maintain new investments. It is indeed imaginable that the municipalities will invest in schools, health centres, and roads in the first few years after debt relief, only to leave the roads half-finished, the schools without teachers and the health clinics without doctors and medical supplies, as a negative external shock reduces available funds.

Vulnerability to external shocks remains Bolivia's main problem, and debt relief will do little to solve that problem. Hard-liners in the government and the private sector consider debt relief relatively unimportant compared to the opening of export markets, which would help put Bolivia on a sustainable growth path with much less dependence on foreign aid. A seaport is also considered a high priority, and the Bolivian president is currently negotiating with the president of Chile on this issue (*La Prensa*, 9 September 2000).

Finally, there are concerns that the debt-relief initiatives will reduce other types of foreign aid. Bolivia is receiving foreign aid amounting to between 7% and 10% of GDP each year, and the much-debated 1% debt relief might conceivably reduce other types of foreign aid by more than one percentage point – leaving Bolivia worse off than it was before the HIPC Initiatives in terms of net flows.

REFERENCES

Antelo, E., "Políticas de Estabilización y de Reformas Estructurales en Bolivia a partir de 1985," in Antelo, E. and L. C. Jemio, eds., *Quince Años de Reformas Estructurales en Bolivia: Sus Impactos sobre Inversión, Crecimiento y Equidad*, ch. 1, La Paz, CEPAL and UCB, 2000, p. 15-98.

Ayala, V. H., "Determinantes de la Inversión privada y Productividad del Sector Hidrocarburos," in Antelo, E. and L. C. Jemio eds., *Quince Años de Reformas Estructurales en Bolivia: Sus Impactos sobre Inversión, Crecimiento y Equidad*, ch. 5, La Paz: CEPAL and UCB, 2000, p. 253-308.

DEI, "Informe 'DEI': Evaluación Política II," Datos, *Estadísticas e Información Srl.* La Paz, 1 y 2 de Julio 2000.

Delgadillo Cortéz, J., *La crisis de la deuda externa y sus soluciones: La experiencia boliviana*, Banco Central de Bolivia, La Paz, 1992.

Gray-Molina, G., W. Jiménez, E. P. de Rada and E. Yáñez, "Pobreza y activos en Bolivia. ¿Que papel desempeña el capital social? *El Trimestre Económico*, México, Julio-Septiembre de 1999, Vol. 66, 3, No. 263, 1999, p. 365-417.

Hernani, W., "La Pobreza en el Área Urbana de Bolivia: Período 1989-1997," Tesis, Departamento de Economía, Univesidad Católica Boliviana, La Paz, Bolivia, 1999.

IMF, "Bolivia: Initiative for the Heavily Indebted Poor Countries (HIPC) Completion Point Document," International Monetary Fund and International Development Association, September 4, 1998.

_____, "Debt Relief for Low-Income Countries: The Enhanced HIPC Initiative," International Monetary Fund, Pamphlet Series No. 51, Washington, D.C., 1999.

_____, "Bolivia: Decision Point Document for the Enhanced Heavily Indebted Poor Countries (HIPC) Initiative," International Monetary Fund and International Development Association, January 13, 2000.

INE, *Base de Datos del Sistema de Indicadores Sociales*, CD-ROM, *Instituto Nacional de Estadística*, Bolivia, 1999.

Jemio, L. C., "Micro- and Macroeconomic Adjustment in Bolivia (1970-1989): A Neostructuralist Analysis of External Shocks, Adjustment and Stabilization Policies," Ph.D. thesis, Institute of Social Studies, The Hague, 1993.

_____, "Reformas, Crecimiento, Progreso Técnico y Empleo en Bolivia," in Antelo, E. and Luis C. J., eds., *Quince Años de Reformas Estructurales en Bolivia: Sus Impactos sobre Inversión, Crecimiento y Equidad*, ch. 7, La Paz, CEPAL and UCB, 2000, p. 355-396.

Jiménez, W. and E. Yáñez, "Pobreza en las Ciudades de Bolivia: Análisis de la Heterogeneidad de la Pobreza 1990-1995," Documento de Trabajo 52/97, UDAPSO, La Paz, 1997.

MDSP, *Primer Censo de Gobiernos Municipales, Ministerio de Hacienda y Ministerio de Desarrollo Sostenible y Planificación*, 1998.

_____, Participación Popular en Cifras, Volumen III, Ministerio de Desarrollo Sostenible y Planificación, *Viceministerio de Planificación Estratégica y Participación Popular, Primera Edición*, January 2000.

Orrelana, W., "Ayuda Externa y Ahorro Interno: El Caso Boliviano (1970-1992)," Documento de Trabajo No. 05/95, Instituto de Investigaciones Socio-Económicas, Universidad Católica Boliviana, La Paz, December 1995.

Prudencio, J. and A. Franqueville, *La incidencia de la Ayuda Alimentaria en Bolivia*, La Paz, UNITAS, 1995.

STDN, *Diálogo 2000: Resumen Ejecutivo, Hacia la Mesa Nacional, Secretaría Técnica del Diálogo Nacional*, La Paz, Bolivia, 2000.

UDAPE, "*Bolivia: Gasto Social y la Iniciativa 20/20*," manuscript, La Paz, December 1998.

United Nations, *United Nations Millennium Declaration* (55/2), 2000.

UNDP, *Human Development Report 2000*, 2000.

VEH, *Energy in Bolivia*, Information Bulletin of the Vice-ministry of Energy and Hydrocarbons, 2, 3, 1999.

Appendix A1. Debt service and non-service, by type of creditor

Year	Debt service (US$ million)				Unpaid debt service (US$million)			
	Multi- lateral	Bilateral	Private	Total	Multi- lateral	Bilateral	Private	Total
1981	41.4	62.8	190.8	295.0	-	-	-	-
1982	46.9	90.1	147.8	284.8	-	-	-	-
1983	60.3	82.5	187.1	329.9	-	-	-	-
1984	89.8	180.4	73.1	343.3	-	-	-	-
1985	116.8	115.9	15.4	248.1	-	-	-	-
1986	135.6	50.0	24.4	210.0	-	-	-	-
1987	114.1	45.0	8.1	167.2	3.2	113.4	0.0	116.6
1988	191.5	41.2	6.2	238.9	0.1	300.5	0.0	300.6
1989	193.4	26.4	6.7	226.5	1.1	156.8	2.7	160.6
1990	202.7	24.8	0.8	228.3	0.0	29.1	7.0	36.1
1991	163.8	30.6	0.8	195.2	0.0	16.2	9.7	25.9
1992	176.2	21.8	8.4	206.4	0.0	14.0	11.4	25.4
1993	194.9	38.4	6.8	240.1	0.0	24.8	13.2	38.0
1994	209.3	57.9	8.7	275.9	0.0	124.5	0.0	124.5
1995	228.9	53.5	4.2	286.6	0.1	81.2	17.1	98.4
1996	251.2	49.2	2.5	302.9	0.0	65.8	17.4	83.2
1997	259.7	58.3	2.8	320.8	0.0	21.7	9.3	31.0
1998	307.9	58.7	3.8	370.4				

Source: Banco Central de Bolivia.

Appendix A2. Price indices for export commodities and imports

Year	Minerals	Tin	Hydro- carbons	Natural gas	Tradi- tional	Non- tradi- tional	Total exports	Total imports	Terms of trade
1980	209.6	257.1	98.2	96.5	164.2	70.9	148.4	59.2	250.5
1981	174.2	215.9	134.6	132.2	158.3	69.5	143.9	63.2	227.7
1982	150.9	195.4	150.3	147.7	151.2	61.7	136.5	67.7	201.7
1983	153.0	197.9	152.3	151.5	153.7	51.1	136.5	66.9	203.9
1984	148.8	187.7	153.2	151.5	152.1	57.4	136.5	69.0	197.8
1985	138.4	179.9	151.3	149.6	146.1	58.9	130.6	74.9	174.4
1986	88.1	97.7	133.6	132.2	114.3	82.3	106.8	71.7	149.0
1987	96.4	108.0	107.1	106.2	105.1	88.7	100.9	76.4	132.0
1988	104.8	113.1	93.3	93.6	101.0	97.2	99.4	80.4	123.7
1989	113.4	137.5	93.0	93.1	105.4	97.9	103.4	88.6	116.7
1990	100.0	100.0	100.0	100.0	100.0	100.0	100.0	100.0	100.0
1991	83.4	91.8	103.2	103.2	90.6	94.8	91.9	105.5	87.1
1992	88.6	101.2	58.7	58.1	78.3	93.3	82.9	108.5	76.3
1993	77.3	86.6	42.6	42.1	65.4	97.1	74.5	110.7	67.3
1994	84.0	90.2	41.8	41.1	69.6	101.2	78.6	114.1	68.9
1995	88.5	102.5	44.6	43.8	73.4	103.4	81.6	118.2	69.0
1996	88.4	102.7	44.9	44.0	73.6	103.6	81.8	121.1	67.5
1997	86.8	94.0	42.5	41.6	71.4	104.3	81.0	120.0	67.5
1998	78.6	93.0	32.9	33.0	62.9	102.1	75.5	118.4	63.7
1999	75.9	88.7	33.0	29.2	61.3	90.3	69.9	117.1	59.7

Source: UDAPE.

Appendix A3. Bolivia's performance relative to the 1997-1998 social development targets

	Base	Target 1997	1998	Observed value 1997	1998
Education					
1. Total expenditure in primary and secondary education/GDP	3.1	3.3	3.5	3.3	3.3
2. Rural coverage-boys	66	67	69	68	81
3. Rural coverage – girls	54.0	56.0	60.0	56.7	77.0
4. Number of girls and boys who finish grade 5 in urban areas	96,000	88,000	91,000	87,000	92,000
5. Number of girls and boys who finish grade 5 in rural areas	60,000	63,000	66,000	63,000	68,000
6. Number of girls who finish grade 5 in urban areas	41,000	43,000	46,000	43,000	46,000
7. Number of girls who finish grade 5 in rural areas	29,000	30,000	32,000	30,000	31,000
8. Number of children 6 years or younger in child development programs	43,667	50,000	80,000	3,013	47,051
9. Number of beneficiary schools implementing quality improvement programs	NA	NA	NA	NA	NA
Health					
1. Percentage of children 5 years old or younger treated for Acute Respiratory Infections within the Maternal and Child Insurance Program	25	43	50	69	69
2. Percentage of children 5 years old or younger treated for severe diarrhea within the Maternal and Child Insurance Program	25	25	36	26.2	29
3. Percentage of births attended by professionals within the Maternal and Child Insurance Program	30	45	56	43.8	49
4. Percentage of children who have completed the vaccination cycle appropriate for their age	78	80	82	86.5	80
5. Share of annual parasite index in endemic malaria areas (1000)	20.7	35.2	20.1	5.3	21.7
6. Percentage of houses fumigated against Chagas in endemic areas	8.0	14.0	25.0	13.4	16.0
7. Percentage of pregnant women in endemic areas undergoing Chagas tests	NA	NA	NA	NA	NA
Rural Development					
1. Number of beneficiaries of water and sanitation projects in rural areas	132,000	132,000	132,000	186,052	216,662
2. Investment in improvement/rehabilitation of rural roads (US$ million)	32.0	32.0	42.0	44.8	40.4
3. Number of hectares subject to official land registry and sanitation (millions)	0.33	1.60	3.50	1.60	3.50

Source: IMF (2000).

Ethiopia's External Debt: The Impact and the Way Forward*

Befekadu Degefe

ABSTRACT

This paper reviews the status of Ethiopia's external debt, identifies the conditions that led to its growth, and suggests means to reduce it. More specifically, the paper examines the conditions under which the objectives of reducing poverty in Ethiopia can be achieved. Not only is the country's debt unsustainable, but also, even though large amounts of debt relief were allowed, they will not be sufficient for the country to fulfill its responsibility toward global poverty reduction goals. Assuming there's no change in income distribution, Ethiopia would have to increase its GDP by more than 8% a year over the next twenty years to allow the country to meet internationally agreed poverty reduction targets. Complete debt forgiveness, accompanied by additional resource inflows will be necessary if an attempt is to be made to meet that objective.

RÉSUMÉ

Cet article passe en revue l'état de la dette de l'Éthiopie, identifie les facteurs responsables de la croissance de cette dette, et propose des mesures pour sa réduction. Spécifiquement, l'article examine les conditions sous lesquelles l'objectif de réduire la pauvreté en Éthiopie pourra être atteint. Il maintient que la dette de l'Éthiopie est non seulement insoutenable, mais que, même des montants excessifs d'allégement de la dette ne pourront permettre au pays d'atteindre les objectifs globaux de réduction de la pauvreté. S'il n'y a pas de changement dans la distribution des revenus, le PIB de l'Éthiopie devrait augmenter de plus de 8% par an pendant les vingt prochaines années pour qu'elle puisse atteindre ses objectifs de réduction de la pauvreté sur le plan international. L'annulation complète de la dette ainsi que des flux additionnels de ressources seront nécessaires si l'on cherche à atteindre cet objectif.

* I would like to thank John Serieux, Senior Researcher, North-South Institute, Ottawa, Canada, for his extensive comments on an earlier version of this paper. All errors remain my responsibility.

INTRODUCTION

Ethiopia comes at or near the bottom of several global rankings. In its various World Development Reports, the World Bank locates it on the lowest rung on a per capita income basis. The United Nations Development Program's Human Development Report ranks it third from the bottom. These are all reflections of the miserable conditions in the country.

These conditions remain despite, and sometimes because of, long-running and significant external assistance that has been, and continues to be, a permanent feature of the country's history. Before 1945, and going as far back as five centuries, the country sought defense-related assistance to protect itself from invasions (Pankhurst 1967). During the post-World War II period, dependence on external assistance increased in intensity and broadened in coverage to include both the defense and economic arenas.

The country's dependence on external resource inflow in the form of credit and grant aid has now reached the stage where it cannot survive without it (Alemayheu and Befekadu 1999). A considerable proportion of government expenditure on the most basic services is made possible by grants and external credit. During the 1990s, external grants and loans financed no less than a quarter of the government's total expenditure.

Despite the many benefits derived from external assistance, the latter has at the same time become a hindrance to the country's development. In particular, the external debt burden has grown to an impossible level, claiming twice what the country earns from its exports of goods and services. If Ethiopia were a company rather than a sovereign country, it would have been declared bankrupt and would have ceased to exist long ago.

The purpose of this paper is to review the status of Ethiopia's external debt, identify the conditions that led to its growth, and suggest means for its alleviation. In particular, the paper examines the conditions under which the International Development Agenda of reducing poverty over a period of two decades would be met.

The essential argument of the paper is that Ethiopia's debt is not simply unsustainable; even the most generous debt relief would not bring the country within reach of meeting its responsibility within the context of global poverty-reduction goals. In fact, much more than complete debt relief would be necessary for any credible attempt at reducing poverty by half over 20 years. Complete debt forgiveness would need to be accompanied by additional resource inflows, as well as a viable policy framework.

The paper has five sections: section I examines the external debt stock, both from a historical perspective and from its current status; section II, the effect of external credit and, more so, external assistance, on the economy; section III, the debt burden using different measures; section IV, the efforts to reduce the debt burden; and section V, the conditions and requirements for meeting the international development objectives of reducing poverty by half over 20 years.

I. ETHIOPIA'S EXTERNAL DEBT

Ethiopia's external debt has changed significantly in magnitude, structure and composition over the years. For comparative purposes, table 1 shows the debt stock and creditors at two critical periods in the country's history over the last 25 years, and for the latest year available.

In 1974, the Imperial regime was overthrown by a military junta (Dergue) whose first budget was issued June 30, 1975.[1] As shown, the stock of external debt the Military regime inherited from the Imperial government as of that date was US$372 million, or 14% of GDP at current prices.

Table 1. Total external debt by major sources (US$ millions)

Creditors	Amount on 30/06/75	%	Amount on 30/06/92	%	Amount on 30/06/99	%
Multilateral	169.3	45.5	1476.8	41.6	2742.7	64.6
IDA	121.1	32.6	944.0	26.6	1641.1	38.7
ADB Group	32.8	8.8	350.1	9.8	846.0	19.9
Others	15.4	4.1	182.7	5.2	255.6	6.0
Bilateral	146.6	39.4	1468.4	41.4	1382.8	32.6
Paris Club	128.6	34.6	761.3	21.5	605.3	14.3
Non-Paris Club	18.0	4.8	707.1	19.9	777.5	18.3
Commercial	55.9	15.3	604.3	17.0	117.2	2.8
NCBED	–	–	–	–	68.5	1.6
EAL	–	320.0	–	–	48.7	1.2
Total (excluding Russia)	371.8	100.0	3549.5	100.0	4242.6	100.0
Russia	–	–	5248.2	59.7	5903.0	58.2
Total (including Russia)	371.8	–	8797.7	–	10145.6	–

Source: Credit and Investment Department, Ministry of Finance.
NCBED = Commercial credit not covered by the debt buyback operation.
EAL = Ethiopian Airlines debt.

---

1. Actually, the fiscal year runs from July 7 of the current year to July 6 of the following year.

Figure 1. External debt 1975-1999

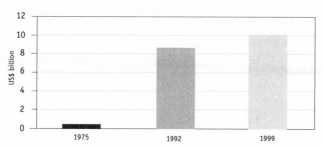

On May 28, 1991, the military government was in turn overthrown by the
Ethiopian Peoples' Revolutionary Democratic Front (EPRDF), whose first
budget was issued June 30, 1992. At that time, the country's external debt
stood at US$3.5 billion and 3.1 billion rubles.[2] In dollar terms, the country's
total debt stock at the commencement of the new regime stood at US$8.8
billion, equivalent to 95% of GDP at current prices. Thus, during its 17-year
tenure, the military government increased the country's total debt 24-fold, at
an annual average growth rate of 21%.

As of June 30, 1999, the total external debt stock had increased to an equivalent of US$10.2 billion, of which US$5.9 billion was owed to Russia and the
balance of US$4.3 billion to other multinational, bilateral and commercial
creditors. This amounts to an annual growth rate of 2% of GDP over the
intervening eight years.

A.   SOURCES OF CREDIT

Although the country's indebtedness to all creditors increased in magnitude
during the last 25 years, the changes in the sources of long-term credit are particularly conspicuous. In 1975, the shares of multilateral, bilateral and commercial debt were 46%, 39%, and 15% respectively. In 1992, the shares of these
sources of credit were 17%, 76% and 7% respectively. The change in the relative share in favour of bilateral at the cost of multilateral and commercial was
due to the colossal (mainly) military credit from the former Soviet Union,
which accounted for nearly 60% of the total external debt stock.

---

2.   3.1 billion rubles is equivalent to about US$5.2 billion (the exchange rate was 0.6 ruble
to US$1 at the time). The total debt given in US$ in table 1 is the sum of these two debts.

Figure 2. Sources of credit in 1975

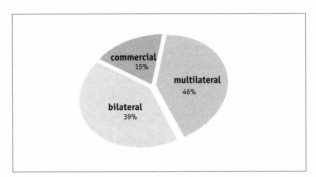

Figure 3. Sources of credit in 1992

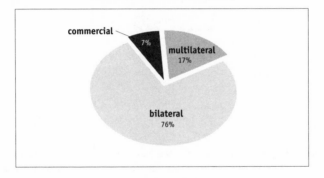

By 1999, the respective ratios had changed to 27%, 72% and 1%. The increase in the proportion of multilateral debt is associated with loans obtained mainly from the World Bank, the IMF and the African Development Fund (ADF), (the soft window of the African Development Bank Group) to finance structural adjustment programs (SAPs).

The sharp decline in the share of commercial credits is the result of the commercial debt buyback operation completed in 1996, as well as the significant reduction in the debt contracted by Ethiopian Airlines as a result of regular and timely repayments. As of June 30, 1999, the debt owed to multilateral creditors totalled US$2.7 billion or 27% of external debt of the country and 65% excluding the amount owed to Russia. Among the multilateral financial institutions, the major sources of credit are the IDA, the soft window of the World Bank Group, and the ADF.

Of the total non-ruble debt, US$1.6 billion or 59.8% of the multinational and 39% of the total debt is owed to the IDA, US$0.8 billion or 31% of the multilateral and 28% of the total non-ruble debt is owed to the ADF, and the remaining US$0.5 billion or 9% of the multilateral or 6% of the non-ruble debt is owed to other multilateral creditors.

Figure 4. Sources of credit in 1999

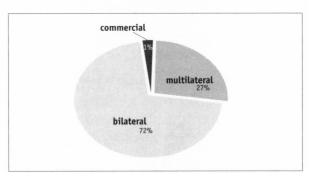

As of June 30, 1999, the total official bilateral debt (excluding the ruble-denominated debt) amounted to about US$1.4 billion, representing 15% of the total external debt and 33% of the debt excluding the ruble-denominated debt. Of this, US$0.6 billion or 44% of the non-Russian bilateral debt was owed to the Paris Club creditor countries, while the balance of US$0.8 billion or 56% was owed to the non-Paris Club creditors. The relative shares of the Paris Club and the non-Paris Club creditors in 1992 were 52% and 48%, respectively. The decline in the share of the Paris Club creditors over the years is due to debt cancellation and rescheduling, whereas the increase in the share of the non-Paris Club creditors is due to the increase in accumulated arrears.

Of the debt owed to the non-Paris Club creditors, the lion's share is the ruble-denominated debt owed to the Russian Federation, which, as of June 30, 1999, amounted to 3.5 billion rubles or US$5.9 billion at the exchange rate of

0.6 ruble to US$1. The debt owed to Libya is also substantial and, as of the same date it amounted to US$243 million, or about 37% of the total non-Paris Club debt (excluding the ruble-denominated debt).

Commercial credits, as of June 30, 1992, stood at about US$604 million or 17% of the total debt (excluding the ruble-denominated debt), of which US$320 million or 53% was Ethiopian Airlines debt. However, over the years commercial credits have continuously declined, and amounted to US$117 million or 2% of the total debt (excluding ruble debt) by June 1999. The main reason for the significant decline in commercial credits was the debt buyback operation, which retired US$226 million, and timely repayments by the national carrier.

Figure 5.   External debt by source in 1999

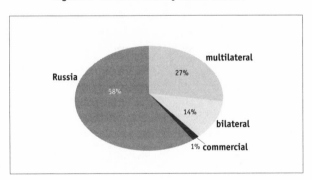

B.   EXTERNAL DEBT BY HOLDERS

All of a country's debt both short and long term, is either public or publicly guaranteed. There is no private sector debt. The country also does not borrow from private financial institutions because its very low credit rating precludes its participation on international capital markets. Private creditors are limited to suppliers' credit, or institutions such as the EX-IM Bank of the US that provides credit for exports from that country.

Examination of the total external debt (excluding the ruble-denominated debt, all of which is held by the central government) by holders shows that the central government is the major user. Furthermore, the external indebtedness of the central government is increasing. At the end of June 1992, the central government's external debt amounted to US$2.8 million or 80% of the total non-ruble debt, while the balance of US$712.2 million or 20% was held by the non-central government public sector, in which the most important entities are public enterprises. As of June 30, 1999, however, the proportions had

Figure 6. External debt by holders in 1992

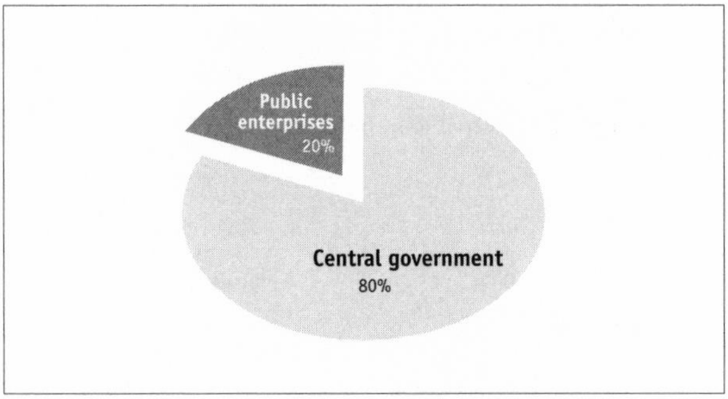

Figure 7 . External debt by holders in 1999

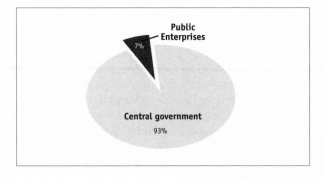

changed and the central government's debt was US$4 billion or 93%. Only US$293.1 million or 7% was owed by parastatals.

The growth in the central government's indebtedness stems from its increasing dependence on external resources for financing the fiscal deficit. This dependence was largely imposed on the government as part of the SAP agreement. That arrangement required it to reduce taxes, and prohibited borrowing from domestic financial institutions to finance its deficits. The reasoning behind the prohibition of central government borrowing from domestic financial institutions derives from the perception of donors that such borrowings would crowd out private sector investment. As a result, a growing share of the deficit, particularly the capital expenditure component, has been financed from external sources since 1992. The volume of domestic borrowing is strictly limited. The financing source is restricted to the non-banking public and is mobilized through the sale of government bonds and treasury bills. In the absence of a capital market, this option for mobilizing financial resources to finance the government deficit has imposed an additional constraint on the government in its effort to expand sorely needed social services,

Table 2. Fiscal out-turn, 1975-1998 (annual averages as % of GDP)

	1975-1984	1985-1990	1992-1998
Revenue	17.4	20.0	15.7
Expenditure	26.1	29.5	24.5
Deficit	8.7	9.5	8.8
Financing			
Domestic borrowing	4.0	4.4	1.0
Foreign financing	4.7	5.1	7.8
Grants	2.1	2.2	3.6
Loans	2.6	2.9	4.2

Source: Own calculation based on World Bank, *African Development Indicators, 2000*.

particularly education and health, and that increased its dependence on external financing.

As shown in table 2, domestic financing of government deficit as a percentage of GDP averaged 4.2% during the military regime and declined to a mere 1% between 1992 and 1998. Foreign financing, however, increased from 4.9% of GDP for the 1975-1990 period to nearly 8% of GDP during the 1992-1998 period.

Obviously, such fiscal policy in general and the limits imposed on government borrowing from domestic sources in favour of external financing have had important repercussions on social conditions and on the country's external debt. Specifically, the reduction of tax rates, particularly on international trade and on business profits, reduced government revenues and increased dependence on grants and credit from abroad. It also forced the government to relinquish its assistance to low-income people in the form of subsidized education, health and basic necessities.

This has sharply increased income inequality in the country, dividing the population into two segments: the extremely rich business class and the majority, who are sinking below poverty. Such developments, unless redressed, can generate resentment and social instability. This aspect of fiscal policy should become a major subject for negotiation in the process of developing the poverty-reducing growth strategy and the post-debt-relief regime because this is likely to continue to increase external debt and the obligations that go with it.

C.   SECTORAL ALLOCATION OF EXTERNAL DEBT

The use of the external resources mobilized should be seen in terms of the source of credit, as well as the time period. Of the US$8.8 billion of debt left behind by the military regime, US$4.7 billion or 53% financed defense activities, while the balance of US$4.1 billion financed relief, rehabilitation and development activities.

By 1999, these proportions had changed. A look at the sectoral allocation of the total debt, excluding the ruble-denominated debt, shows that as of June 30, 1999, 37% had originally been allocated to public administration and social services, 13% to transport and communication, 11% to agriculture, 10% to industry, 10% to mines, energy and water, and the remaining 10% to others.

D.   NATURE, TERMS AND CONDITIONS OF LOANS

Ethiopia's status as an IDA country, means that external loans are predominantly concessional, with low interest and long maturity and grace periods. Concessional long-term debt from all sources increased from 55% in 1970 to over 90% in the late 1990s. While bilateral debt was heavily biased in favour of concessionality from the beginning, a major shift was observed in multilateral loans, whose share of concessional loans increased from a third of the total in the 1970s to an average of 90% in the 1990s.

The terms by which the country acquired loans over the last few years, particularly since the introduction of the reform program, have also evolved significantly. The average maturity period of new financing increased to 41 years

Table 3. **Long-term debt by source (US$ millions) and concessionality (%) 1970-1998**

Debt type	1970	1980	1990	1992	1994	1996	1997	1998
Long term, total	169	688	8483	9003	9571	9485	9427	9618
Concessional	93	563	7537	7858	8521	8696	8633	8742
Concessional (%)	55.0	81.8	88.9	87.3	89.0	91.7	91.6	90.9
Multilateral	70	340	1268	1503	2132	2486	2460	2629
Concessional	23	282	1151	1367	1970	2278	2233	2391
Concessional (%)	32.8	82.9	90.8	89.4	92.4	91.6	90.8	88.2
Bilateral	70	299	6638	6735	6785	6644	6614	6639
Concessional	70	281	6386	6491	6515	6418	6400	6423
Concessional (%)	100.0	94.0	96.2	96.4	96.6	96.6	96.8	96.8
Non-concessional	76	125	946	1145	1086	789	794	876
% of total	45.0	18.2	11.1	12.7	11.0	8.3	8.4	9.1

Source: World Bank, *Global Development Finance, 2000.*

in 1998 from 19 years in 1980, and 22 years in 1990 (World Bank 2000, p. 237). The grace period improved from an average of 4 years between 1980 and 1990 to 10.1 years by the end of the decade. Interest rates on average declined from nearly 7% in 1990 to 0.6% in 1998. The grant element followed the same trend, increasing from an average of 50% during the 1980s to 75% in the 1990s.

E.   CURRENCY COMPOSITION OF EXTERNAL DEBT

Classification of the total external debt, including the ruble-denominated debt by contracting currencies, as at June 30, 1998, shows that about 58% of the debt was contracted in Russian rubles, and 28% in US dollars. The balance of

Table 4. **Average terms of new commitments (all creditors)**

Terms	1970	1980	1990	1992	1994	1996	1998
Interest rate (%)	4.4	3.6	6.6	1.0	1.1	2.2	0.6
Maturity (years)	31.8	19.2	21.7	40.0	40.3	30.4	40.6
Grace period (years)	6.6	3.8	3.5	9.8	9.3	7.6	10.1
Grant element (%)	43.3	39.5	23.7	73.6	71.6	62.1	81.3

Source: World Bank (2000, p. 237).

Table 5.   Currency composition of long term debt (%)

Currency	1970	1980	1990	1992	1994	1996	1998
Deutsche mark	2.7	8.1	1.9	1.9	2.2	2.2	1.8
French franc	0.0	0.0	0.2	0.1	0.0	0.1	0.1
Yen	0.0	2.5	0.5	0.3	0.4	0.2	0.2
Pound sterling	2.1	2.3	0.3	0.2	0.1	0.2	0.2
Swiss franc	0.2	0.1	0.1	0.1	0.1	0.1	0.1
US dollars	41.8	64.5	24.2	27.6	29.2	26.8	28.1
SDR	0.0	0.0	0.2	0.2	0.2	0.2	0.2
Russian ruble*	0.0	15.1	59.7	56.2	55.7	59.2	57.8
All other currencies	53.2	7.4	12.9	13.4	12.1	10.8	11.5

* Author's calculation for Russia; for the others, World Bank (2000).
Source: World Bank, *Global Development Finance 2000*, Country Tables, 2000.

12% of the debt was contracted in an assortment of other currencies, of which the German mark is the most significant.

Table 5 is important not so much for the figures but as an indicator of tied aid, albeit indirectly. With the exception of the US dollar and Special Drawing Right (SDR), a conclusion could be made with regard to the source of imports financed by the loans. The Russian ruble denominated debt financed imports from that country, the most significant of which were defense related. The US-dollar-denominated debt needs to be broken down into credit from the US, which finances goods and services sourced from the US, and those granted by

Table 6.   Flows of external assistance to Ethiopia in 1970-1998, excluding Russian debt (US$ millions)

	1970	1980	1990	1998
Flows on debt				
Disbursement	28	119	378	163
Principle repayment	15	17	177	69
Net flows on debt	13	102	201	94
Interest payment	6	28	59	50
Net transfers on Debt	7	74	142	44
Net transfers as % of GDP	0.3	1.8	1.8	0.7
Flows on grants				
Grants (e.g. technical cooperation)	6	125	604	418
Without grants in kind as % of grants	10	20	31	42
Grants as % of GDP	0.3	3.0	7.9	6.6
Technical cooperation	20	4.4	254	118
Technical cooperation grant as % of GDP	0.9	1.1	3.1	7.3
Total flow	33	243	1,000	580
As % of GDP	1.5	5.9	12.8	14.6

Source: World Bank, *Global Development Finance 2000*.

other creditors, particularly the multilateral institutions whose loans are usually in US dollars.

As shown in table 6, most of the grants come in the form of commodities or technical assistance. Although details of how the credits from bilateral sources are financed or how they were used, are not available, it is most likely that a significant percentage is tied to the purchase of commodities from lending countries.

II. IMPACT OF EXTERNAL RESOURCE FLOWS

Ethiopia has been a beneficiary of external assistance since the eve of World War II. This assistance has come mainly in three ways – short- and long-term loans, grants and technical assistance. A sampling of these flows appears in table 6. Total net resource flows to the country increased from less than 2% of GDP in 1970 to almost 15% of GDP in 1998. Although long-term debt disbursed was increased in the 1990s, net transfers (or the amount of resources actually received by the country) were on the decline. In 1970, disbursement was 1.3% of GDP, but net transfer was only 0.3%. In 1980, disbursement amounted to 2.9% and net transfer was 1% only. In 1990, disbursement was 4.7% and net transfer 1.7% of GDP. In 1998, disbursement and repayment declined to 2.6% and 0.7%, respectively. The difference between disbursement and net transfers is debt-service payments.

The largest share of resource transfer from donors to Ethiopia comes in the form of grants excluding technical assistance. Over the last three decades, this has grown from less than 1% of GDP to nearly 8% in 1990, declining to about 7% in 1998. Technical cooperation grants are also very important and increased from 1% in 1970 to more than 7% of GDP in 1998.

How have these flows affected the country? Research attempting to link external assistance to growth, savings and the government's fiscal position remains controversial. Two recent papers have attempted to evaluate that impact (Befekadu 1992; Alemayehu and Befekadu 1999). Befekadu (1992) showed that there was a positive correlation between external resource inflows and economic growth between 1960 and 1974, but a negative correlation between 1975 and 1988. The different outcome was explained by the different policy regimes pursued by the two governments – the market-oriented imperial regime and the socialist policies of the military government. Alemayehu and Befekadu (1999) used an error correction model (ECM), the results of which showed a positive long-run relationship between aid and growth, although the correlation was negative in the short run.

But even if the econometric models failed to establish significant correlation between growth and external assistance, the benefits of foreign resource inflows, including long-term credit, should neither be underrated nor diminished. Much life has been spared, more adults and children educated, productivity enhanced and critical infrastructures such as roads, communication facilities and power generating plants built. To maximize the benefit from resource inflows, donors would need to improve the nature and quality of aid, and the country should upgrade its debt management.

It has become an established truism that countries' GDP and foreign exchange earnings would need to grow at rates faster than the rates of growth of external debt if they are to avoid falling into the debt trap. Real GDP growth in excess of external debt means that the debt will be retired from the extra income generated by higher growth. An additional requirement for countries such as Ethiopia, whose currencies are inconvertible, is the need to convert the growing domestic goods and services to foreign exchange through increased export of goods and services to pay the debt.

In Ethiopia's recent history, these two requirements were consistently violated, and the result was the excruciating debt burden. As shown in table 8, long-term debt increased 11 times faster than real GDP growth, and 9 times faster than export growth, while per capita income fell by more than 1% per year during the tenure of the military regime. Among the factors that gave rise to such inordinate and asymmetrical growth were inappropriate policies and the wrong use of the resources so mobilized (Befekadu 1992). The economic policies of the military junta included the nationalization of private property, administrative rather than market-based resource allocation, the suppression of the private sector in favour of state enterprises and cooperatives.

The huge defense-related loans from the former Soviet Union had a decisively adverse impact on growth. Their intensive use diverted human, physical and financial resources in waging wars in which large numbers of potentially productive young people were killed and maimed, and social and economic

Table 8.   Growth rates of GDP, exports, debt and population, 1975-1999

Period	GDP	Export	Long term debt	Population
1975-1991	1.9	2.8	20.5	3.1
1992-1999	4.3	8.4	2.1	2.9

Source: Author's calculations.

infrastructure was destroyed, generally disabling productive capacity in the areas of conflict.

The current government has reversed the policy stance of the military regime and has initiated extensive reforms. GDP and export earnings are located on a higher growth trajectory. Per capita income is on a positive trend, and the rate of growth of external debt has been dramatically reduced. Two points that need to be made at this juncture are that the current debt burden is the making of the previous regime and that recent reduction in the rate of growth of debt is partly due to the debt forgiveness and restructuring, as well as the slowing down of the rate at which new debts were contracted.

The positive contribution of external borrowing notwithstanding, it is important to note that there is a limit beyond which it has negative effects on the economy. In two recent papers, Elbadawi et al. (1997a, 1997b) generated a Laffer curve of debt establishing a critical threshold beyond which debt impacts negatively on growth and investment. On the basis of their results, debt in excess of 97% of GDP is likely to have a negative impact on investment and growth. With respect to the private sector investment, they posit that a debt to GDP ratio greater than 33.5% would generate a depressive effect by reducing investment.

In the Ethiopian experience, both of these thresholds have long been surpassed and have assumed impossible magnitudes. The impact of the debt burden is most acutely felt by the private sector, whose investments are crowded out by the servicing of foreign debt, and existing plants remain underutilized due to a shortage of foreign exchange. Even where foreign exchange is obtained through the competitive market, the resulting depreciation of the domestic currency renders domestic plants uncompetitive relative to imports. The net effect is that the servicing of foreign debt reduces the supply of foreign exchange, which in turn reduces the volume of strategic inputs (including capital goods, raw materials, and spare parts) that would have contributed toward pushing the economy to the full employment frontier.

III. DEBT BURDEN AND SUSTAINABILITY OF DEBT

External borrowing has had two important effects on Ethiopia's economy and on the welfare of the people. First, it has increased the volume of resources available both for consumption and investment as shown above. Second, the negative effect of external debt is the growth of the volume of repayments (interest and principal) beyond the country's capacity, which has resulted in the gradual build-up of arrears. The responsibility of meeting its international obligations, while at the same time satisfying the population's basic needs and laying the minimum developmental infrastructure for future generations, has become an impossible task.

The issue of what constitutes debt sustainability and how it should be measured is a contentious one (Cohen 1988). There are essentially three basic postulates of sustainability: those of creditor countries and institutions, those of the NGO community, and those of the national social planners, the objective being to realize the international development goals. We will deal with the first concept in this section and consider the latter two in the following section.

The idea of sustainability held by creditors presumes that, by eliminating arrears, rescheduling, and debt-reduction measures, the country can meet its debt-service obligations (i.e. equating debt service paid and debt service due). The strategy for realizing that objective also targets increased export earnings and import contraction such that sufficient foreign exchange surplus is generated to service the debt.

While this general idea governed the relationship between debtor and creditor, countries and institutions, an agreed upon quantitative measure of a sustainable level of debt did not exist until the HIPC Initiative was launched in 1996. This initiative defined a sustainable debt level for poor countries as one

Table 7.   External debt burden indicators for Ethiopia

Debt burden indicators	1980	1992	1993	1994	1995	1996	1997	1998
Debt service as % of export								
Scheduled	7.6	376.8	363.5	213.2	150.9	145.4	175.3	192.6
Actual	7.6	23.9	18.5	19.8	19.1	42.2	9.6	11.3
Debt/export ratio (%)	159	2037	1889	1788	1277	1225	968	984
Debt/GDP ratio	17	169	158	209	180	169	159	160

Source: World Bank, *Global Development Finance 2000*, Export of Goods and Services, 2000.

where the NPV of debt to exports ranged between 200% and 250%, with an annual debt service of up to 20-25% of exports.

In 1999, creditor countries and institutions revised the original HIPC threshold. HIPC II broadened the vista by increasing the volume of debt relief to be provided, shortening the process and earmarking the proceeds for poverty reduction. Excluding countries that are eligible for HIPC II through the fiscal window, the entry point was reduced to an NPV of debt-to-export ratio of 150. Table 7 provides the essential measures of the debt burden in Ethiopia in recent years.

The table clearly shows that Ethiopia's debt burden, measured by any standard, is unsustainable. In the 1990s, the debt-to-GDP ratio averaged close to 170. The debt-to-export ratio averaged more than 1,400, although it declined late in the decade because of higher export earnings and reduced debt through debt relief. The scheduled debt service would have claimed twice the annual foreign exchange earnings from the export of goods and services, a clearly untenable situation.

IV. EFFORTS AT REDUCING THE DEBT BURDEN

It is clear that the debt burden needs to be reduced, given the above parameters, if only for want of resources to meet debt-service obligations. Faced with the impossibilities of meeting scheduled payments, the government pursued four basic coping strategies. The first was to reduce payment. In this, the government pursued a very selective strategy, meeting all the obligations of the multilateral institutions and those of the Paris Club creditors, with the exception of Russia (table 9).

As a result of the gap between the scheduled and actual debt-service payments, arrears have been building up in recent years. Until 1989, Ethiopia had no arrears, but starting in 1990, the country began to fall behind in meeting its contractual obligations of repaying its debt. As in the discussion of the debt stock, it would be useful to relate the arrears into their respective US dollar- and Russian ruble-denominated debts.

When the new government assumed office in 1992, the accumulated arrears amounted to US$490 million and 996 million rubles (equivalent to US$1.7 billion), all of it owed to the non-Paris Club creditors. By June 1999, arrears had risen to US$668 million and to 3.3 billion rubles (or US$5.5 billion). Arrears of the US dollar-denominated debt had increased by 36%, while arrears in rubles debt had risen by 231% between 1992 and 1999. Arrears in the total debt stock increased from US$2.2 billion to US$6.1 billion, or 187%.

Of the total arrears by the middle of 1999, US$4.8 billion or 79% were arrears on principal and US$1.3 billion were interest payments. Of the total US dollar-denominated arrears, US$568 million or 85% was to be repaid by the central government while the rest – US$100 million was the responsibility of the rest of the public sectors. Out of the total arrears in rubles, 2.8 billion rubles (85%) was defense credit, whereas the balance of 0.5 billion rubles (15%) was development loans.

Table 9.   Nominal and net present value (NPV) of external debt outstanding
            at end of June 1998 (US$ millions)

	Principal	Arrears	Total
Total nominal debt stock	**4,778.4**	**5,203.6**	**9,981.9**
Multilateral	2,850.5	0.0	2,850.5
Bilateral official	1,857.8	5,203.6	7,000.0
Paris Club	1,712.8	4,563.4	6,276.2
(without Russia)	(1,077.4)	(4,563.4)	(5,640.8)
Non-Paris Club	145.0	5,78.7	723.7
Commercial creditors	70.1	61.4	131.5
NPV of total debt	**2,821.4**	**5,203.6**	**8,025.0**
Multilateral	1,448.2	0.0	1,448.2
Bilateral official	1,302.0	5,203.6	6,505.6
Paris Club	1,220.4	4,563.4	5,783.8
(without Russia)	(721.8)	(4,563.4)	(5,285.3)
Non-Paris Club	81.6	578.7	660.4
Commercial Creditors	71.2	61.4	132.6

Source: World Bank.

The second strategy was to increase foreign exchange earnings. To this end, the government implemented reforms that would have a positive impact on the tradable sector. In 1992, the currency was devalued by 41% to make the country's exports more competitive. This policy was accompanied by institutional reforms that included the dismantling of state enterprises engaged in the purchase and export of exportables, and the elimination of price controls. These reform measures have had a positive impact on foreign exchange earnings. Between 1992 and 1999, exports averaged an annual increase of 11%.

The third avenue was to negotiate with creditors for debt reduction. In view of reducing the country's external debt service obligations and the debt overhang, debt-reduction measures have already been taken. Specifically, two debt-relief negotiations with the major Paris Club creditor countries and a debt buyback operation have been completed successfully, and bilateral negotiations with the non-Paris Club creditor countries have been initiated.

A.   PARIS CLUB I AND II DEBT RESTRUCTURING

The first round of Paris Club meetings with creditor countries for the restructuring of the debt was held in 1992. At this meeting, the terms applied to restructure the debts were London terms or Enhanced Toronto terms, which allows a 50% reduction in NPV terms on all eligible pre-cut-off date Paris Club debts. The agreed upon cut-off date for restructuring was to be 31 December 1989, with consolidation period of 35 months covering the period from 1 December 1992 up to 31 October 1995. As a result of the first round of Paris Club debt restructuring, arrears up to 30 November 1992 amounting to US$208 million and repayments due during the consolidation period amounting to US$165 million with a total of US$373 million were restructured. Out of this, US$102 million (or 27%) was cancelled while US$ 271 million (or 74%) was rescheduled.

Although the first round of the Paris Club restructuring provided relief to the debt-distressed economy, it was insufficient to render the stock of debt sustainable. Aware that this heavy debt burden would hinder the successful implementation of the reform program, a second approach was made to the Paris Club creditor countries in 1997. The fact that the country had established a good track record during the previous three years and that the fourth Policy Framework Paper (PFP) and the first ESAF arrangements with the IMF were in place, provided the basis for restructuring. The consolidation period was 34 months, from January 1, 1997 to October 21, 1999. The term applied was Naples term, which allows a 67% reduction in NPV terms on all eligible debts.

As a result of the second Paris Club debt restructuring, debt relief worth US$164.8 million was obtained. Out of this, US$40 million was cancelled, while the remaining US$125 million or 76% was rescheduled. Of the total relief, US$52 million was arrears and US$113 million was debt service due during the consolidation. Under these two debt-restructuring programs, the total debt relief obtained was US$538 million, and out of this US$142 million or 26% was cancelled and US$396 million was rescheduled.

B.   THE RUSSIAN FEDERATION DEBT

The debt owed to the Russian Federation was denominated in both rubles and US dollars. The loans denominated in US dollars had been cleared through the IDA-financed commercial debt buyback operation. The ruble-denominated debt at the end of June 1999 amounted to 3.5 billion rubles or about US$5.9 billion (using the exchange rate US$1 = 0.6 ruble, which was set by the Central Bank of the Russian Federation to evaluate the Russian claim on other countries). This debt represents about 80% of the total bilateral debt and 58% of the country's total debt stock. In order to resolve the debt issue with the Federation, the Ethiopian government held a series of negotiations. Since the Russian Federation became a member of the Paris Club, it has cancelled 80% of the debt and agreed to reschedule the remaining 20% on Paris Club Naples terms. Accordingly, US$4.7 billion have been cancelled, bringing it down to a balance of US$1.2 billion.

C.   OFFICIAL NON-PARIS CLUB CREDITORS

Unlike the Paris Club creditor countries, no official forum exists for restructuring debts from the non-Paris Club creditor countries. Their status remains unclear. Bilateral negotiations will most likely be required to resolve that issue.

D.   COMMERCIAL CREDITORS

As of the end of June 1992, debts owed to commercial banks, including suppliers' credit, amounted to US$604 million, representing about 17% of the country's total debt. Starting in 1993, a debt-buyback operation was launched with the assistance of the World Bank and other bilateral donors.

In April 1996, the debt-buyback operation had been finalized, and as a result, US$226 million of eligible principal (excluding US$30 million in interest, which was written off) had been retired at a total cost of US$18 million. The buyback price had been 8 cents per dollar and the operation covered about 80% of the debts included in the program.

Table 10.   Income, debt service and expenditure on education and health per capita, 1980-1998 (US$)

	1993	1994	1995	1996	1997	1998
GDP per capita	100	93	100	106	107	106
Debt per capita	183	183	187	180	174	173
Debt service per capita	5.4	4.6	4.6	4.4	4.0	7.3
Exp. on education per capita	2.8	3.3	3.4	3.9	3.7	3.8
Exp. on health per capita	1.0	1.1	1.3	1.4	1.5	1.7

Source: author's calculation based on World Bank and National Data.

The fourth strategy has been one assumed by the government for lack of choice – low budgetary outlays for social development, particularly education and health.

During the 1990s, per capita income averaged US$102 while per capita debt averaged US$180. Debt service claimed a steadily increasing share of government expenditure, growing from 5% in 1980 to more than 11% in 1998, while it averaged US$5 on a per capita basis. Total (recurrent and capital) expenditure per capita on education and health was lower than the annual per capita debt-service payments. Per capita expenditure on education averaged less than US$3, while that on health amounted to US$1.3 per person per year.

Table 11. Comparative development indicators, 1998

	Ethiopia	SSA	LLDC's	World
HDI	0.309	0.464	0.435	0.7120
Life Expectancy	49.4	48.9	51.9	66.9
Male	42.5	47.6	51.2	64.9
Female	44.4	50.3	52.9	69.1
Adult Literacy	36.3	58.5	50.7	78.8
Male	42.1	68.0	61.4	84.6
Female	30.5	51.6	41.0	73.1
Combined enrollment	26	42	37	64
Male	32	46	42	67
Female	19	37	32	60
GDP per capita (PPP$)	574	1607	1064	6526
Male	764	2079	1356	8587
Female	383	1142	771	4435

Source: UNDP, *Human Development Report,* 2000.

The important point here is that the country spends more on servicing the debt than it does on recurrent and capital expenditures on education and health. For a society that suffers from inordinate illiteracy and one of the lowest life expectancies at birth in the world, its actual debt repayment is staggering. The human conditions in Ethiopia at the end of the millennium are summarized in table 11.

Table 11 paints an unflattering picture of human development in Ethiopia at the end of the millennium. The indicators are not only low in and of themselves but they also compare abysmally to the rest of the world, sub-Saharan Africa (SSA) and the 43 countries designated by the UN as the least developed (LLDC).

The Human Development Index (HDI) is only 43% of the world average, 34% lower than that for SSA and 30% lower than the LLDC average. The adult (15 years and above) literacy rate is less than half the world average, and 62% and 72% of the SSA and LLDC averages, respectively. The combined primary, secondary and tertiary gross enrollment does not accommodate 74% of the appropriate school age children, while the purchasing power adjusted per capita GDP is less than a tenth of the global average, a third of SSA level, and half of the per capita income of LLDCs.

The government has been meeting the partial repayment from the resources that it ill-affords. It would have been more equitable to spend these resources on social development.

E.   SUSTAINABILITY OF DEBT AFTER DEBT RELIEF

The debt relief that Ethiopia received from the first and second round of Paris Club debt restructuring and the commercial debt-buyback operations have led to a reduction in scheduled debt-service ratios. However, the impact of these debt-relief operations on the economy has been insignificant.

Table 12.   Debt burden indicators before and after debt relief
(US$ millions)

Debt burden indicators	1997	1998	1999
Debt service before relief (US$)	430.2	212.2	217.4
Debt service after relief	86.2	172.8	178.2
Total debt before relief	117.4	4,322.1	4,286.1
Total debt after relief	073.4	4,282.7	4,242.6
Export of goods & services	9.0	538.0	570.0
Debt service ratio before debt relief (%)	77.0	39.4	38.2
Debt service ratio after debt relief	69.1	32.1	31.3
Debt-to-export ratio before relief (nominal) (%)	736.6	803.4	751.9
Debt-to-export ratio after relief (nominal)	2.7	796.0	745.1

Source :   Ministry of Finance, Credit and Investment Department.
Excluding Russian Debt.

Even after debt relief, Ethiopia's external debt burden remains much higher than the sustainability ratio set out by the World Bank and IMF. Debt service ratio after debt relief declined to 31% of exports compared to 38% before the debt relief. The debt-to-export ratio fell by less than 1% following relief. In other words, the debt relief was too little to have had a significant impact on the debt burden.

To reduce the volume of debt to the globally acknowledged sustainability level of 150% of exports, it would be necessary to cancel close to US$4 billion of the outstanding debt in 1999.

V. DEBT AND CONDITIONALITY: THE PUBLIC'S VIEW

At the time of the writing of this paper, Ethiopia had yet to develop a PRSP as the basis for negotiations (and for defining the magnitude and the nature of debt relief) with creditor countries and institutions. Although donors believe this is to be accomplished thorough an all-inclusive public discussion, based on past experience, the government will likely initiate and complete the process without consulting the public.

In the absence of the PRSP to underpin and anchor public assessment of the specific modalities and conditions relating to debt relief, a broad range of public opinion was solicited with regard to external debts and the conditionalities that accompany debt relief in general. The survey had two basic objectives. The first was to develop an understanding of the degree of awareness of the broad range of social strata on these two issues, and the second was to develop some ideas as to how they were assessed. A simple questionnaire was developed and presented to the individuals from various interest groups, and institutions, representing a cross section of society.

The sample was drawn from representatives of six groups:
- government officials in the ministries of Finance; Economic Development and Cooperation; the National Bank of Ethiopia, and the Central Bank;
- people in the business community;
- NGOs, such as Christian Aid and Oxfam;
- academics at Addis Ababa University – departments of business, economics, and political science;
- people on the street; and
- labour leaders.

From each group, 12 people were randomly selected, making up a sample of 96 (76 males and 20 females). They were asked to reflect on each of the following statements:
- The external debt of the country inhibits growth.
- The external debt negatively affects my welfare.
- The external debt should be written off completely.
- The conditions attached to relieve the debt burden are harmful to the economy.

They were to evaluate them with one of the responses: strongly agree; agree; weakly agree; weakly disagree; disagree; or strongly disagree.

The responses are summarized and evaluated below.

1.   *Government officials*

They are the most knowledgeable and yet the most unsure of their position. Perhaps due to their profession, being all economists, they are most uncertain and most inconsistent in their responses.

On the impact of debt on growth, two thirds of them agreed that it inhibits growth against one third. Those who disagreed maintained that the extra resources from borrowing, if used wisely, should have boosted investment, hence growth. This did not happen because the country had failed to use these

Table 13. Position of economists working for government (% of respondents)

Questions	Strongly agree	Agree	Weakly agree	Weakly disagree	Disagree	Strongly disagree
(1)	17	25	25	17	8	8
(2)	25	17	33	17	8	–
(3)	8	25	17	17	8	25
(4)	8	17	8	25	17	25

resources properly. On the current debt and growth, they maintained that if resources were properly managed, the country could honour its commitments and at the same time invest in priority areas that have the potential to kick-start and sustain high rates of GDP growth.

At a more personal level, 75% agreed that external debt affects their own welfare because the debt-service obligation compromises the government's capacity to increase salaries.

Opinion on debt forgiveness was equally divided. Those viewing debt forgiveness as inappropriate explained their position with regard to the willingness of creditors to extend loans in the future, given that the country cannot do without external assistance.

With respect to conditionality, two thirds of them, although in favour of the appropriate type of conditions, were against the type that is operationalized by the Bretton Woods institutions and bilateral governments. They are convinced that for an economy that is located well inside the production possibility frontier, the appropriate conditionality should be a type that would expand rather than constrain both the demand and the supply side. The current condition assumes the economy is at full employment and that excess demand results in inflation. This is not the case for economies such as Ethiopia's.

In particular, the economists believe that the current strategy imposed by the donors is poverty increasing rather than poverty reducing. They specifically point to constraints on growth due to tight monetary and fiscal policies, and the continued depreciation of the domestic currency, which is not only inflationary but also drives up the prices of imported capital goods and thus reduces investment and capacity utilization.

2. The Business Community

The business community was divided into three categories: industrialists, importers and exporters. Importers and industrialists were generally definitive about their stance on debt.

Industrialists were in total agreement, although with differing intensity, that external debt is harmful to the country's economy. They explained this in relation to their inability to obtain foreign exchange for the importation of capital goods, raw materials, intermediate inputs and spare parts. They associate the shortage of foreign exchange with debt servicing. They also maintained that external debt affects their personal well-being, and recommended that the country's debt be written off.

Table 14. Position of industrialists on debt and conditionality (% of respondents)

Questions	Strongly agree	Agree	Weakly agree	Weakly disagree	Disagree	Strongly disagree
(1)	67	25	8	–	–	–
(2)	83	17	–	–	–	–
(3)	100	–	–	–	–	–
(4)	100	–	–	–	–	–

They are vehemently opposed to conditionality related to liberalization because, in their view, this robs them of the domestic market. Liberalization of external trade has allowed imports to compete unfairly against their products, which suffer a high cost of production due to the high interest rates occasioned by the tight monetary policy and the depreciation of the domestic currency. They are vexed that the government allows the use of scarce foreign exchange to import socially useless and harmful commodities while they cannot import inputs to make full use of existing capacity.

Importers have a markedly different opinion on debt and conditionality. An overwhelming majority believe that external debt harms growth and has a negative impact on their personal welfare. Less debt means more foreign exchange for the import of goods and services and, therefore, a better business environment for them.

They are, however, in favour of conditionality, and more so, liberalization, because they are now limited only by their capacity to import compared to the military junta's policies of prohibiting private importers and a long list of

Table 15. Position of importers on debt and conditionality (% of respondents)

Questions	Strongly agree	Agree	Weakly agree	Weakly disagree	Disagree	Strongly disagree
(1)	25	33	25	2	10	5
(2)	8	17	50	17	8	–
(3)	17	50	33	–	–	–
(4)	8	17	8	33	17	17

Table 16. Position of exporters on debt and conditionality (% of respondents)

Questions	Strongly agree	Agree	Weakly agree	Weakly disagree	Disagree	Strongly disagree
(1)	8	25	33	33	–	–
(2)	–	8	50	25	8	8
(3)	8	8	50	25	8	
(4)	–	–	–	8	42	50

goods. But they complain about the gradual depreciation of the domestic currency because this increases the cost of imports denominated in domestic currency.

Exporters also support liberalization, but they are not as certain about external debt as they are about conditionality. They credit the dismantling of price controls, removal of the prohibitions on private sector involvement in the export of goods and services (in favour of state enterprises and cooperatives), and an end to the compulsory surrender of foreign exchange earned to the central bank, to the conditionality imposed on the government by the IMF.

As a group, they do not feel strongly about the effect of debt on growth or their personal welfare. The majority agree that external debt negatively affects growth, not because they understand the intricate and complex transmission mechanism from one to the other, but because they think of their own status when personally indebted.

3. The NGO community

The NGO community is most explicit on debt and conditionality. NGOs assert that external debt and the conditions that are attached to any relief and further assistance are inimical to growth and poverty reduction. Specifically, they hold the creditor countries and institutions responsible for the extreme and growing poverty of the people.

Table 17. Views of the NGO community on debt and conditionality (% of respondents)

Questions	Strongly agree	Agree	Weakly agree	Weakly disagree	Disagree	Strongly disagree
(1)	17	25	25	17	8	8
(2)	25	17	33	17	8	–
(3)	8	25	17	17	8	25
(4)	8	17	8	25	17	25

NGOs go the distance to allege that their personal welfare is affected by the restraint imposed on them by the debt and conditionality, not in financial terms, but psychological terms, the frustration they experience in living and working in a poor society that is forced to adopt an inappropriate strategy and becomes incapacitated by the debt burden. They maintain that the only viable solution to the debt problem is the complete write-off, and the freedom for each country to prepare its own development strategy.

4. The academic community

The sample from the academic community was drawn from the departments of economics and political science and international relations. The political scientists categorically condemned the creditor countries and institutions. They strongly believe that the external debt is an instrument for neocolonialism and that the conditions are a means of control. They would like to see the debt written off and want the IMF to stop meddling in the country's affairs.

The staff of the Department of Economics had a rather mixed opinion. They saw the debt burden as a constraint on the development process, but they did not support a debt write-off because this would adversely affect future resource flows.

Table 18.   Views of members of the department of economics at Addis
            Ababa University on debt and conditionality (% of respondents)

Questions	Strongly agree	Agree	Weakly agree	Weakly disagree	Disagree	Strongly disagree
(1)	100	–	–	–	–	–
(2)	100	–	–	–	–	–
(3)	8	17	50	8	17	–
(4)	100	–	–	–	–	–

They all agreed that the debt burden affects their welfare, since it affects the growth of the economy and therefore their salary, in real terms, as well as in absolute terms.

They also agreed that the conditions attached to debt relief and external assistance are inappropriate. Given the structure and level of development of the economy, as well as the skills and knowledge base of the society, they found trade liberalization and globalization inappropriate for the industrialization of the country. They were also against the forced withdrawal of the government from the economy, in a country where the private sector is still weak.

5.   People on the street

People from the street are generally unaware of the existence of external debt, but all agreed that any debt is bad and must be paid off. This is their personal view about debt in general, including their own debt. That the general public is unaware and is ignorant of the external debt and its burden is not surprising, since the government has neither disclosed nor discussed these issues with the public to this point.

Conditionality was generally condemned. Public awareness in this regard was high following the complete withdrawal of World Bank, IMF and bilateral assistance from some Western countries because of the war with Eritrea, a fact that was well publicized by the government.

6.   Labour leaders

Labour leaders are not really aware of the debt and the debt burden, but are totally against conditionality because of privatization and the retrenchment effect – when firms are privatized, it is usually accompanied by layoffs, which labour leaders oppose.

The general conclusion emerging from the survey is that, for a variety of reasons, and more so vested interest, both the debt burden and conditionality are not appreciated by the public in Ethiopia. The only group that was able to relate the two to poverty are the NGO community and people working in the ministries of Finance and Economic Development and Cooperation.

VI. THE SOCIAL PLANNERS' VERSION OF SUSTAINABILITY

The social planners' version of sustainability goes beyond the understanding of the creditor countries and institutions, and focusses on the welfare of the people in the debt-distressed countries. In this respect, there are two distinct versions of what we would refer to as the "social planners" idea of debt sustainability – that of the NGO community and that of the OECD countries.

The NGO position is encapsulated within the Jubilee 2000, a coalition of NGOs. The point of departure for the Jubilee 2000 position on debt sustainability is the human development need (World Bank 2000). While the creditors are called upon to operationalize the various debt-relief proposals that offer considerably larger relief than those on the ground, they also require HIPC countries to use the proceeds to reduce poverty.

The NGO proposals can be divided into two types. The first calls on creditor countries and institutions to write off the debt in its entirety. The second approach, the most important proponents of which include UNICEF and OXFAM International (2000), accept the HIPC II arrangement in principle but would like to have it revised to meet the challenges of reducing poverty. Among the major revisions they want to be embodied are:

- determine eligibility criteria on the basis of a more integrated approach and in which poverty-reduction concerns are placed at the centre of macroeconomic policy design;
- anchor debt-sustainability analysis on the fiscal, rather than export, variables since from the human development perspective, budget revenue is a more relevant factor than exports;
- provide debt relief more quickly and deeply by reducing the time span between decision and completion points to a maximum of two years;
- provide interim debt relief by the international financial institutions in advance of completion points to reduce cash flow burden and "front-loading" them in the early years.

The reduction of poverty in the developing countries is also a concern of the OECD countries which initiated the international development agenda, which gave rise to the International Development Targets (IDT). The international development agenda is a synthesis of major global initiatives of the first half of the 1990s. It was first defined as a new agenda for developing cooperation by the DAC of the OECD in its report "Shaping the 21st Century: the Contribution of Development Cooperation." These goals are articulated as:

- reduce the proportion of the people living in poverty by half by 2015;
- implement universal primary education by 2015;
- make progress toward gender equality and empowering women by eliminating gender disparities in primary and secondary education by 2005;
- reduce infant and child mortality rates by two thirds by 2015;
- reduce maternal mortality ratios by three quarters by 2015;
- provide access for all who need reproductive health services by 2015;
- implement national strategies for sustainable development by 2005 so as to reverse the loss of environmental resources by 2015. (OECD 2000)

The social planner's perspective on debt emerges from its target of realizing the international development goals. Thus the planner's objective function is defined by the fundamentals of reducing poverty by half; gender-sensitive universal primary education; reduction of infant, child and maternal mortality; provision of reproductive health care and environmentally sustainable development strategy.

Table 19. The challenge facing the Ethiopian social planner and the donor community

	Baseline (1998)	Target (2020)
People not expected to reach age 40	42.1%	21.1%
Percent of age group not enrolled in primary school	64.8%	32.4%
Infant mortality	110/1000	55/1000
Under 5 mortality	173/1000	86.5/1000
Maternal mortality	110/100,000	55/100,000
Population below the national poverty line	46%	23%

Source: UNDP, *Human Development Report,* 2000; and national data sources.

An obvious point of departure for an Ethiopian planner, as the case would be for planners in any country, is the quantifiable specification of the challenges to be met, the time horizon during which it is to be achieved and the resources required. The specific challenge facing the national social planner and the donor community is that of meeting the IDT shown in table 19.

Because the international development goals would most likely not be met by 2015 as originally envisaged, we have extended the target period to 2020.

In 1998, 42% of the population was not expected to survive to age 40, while 66% are not expected to survive to age 60. Of 1,000 children born alive, 110 did not celebrate their first birthday. Of the 1,000 that survived their first year, 173 did not celebrate their 5th birthday. Nearly one mother in 100,000 dies in the delivery process.

On a national poverty line income of Birr 10,175 (US$165 per year or US$0.45 per day), 48% of the rural, 33% of the urban and 46% of the total population are designated as poor. If the poverty line is based on the internationally accepted US$1 a day, the proportion of the population below this line would increase to 60%. Of the primary school age children, nearly 65% do not attend school. While the female adult literacy rate is 31%, only 27% of primary school age girls attend school (MEDEC 1999).

Environmental degradation is advancing at an alarming rate, estimated at a permanent loss of 0.5% of forest land per year (UNDP 2000). The occurrence of severe drought has decreased to every 7 rather than the usual 10 years of the earlier periods. The environmental degradation is due to population increase and the ensuing higher demand for agricultural land and for fire wood, which provides no less than 90% of energy consumed annually.

Thus the challenge faced by national social planners and the donor community to meet the IDT in Ethiopia is daunting. The key question is what does it take to meet these objectives?

A. REDUCING POVERTY BY HALF

The point of departure for this section of the paper is the international development agenda (IDG) of improving the conditions of life in the poor countries over a 20-year period. Although the IDG was expected to have been initiated in 1995 and run to 2015, developments so far do not favour the meeting of these objectives by the original target date. For this reason, we have taken 2001 as the starting date, to run to 2020.

Furthermore, while the IDG covers a wide area of the human condition in the developing countries, we only focus on poverty. The motivation for this singular target is based on the consideration that the other components could be met through poverty reduction or are a means to poverty reduction. For example, the literacy rate could increase if poverty were reduced and the population were more literate; the higher the productivity, the faster the poor would exit from the poverty trap. Similarly, infant, child and maternal mortality would decline as the income of the poor increases, enabling them to spend more on nutrition and health care.

Given the 46% of the population below the national poverty line in 1999, reducing that amount by half over 20 years requires an annual reduction of 3.4% over the target period. The next question is at what rate does the economy need to grow over the target period? To obtain the required growth, we would have to obtain the growth elasticity of poverty (i.e. the amount by which poverty declines for every 1% increase in GDP).

Our calculations (appendix 1) show that in order to reduce the proportion of the poor from 46% in 1999 to 23% in 2020, it would be necessary to attain and maintain an 8.5% GDP growth rate per year over the target period, assuming an annual population growth rate of 2.9%. Alternatively, at a lower rate of population growth of 2% per year, the required annual GDP growth rate would be 7.6%.

B.   NECESSARY CONDITION TO ATTAIN AND SUSTAIN POVERTY REDUCING GROWTH RATE

Attaining and sustaining an 8.5% growth rate over the target period seems to be very high given past performances and experiences, but it is not an impossible task. A cursory review of GDP growth over the last eight years shows that the actual performances surpassed the required growth rate on a number of occasions. The problem is not one of attaining or even surpassing an 8.5% growth rate as much as one of sustaining at that level. Therefore, the issue is what needs to be done to attain and maintain this growth rate and reduce poverty by half over the next two decades.

Two fundamental issues need to be addressed in this respect, namely, resources and creating an optimal environment. These will be discussed sequentially.

C.   INVESTMENT REQUIRED

Despite the trenchant and empirically convincing criticism by Easterly (1997), the Harrod-Domar model will be used to estimate the resources required to attain and sustain the poverty-reducing rate of growth. The Harrod-Domar growth model in continuous time frame is given by the following set of equations.

Production function: $Y = \min(K/v,\ L/u)$ (1)

Saving function: $S = sY$ (2)

Saving-investment equilibrium condition: $I = dK/dt = S$ (3)

In these equations, Y is GDP; K is capital stock; L is labour; s is saving; I is investment (which is equal to the change in capital stock) over time; v is capital output ratio; and u is labour output ratio.

When capital is the scarce factor in the economy, production is determined by the available capital:

$$Y = K/v \qquad (4)$$

Differentiating equation (4) with respect to time, and substituting equation (2) and (3) yields the growth rate as:

$$(dY/dt)(1/Y) = g = s/v \qquad (5)$$

Given a required growth rate (g′) to reduce poverty by half over the target period and the capital-output ratio, the necessary investment to achieve this rate of growth would be:

$$I/Y = S/Y = s = vg'$$

The incremental capital output ratio of 5.2 was obtained by averaging the annual values over 1992-99. From the simple model developed in the appendix, the growth rate required for achieving a 50% reduction in poverty over the next 20 years is 8.5%. Substituting for v and g yields the annual investment requirement of 44.2% of GDP per year over the target period (if poverty is to be reduced by half over the target period).

At the lower bound population growth rate (of 2%) the required investment would amount to 39.5% per year. This means, in effect, that an annual investment rate of between 40% and 44% of GDP would be required if poverty is to be reduced by half over the next two decades.

D.   RESOURCE REQUIREMENT

The traditional sources of financing investment are domestic saving, ODI flows including long-term credit, and FDI. The average level of these sources of financing are discussed below.

Gross domestic savings over the 25 years averaged 6.5%. Net ODI flows have been increasing and averaged 11% during the period under review. Because of the xenophobic policy of the military regime, the country had no FDI during its 17-year tenure, and it only picked up under the current government.

What is evident from table 20 is that the resources required to finance the required volume of investment are beyond the country's capacity to mobilize either from domestic sources or from abroad. Specifically, if one assumes that the average of the 1990s savings, ODI and FDI, would be available in the future and that these resources and more so the ODI are used to finance investment (which is unlikely given the nature of flows), no more than 28% of the required investment would be covered, leaving a gap of 16% of GDP. Under the alternative scenario of lower population growth, the resource gap would amount to 12 % of GDP.

Table 20. Savings, investment and FDI, 1975-1998

	1975-84	1985-90	1990-98
Gross domestic savings	6.4	7.2	5.7
Net ODI flows	5.1	10.0	17.0
FDI	0.0	0.0	5.4

Sources: World Bank (2000) and UNCTAD (1999).

E.   CLOSING THE FINANCING GAP

If Ethiopia is to meet the international development goals, the above observations show that it is beyond its capacity to finance the required investment. Admittedly, the 44% of annual investment is on the high side, but even if this was reduced to 33% as in the East Asian countries, this would still leave a gap of 5% of GDP. If the debt is to be written off in its entirety, the resources that would be freed from servicing the debt would cover only 2% of GDP after debt relief.

The point here is that, if Ethiopia were to meet the international development goal of reducing poverty by half over the next two decades, it would need more resources than would be released by writing off the entire debt, but this need would only be during the initial years of the program. Assuming that domestic savings would grow at a rate equal to the increase in GDP (i.e. 8% per year), over the target period, it would amount to 27% of GDP, thus enabling the country to finance the bulk of its investment requirements.

This would reduce the country's dependence on external assistance, while liberating a good portion of its population from excruciating poverty.

F.   CREATING AN ENABLING ENVIRONMENT

Mobilizing resources for poverty-reducing growth is a necessary but not a sufficient condition. The sufficient condition would be to develop a poverty-reducing strategy and create an enabling environment.

As the poorest of the poor countries, Ethiopia's development challenge is to reduce and eventually eliminate absolute poverty. The government has taken this objective as its centre piece in the articulation of its development priorities. Although there is as of yet no PRSP, Ethiopia's Agriculture Led Industrialization Development Strategy (ALIDS) has the basic objective of reducing rural poverty by increasing agricultural production and productivity. The strategy is operationalized through the provision of fertilizers, improved seeds, chemicals to small holders and improving the marketing of the proceeds. These inputs are provided on credit.

Although the government is the major player, there are other participants, including NGOs and the donor community. The latter play a critical role by providing the necessary credit for the purchase and transportation of fertilizer, chemicals and other inputs.

While the efforts of the government and the donor community to address the plight of the rural poor through agricultural development are laudable and have shown tangible results, they are nevertheless moving slowly. Attempts at alleviating the plight of the poor are overwhelmed by the pressing needs of the population.

Creating an enabling environment has the additional potential of helping mobilize resources. In particular, there have been massive outflows of both human and financial capital, which if reversed, could add to the availability of resources. Furthermore, an enabling environment would increase FDI.

To this end, the government should continue to deepen its policy reforms, develop a coherent poverty-reducing growth strategy and operationalize these without delay.

CONCLUSION

This paper has attempted to document the extent of Ethiopia's external indebtedness, examine the benefits and constraints it generated, and the conditions under which the international development agenda of reducing poverty by half was to be realized. Despite the empirically established positive impact external credit and assistance have had on the economy and the welfare of the people, it has imposed a burden on the country that the latter cannot shoulder.

While the country has benefited from two rounds of debt cancellation and restructuring under the different arrangements, these arrangements did not yield results that would have reduced the debt burden to a level that is acknowledged by the international community to be sustainable. More debt reduction would be necessary to bring the debt to a sustainable level and capacity to pay based on its annual foreign exchange earnings from the export of goods and services.

Furthermore, and even if the debt is entirely written off, the country would still need additional assistance if it were to kick-start and sustain a level of GDP growth in order to reduce poverty by half over the 20 years, as envisaged in the global development agenda.

In this respect, the objective of reducing poverty by half over 20 years implies that the GDP would have to increase at a rate exceeding 8% over the target period. This result is obtained on the basis of growth elasticity of poverty, given that the current poverty line and income distribution remain constant over the target period.

REFERENCES

Alemayehu, G. and B. Degefe, Management Transition from Aid: Dependence in Ethiopia, in Lancaster, C. and S. Wange, eds., *Managing Transition from Aid in SSA*, Macmillan, 1999.

Ali, A. A. G., "The Challenge of Poverty Reduction in Africa," Discussion paper Series, ESPD/DPS/98/1, Addis Ababa, UNECA, 1998.

Ali, A. A. G. and E. Thorbecke, "Poverty in Sub-Saharan Africa: Magniture and Characteristics," unpublished paper, Nairobi, African Economic Research Consortium (AERC), 1998.

Amoako, K., and A. A. G. Ali, *Financing Development in Africa: Some Explanatory Results*, AERC, Nairobi, 1998.

Befekadu, D., "Growth and Foreign Debt: The Ethiopian Experience 1964-86," Research Paper No. 13, Nairobi, AERC, 1992.

Burnside, C. and D. Dollar, "Aid, The Incentive Regime and Poverty Reduction," draft paper, Washington, D.C., World Bank, 1999.

_____, "Aid, Policies and Growth," Policy Research Working Paper 1777, World Bank Development Research Group, Washington D.C., World Bank, 1997.

Chenery, H. and A. MacEwan, "Optimal Patterns of Growth and Aid: The Case of Pakistan," *Pakistan Development Review*, 1996.

Chenery, H. and A. Strout, "Foreign Assistance and Economic Development," *American Economic Review*, 56, 4, 1996, p. 679-733.

Chenery, H. and M. Bruno, "Development Alternatives in an Open Economy: The Case of Israel," *Economic Journal* , 72, 1962, p. 79-103.

Cohen, D., "The Management of the Developing Country Debt: Guidelines and Application to Brazil," *World Bank Economic Review*, 2, 1, 1988.

Collier, P. and D. Dollar, "Aid Allocation and Poverty Reduction," Working Paper 2041, Washington, D.C., World Bank, 1998.

Griffin, K., "Foreign Capital, Domestic Savings and Economic Development," Bulletin of the Oxford University Institute of Economics and Statistics, 1970.

Griffin, K. and J. Enos, "Foreign Assistance, Objectives and Consequences," *Economic Development and Cultural Change*, 1970.

Heller, P. S., "A Model of Public Fiscal Behaviour in Developing Countries: Aid, Investment and Taxation," *American Economic Review*, 1975.

MEDEC, *The Poverty Situation in Ethiopia*, Addis Ababa, 1999.

Mosley, P., J. Hudson and S. Horrell, "Aid, the Public Sector and the Market in Less Developed Countries," *The Economic Journal*, 1987.

Mukherjee, C., H. White and M. Wuyts, *Econometrics and Data Analysis for Developing Countries*, London, Routledge, 1998.

OECD, "Progress Towards the International Development Goals," Report prepared by the Staff of the IMF, OECD, UN and the World Bank, 2000.

Pankhurst, R., *Economic History of Ethiopia*, Addis Ababa, Haile Selassie University Press, 1967.

UNICEF and OXFAM International, *Debt Relief and Poverty Reduction: Meeting the Challenge*, 2000.

UNDP, *Human Development Report*, New York, Oxford University Press for UNDP, 2000.

Weisskopf, T. E., "The impact of Foreign Capital Inflow on Domestic Savings in Underdeveloped Countries," *Journal of International Economics*, 1972.

White, H., "The Macroeconomics Impact of Development Aid: A Critical Survey," *Journal of Development Studies*, 1992.

World Bank, *Heavily Indebted Poor Countries Initiative: Perspectives on the Current Framework*, 1999, www.worldbank.org/hipc.

_____, *Global Development Finance: Country Tables*, Washington D.C., World Bank, 2000.

APPENDIX 1

CALCULATING THE GROWTH RATE

To obtain the required growth, it would be necessary to obtain the growth elasticity of poverty (the amount by which poverty declines for every 1% increase in GDP).

To this end, we start with a generalized form of poverty function as given in equation (1) below.

$$P = P(\mu, z, m) \tag{1}$$

where, P is an index of poverty, μ is mean per capita income, z is the poverty line, m is a measure of income inequality, say the Gini coefficient.

The change in P can be written as:

$$dP = \frac{\partial P}{\partial \mu} d\mu + \frac{\partial P}{\partial z} dz + \frac{\partial P}{\partial m} dm \tag{2}$$

Since P is homogeneous of degree zero with respect to μ and z, we have, by Euler's theorem:

$$\frac{\partial P}{\partial z} z + \frac{\partial P}{\partial \mu} \mu = 0$$

Equation (2) could be written as follows:

$$dP = \frac{\partial P}{\partial \mu} d\mu - \frac{\partial z}{\partial \mu} \frac{\mu}{z} dz + \frac{\partial P}{\partial m} dm \tag{3}$$

Growth rate in P is given by:

$$\frac{dP}{P} = \frac{\partial P}{\partial \mu} \frac{\mu}{P} \frac{d\mu}{\mu} - \frac{\partial P}{\partial \mu} \frac{\mu}{z} \frac{z}{P} \frac{dz}{z} + \frac{\partial P}{\partial m} \frac{m}{p} \frac{dm}{m} \tag{4}$$

Rearranging the terms, we have:

$$\frac{dP}{P} = (1 - \varepsilon) \eta \frac{d\mu}{\mu} + v \frac{dm}{m} \tag{5}$$

where,

$$\varepsilon = \frac{\partial z}{\partial \mu}\frac{\mu}{z}$$

$$\eta = \frac{\partial P}{\partial \mu}\frac{\mu}{P}$$

$$v = \frac{\partial P}{\partial m}\frac{m}{P}$$

Invoke the Kuznets' elasticity:

$$\kappa = \frac{\partial m}{\partial \mu}\frac{\mu}{m}$$

So that :

$$\frac{dP}{P} = \left(\left(1-\varepsilon\right)\eta + v\frac{dm}{d\mu}\frac{\mu}{m}\right)\frac{d\mu}{\mu} \qquad (6)$$

$$\frac{dP}{P} = \left(\left(1-\varepsilon\right)\eta + v\kappa\right)\frac{d\mu}{\mu} \qquad (7)$$

In the case of Ethiopia, based on parameters derived from an econometric equation fitted by Ali (1998) to cross-section data of the least developed African countries using the Summers and Heston mean per capita income for Africa, our calculations reveal that a 1% growth in GDP would reduce poverty by 0.76.

Furthermore since

$$dP/dt = -3.4 = \beta(g-n)\,1/p$$

where g is the growth rate of GDP, n is the rate of population growth, and b is the growth elasticity of poverty, substituting for β gives the necessary growth rate of 5.6% which is capable of reducing poverty at an annual rate of 3.4%.

This rate of growth assumes that the rate of population increase is zero. To get the growth rate that accounts for population growth, we add the annual increase in population of 2.9% to obtain total growth rate of 8.5% per year.

If it is assumed that the population would increase at a lower rate of 2% per year, given the HIV/AIDS pandemic, the necessary rate of GDP growth to reduce poverty by half over the next two decades would be 7.6% per year.

Nicaragua and the HIPC Initiative: The Tortuous Journey to Debt Relief

Ligia María Castro-Monge

ABSTRACT

This paper examines Nicaragua's experience with the Enhanced HIPC Initiative. Particular attention is paid to the country's experience leading up to the decision point of the Initiative, the magnitude of resource flows resulting from debt relief, and the attitudes of various sectors of the population to debt relief. The research reported here indicates that, though the HIPC Initiative will result in a substantial reduction in Nicaragua's foreign debt, the expected amount of debt forgiveness does not match, either in terms of magnitude or implied discount, some earlier debt reduction operations. Further, the flow of debt relief envisaged would represent a less than 20% enhancement of recent aid flows. While there is general support in Nicaragua for debt reduction and the associated public consultation, what is seen as a top-down, overly limited, and hasty consultation process has come in for severe criticism from several sectors of Nicaraguan society. Beyond debt relief, many Nicaraguans view greater access to developed-country markets, and more innovative and coordinated approaches to development financing, as indispensable to long-term poverty reduction.

RÉSUMÉ

Cet article examine l'expérience du Nicaragua par rapport à l'Initiative PPTE renforcée. L'expérience du pays jusqu'au point de décision de l'Initiative, l'ampleur des flux de ressources provenant de l'allègement de la dette, l'attitude des différents secteurs de la population par rapport à l'allègement et la conditionalité de la dette, ainsi que quelques points de vues locaux concernant la marche à suivre au-delà de l'allègement de la dette, sont examinés en détail. Même si l'Initiative PPTE va entraîner une importante réduction de la dette extérieure du Nicaragua, l'annulation attendue ne surpasse pas, soit en ampleur ou en escompte implicite, les montants précédents de réduction de la dette. De plus, l'allègement attendu n'équivaudrait qu'à une augmentation de moins de 20% des flux récents d'aide. Même si la réduction de la dette, ainsi que les consultations avec le public reçoivent beaucoup d'appui au Nicaragua, le processus de consultation a été l'objet de critiques de la part de différents secteurs de la société, notamment parce qu'il adopte une approche descendante, et qu'il est trop limité et rapide. Au-delà de l'allégement de la dette, les Nicaraguayens perçoivent un plus grand accès aux marchés des pays développés ainsi que des approches plus innovatrices et coordonnées au financement du développement, indispensables à la réduction permanente de la pauvreté.

INTRODUCTION

Nicaragua has experienced rapid transitions through three distinct political regimes – from a dictatorship to a communist regime, and then to a democracy. The period of communist rule was particularly disastrous on the economic front. These wrenching political, economic and social changes left a legacy of high levels of external debt; low levels of income, production and exports; low social indicators; and a culture of mistrust throughout the country, that impedes collective action and breeds a sense of hopelessness.

In the last decade, Nicaragua has made an extraordinary effort and achieved great progress on the economic front, but these results have not yet translated into important benefits on the social front. One factor that shuts out a large part of the population from potential access to the fruits of economic gain, is the high external debt burden that every Nicaraguan must shoulder (approximately US$1,300 with a GDP per capita of only US$450).

Although debt relief is a necessary condition for Nicaragua to move up the ladder of economic and human development, it is not a sufficient condition. The amount of investment needed to bring Nicaragua's economic and social indicators up to the levels of those of Costa Rica – the most developed country in the region – far exceeds the resources that will be released through debt relief. It would require additional grant aid, foreign direct investment (FDI), and new concessional financing of programs and projects to give Nicaragua a chance for a successful take off.

This paper examines Nicaragua's experience with the heavily indebted poor country (HIPC) Initiative. Particular attention will be paid to the attempt to establish a link between poverty reduction and debt relief, the magnitude of the debt-relief dividend, the extent of the removal of the debt overhang, and the attitudes of the country's leadership toward the debt relief and related conditionality. More generally, this paper tries to determine how the Enhanced HIPC Initiative compares with previous debt-relief experiences for Nicaragua and, therefore, whether its substance validates the greater attention it has received from the international community.

I. ECONOMIC MANAGEMENT, SOCIAL PROGRESS AND THE EXTERNAL DEBT PROBLEM: A BRIEF SITUATIONAL ANALYSIS

A.   ECONOMIC MANAGEMENT AND PERFORMANCE (1990-1999)

Since 1990, with the re-establishment of peace and the restoration of democracy, Nicaragua has made substantial progress in reducing macroeconomic imbalances and reconstructing a market-based economy. As a result, output growth has resumed and inflation has declined; investment (both public and private) and capital formation have recovered, and national saving has become positive (table A1, Appendix). In late 1997, the government adopted a medium-term economic and structural reform program for 1998-2000. In March 1998, the program was supported by a three-year Enhanced Structural Adjustment Facility (ESAF) with the IMF.[1]

Policy implementation strengthened under the ESAF compared to previous years. Nicaragua's economic performance during the first nine months of 1998 was strong. In October, however, Hurricane Mitch hit the country, severely damaging physical infrastructure, housing and crops. Losses were estimated at US$1.3 billion. As a result, real GDP growth slowed, inflation rose and the external current account deficit increased (the larger deficit was covered by the higher official and private capital inflows). In the public sector, revenues increased, expenditure growth was contained, and the finances of public enterprises improved. Thus, despite revenue losses and the acceleration of spending post-Mitch, the overall deficit decreased (compared to 1997 levels) and public sector saving rose. In addition, progress was made in implementing structural reforms.

In early 1999, a new economic program for 1999-2001 was adopted to address the adverse effects of Hurricane Mitch. The program's main objective was to improve social conditions and alleviate poverty, while advancing toward macroeconomic stability. The program's quantitative targets were to be achieved through the implementation of:

- macroeconomic policies;
- a comprehensive set of "second-generation" structural reforms to create conditions for high rates of sustained economic growth, by increasing efficiency and promoting saving and private investment;

---

1. The ESAF has since been renamed the Poverty Reduction and Growth Facility (PRGF).

- social policies and poverty-alleviation programs focussed on promoting economic growth with equity, investing in human capital, strengthening the social safety net and promoting rural development;
- rural-sector policies, aimed at promoting rural development and raising the productivity of small farmers.

Indicators for 1999 show a strong economic recovery. Real GDP growth accelerated and reached 7% as a result of strong growth in domestic demand, driven by the reconstruction effort. Inflation fell to 7%; national saving reached 9.5% of GDP; and open unemployment declined to 11%. However, the fiscal deficit rose above program projections; there were delays in some structural adjustment measures; and concerns about governance remained.

During 2000, the government implemented a policy package to bring performance back to a path of fiscal and external-sector viability, took steps to improve governance, adopted actions to improve the overall wealth of the banking system and increase confidence, and implemented the first stage of the privatization of the state-owned electricity company (distribution units).

B.   POVERTY AND SOCIAL PROGRESS

Nicaragua is one of the poorest countries in the Western hemisphere. Although better than the average for other HIPCs, its social indicators are among the weakest in the Latin American and Caribbean region.[2] Based on the consumption index, almost one half (47.9%) of the population is poor (2.3 million people), of which 17.3% are extremely poor (830,000 people). Measured by the unsatisfied basic needs method, poverty is estimated at 72.6% and extreme poverty at 44.7%. Based on the income-distribution method, overall poverty is 60% and extreme poverty is 33.5%. Judged by relative levels of consumption, in 1998 the level of poverty was 2.4 percentage points lower than it was in 1993; and extreme poverty, 2.1 percentage points lower (Appendix: table A2). Despite these reductions, however, the absolute numbers of both the poor and the extremely poor rose, meaning that population growth has outpaced poverty reduction.

The most recent Human Development Index (based on data for 1998) ranks Nicaragua 116th out of 174 countries (UNDP 2000). During the period 1975-1998, the country had mixed results in the generally measured areas of human development. Although it experienced better than average increases in life expectancy, it was behind the low-income country average in improving

---

2. According to the Human Development Index 2000, in the Americas, only Haiti and Guatemala are weaker than Nicaragua.

Table 1. Nicaragua: selected economic indicators

Variable	1997	1998*	1999*
Economic activity and employment			
GDP growth (%)	5.1	4.1	7.0
GDP per capita growth (%)	2.3	1.3	4.3
Open unemployment rate	14.3	13.2	10.7
Underemployment rate	12.2	11.6	12.3
Prices, interest rates and exchange rate			
Inflation (annual %)	7.3	18.5	7.2
Loans interest rate (%, córdobas, short term)	21.6	21.9	21.3
Savings interest rate (%, córdobas)	8.6	8.7	8.5
Devaluation (annual %)	12.0	12.0	10.0
Public finances (NFPS, % GDP)**			
Tax revenue	27.3	30.1	29.5
Current expenditure	26.1	27.4	25.5
Fixed capital formation	9.1	8.6	12.2
Current surplus	6.5	8.4	8.4
Overall deficit before donations	-7.2	-4.2	-11.9
External financing	8.6	11.3	18.1
External sector (millions US$)			
Exports FOB	625.9	573.2	543.8
Imports FOB	1,329.3	1,383.6	1,683.2
Current account deficit (% GDP)	-41.2	-38.4	-47.3
Gross international reserves	387.1	356.6	512.9
External debt	6,001.0	6,287.1	6,498.9

Notes: * Preliminary figures.
          ** Non-Financial Public Sector.
Source: *Banco Central de Nicaragua* Web site.

literacy rates (table 2). Nicaragua allocates a relatively high share of GDP to the social sectors (12.5% on average for the period 1993-1999, 17.2% in 1999); however, given the country's low average income, annual social expenditure per capita remains extremely low (US$78.8).

The Living Standards Measurement Surveys (LSMS) of 1993 and 1998, and the Health and Population Surveys of 1995 and 1998, indicate that poor and extremely poor households have one or more of the following characteristics:

- rural location (particularly Atlantic coast);
- engaged in agriculture;
- absence of a social safety net;
- larger than average household;
- high fertility rates among female adolescents;
- fewer than the four years of schooling required to acquire useful cognitive ability (3.1 on average for the poor, 2.3 for the extremely poor);
- limited access to safe water, sanitation and health services (Government of Nicaragua 2000, p. 4).

Table 2.   Progress in social development

Social Development Measure	1970	1980	1990	1998
Nicaragua				
Life Expectancy at birth	53.9	58.7	64.5	68.4
Adult Literacy Rate	56.9	61.1	64.9	67.9
Low Income Countries				
Life Expectancy at birth	53.5	-	61.5	63.5
Adult Literacy Rate	42.8	52.7	62.7	68.7

Source: World Bank, *World Development Indicators 2000.*

These characteristics mean that the poor are vulnerable and are highly exposed to terms of trade shocks, natural disasters, illness, theft, fire, and loss of crops. The poor are also conscious of their vulnerability. A qualitative study for the World Bank (2000) found that people who are poor view poverty as a lack of access to the social benefits enjoyed by the non-poor, and the absence of economic and political power to influence decision-making processes that affect their lives.

C.   THE EXTERNAL DEBT PROBLEM

The origin of Nicaragua's external debt problem can largely be traced back to the economic strategy of the Sandinista regime in the 1980s. It resulted from the intensive use of external borrowing and the depletion of international reserves to finance unsuccessful projects, consumption, and the ongoing internal conflict. Despite the low debt-servicing rates and the rapid accumulation of arrears during the 1980s, the external debt grew steadily at an average annual rate of 17.8% (Appendix, table A3 and figure 1). FDI was non-existent. Starting in 1991, in an attempt to normalize relations with the international financial community, debt-service payments were increased substantially (average annual payments increased from US$137.7 million for the period 1980-1989 to US$255.6 million in the years 1990-1999 [Appendix A5]).

An examination of some simple correlation measures suggests that debt-service payments came at some cost to domestic spending on social and physical investment. The correlation coefficient between government expenditures on education and health, and debt service (actual payments), both measured as a percentage of GDP, is -0.26 for the 1990s (-0.36 if the extraordinarily high level of debt service in 1991 is replaced by the average payment for the decade). Likewise, the correlation coefficient between government expenditure on social sectors and debt service, both measured as a percentage of GDP, is -0.32 for the 1990s (-0.20 if debt service for 1991 is substituted by the

Figure 1. Nicaragua: Evolution of external debt

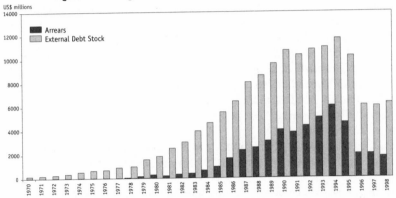

average payment for the decade). The correlation coefficient between government capital expenditure and debt service, both measured as a percentage of GDP, is -0.22 for the 1990s (if debt service for 1991 is substituted by the average payment for the decade, the correlation coefficient changes sign and has a value of 0.25).

Until the original HIPC Initiative was launched in 1996, multilateral creditors rarely rescheduled, refinanced, or forgave debt. Debt reprieves came largely from bilateral and/or commercial creditors. In that regard, Nicaragua's experience was quite typical. The country had three rescheduling agreements with the Paris Club in the 1990s. In December 1991, Nicaragua obtained flow rescheduling on London terms (50% NPV reduction),[3] and in March 1995 and April 1998, flow rescheduling on Naples terms (67% NPV reduction).[4] In December 1998, after Hurricane Mitch hit Nicaragua, Paris Club creditors deferred all debt service payments due during the remainder of the consolidation period. In addition, several Paris Club creditors forgave all or part of their debt claims on Nicaragua and, through the Central America Emergency Trust Fund created in December 1998, several bilateral donors financed a significant part of Nicaragua's debt-service payments to multilateral institutions.

---

3. Net present value (NPV) is the sum of all future debt-service payments discounted at a market rate of interest. Therefore, debt incurred on concessional terms will have a lower NPV than its face value might suggest.

4. As is typical of Paris Club debt operations, only pre-cut off date debt was eligible for rescheduling or reduction.

In 1995 and 1996, rescheduling and debt-reduction agreements were reached with several non-Paris Club official bilateral creditors (Mexico, the Czech Republic and Russia before its accession to Paris Club membership) that provided debt reductions of 92% of NPV (Appendix: table A6).[5] In December 1995, a commercial debt buyback was concluded with commercial creditors. The buyback terms represented a 92% discount on eligible debt. In addition, in September 1997, a rescheduling agreement, which involved the forgiveness of US$104 million in arrears, was reached with the Central American Bank for Economic Integration (CABEI).[6]

II. NICARAGUA'S EXPERIENCE WITH DEBT RELIEF IN THE CONTEXT OF THE HIPC INITIATIVE

Nicaragua was declared eligible for assistance under the HIPC Initiative in September 1999. The preliminary Debt-Sustainability Analysis (DSA) prepared jointly by the staffs of the IMF and the IDA, in consultation with the national authorities, revealed that the country's debt-burden indicators at the end of 1998 were among the highest recorded by HIPC (IMF and IDA 1999).

Originally, with the move to floating decision points under the Enhanced HIPC Initiative, Nicaragua was scheduled to reach its decision point at the end of 1999, but it did not do so until December 2000. The one-year delay stemmed from Nicaragua's failure to meet certain ESAF (now PRGF) related targets, and concerns of the international community regarding progress in improving governance, transparency and accountability in the management of public finances.

Few of the initiatives the country had difficulty fulfilling were directly related to poverty reduction or debt relief, but, as part of the PRGF, their fulfilment remained part of the precondition for debt relief. However, these were not the only impediments to expeditious debt relief.

At the Consultative Group for Nicaragua, held in Washington, D.C., on May 23 and 24, 2000, the donor community clearly stated that it would not provide any additional funding to Nicaragua, unless there were unequivocal signs of good government performance, efforts at poverty reduction, and a fight against corruption. This position, supported by most of the bilateral delegations, was

---

5. A similar agreement was reached with the Slovak Republic in 2000.

6. This agreement rests on the assumption that it will be counted as part of CABEI's interim assistance under the HIPC Initiative.

summarized by Miguel Martínez, IDB's manager for the region: "Nicaragua faces the challenge of showing the goodness of the new institutional systems, and that there is zero tolerance on corruption."[7] More specifically, on those dates, the donor community was expecting a prompt resolution of several corruption cases, particularly the one against Byron Jeréz, the former General Director of Revenues.[8]

Another important impediment to an early decision point was the issue of funding for the contribution of the regional financial institutions (for debt reduction), particularly the IDB and CABEI. However, by late 2000 these difficulties had been resolved satisfactorily.

Ultimately, Nicaragua's final arrival at the decision point was due less to the resolution of all outstanding concerns than to the creditor community's desire to ensure that at least half of the HIPCs had reached that point by the close of 2000. But, clearly, since these issues have little to do with the future use of debt relief for poverty reduction (the stated primary condition for debt relief), this did not represent a policy reversal. Rather, it reflected a decision (by the creditor community) to overlook the myriad of hurdles, based on only tangentially relevant conditions, that the creditor community had put ahead of debt relief.

III. THE EXPECTED DIVIDENDS FROM DEBT RELIEF

As mentioned earlier, during the 1980s, Nicaragua's external debt stock grew steadily, both as a result of the rapid accumulation of arrears and new financing (figure 1). However, in 1991, debt-service levels began increasing substantially (Appendix: table A5). The resources for debt servicing came, in part, from official transfers and loans received by the government.[9]

Table 4 shows the evolution of the ratios of actual payments of principal and interest to expected debt service for the last decade.[10] The average annual payments for 1990-1994 and 1995-1999 were remarkably similar, both approximating US$255 million. However, the average ratio of debt service

---

7. *La Prensa*, "Donantes enfáticos: Cero ayuda extra," 25 May 2000. The new institutional system refers to the changes introduced by the recent constitutional amendments and the reforms to the electoral act, which were the result of the pact between Sandinistas and Liberals.

8. *La Tribuna*, "Donantes esperan resolución de Contraloría. Grupo de seguimiento preocupado por caso Jeréz," 2 June 2000.

9. In fact, 30% of external resources went to amortizing of the external debt in 1999 (Government of Nicaragua, *A strengthened poverty reduction strategy*, August 2000, p. 16).

10. Ratios for the 1980s could not be calculated due to limited data on scheduled debt-service amounts for that period. However, we do know that these ratios were low because of the extremely low payment amounts despite the large and increasing debt load.

Table 3.   Net official capital balance (US$ millions)

Year	Amount	Year	Amount
1990	55.9	1995	-150.6
1991	131.9	1996	23.0
1992	-66.9	1997	115.6
1993	-164.2	1998	334.9
1994	-440.5	1999	505.5

Source: *Banco Central de Nicaragua*, Web site.

Table 4.   Debt service expected versus debt service paid (US$ millions)

Concept	Average 1990-1994	Average 1995-1999
Expected debt service	**1,105.4**	**515.6**
Principal[1]	832.5	348.4
Interest [2]	273.0	167.2
Paid debt service	**256.1**	**255.2**
Principal[3]	159.3	163.4
Interest[3]	96.8	91.8
Ratios: paid/expected (%)		
Debt service	20.7	56.3
Principal	16.9	55.3
Interest	35.7	59.8

Source: Calculations made by the author with data from the *Banco Central de Nicaragua*, Web site.
Notes: 1. Includes paid, renegotiated and unpaid principal.
          2. Includes paid, renegotiated, unpaid and capitalized interest.
          3. Real service of the public sector. This does not include interest capitalization and payments
             with exports (pre-financing).

paid to expected debt service increased from 20.7% for 1990-1994 to 56.3% for 1995-1999 because of the debt-reduction agreements reached in 1995-1996 with several non-Paris Club official bilateral creditors, and the commercial debt buyback of December 1995.

According to the World Bank and IMF's DSA of December 2000 (IMF and IDA 2000), at the end of 1999, the NPV of Nicaragua's total external debt was approximately US$6.5 billion (Appendix: table A4), and the NPV after full application of traditional debt-relief mechanisms was about US$4.5 billion. The DSA's baseline scenario estimates Nicaragua's needed assistance in NPV terms at US$3,267 million. This would amount to a 72% reduction in the

NPV of (old) debt after the full use of traditional debt-relief mechanisms.[11] The anticipated average annual flow of debt relief between 2001 and 2019 is US$190.4 million. The anticipated average for 2001 to 2015 (an important year in the global poverty-reduction agenda) is US$194.2 million.[12]

The average annual debt-service requirement, after HIPC debt reduction, is expected to be US$140.8 million (for 2001-2015), a reduction of 58% from the average pre-HIPC relief level of US$334.9 million. However, when compared with Nicaragua's average debt-service payment levels of US$255.2 million during 1995-1999, the reduction in expected debt-service payments implies an average budgetary saving of only US$114.4 million (a 44.8% reduction). In effect, while the reduction in debt-service obligations offered by HIPC debt relief is substantial, the reduction in average debt-service payments compared to recent payment levels (the much ballyhooed debt-relief dividend) is more modest. In fact, based on these estimates, the average debt-relief dividend (or the average reduction in debt-service payments compared to the most recent levels) for Nicaragua is only 58.9% of the flow of debt relief.

The average annual debt-relief dividend of US$114.4 million, if added to estimated social spending in 2000, would have led to a 26.2% increase. In fact, it is anticipated that in 2001-2003, average social spending will increase from a previously anticipated average of 16.3% of GDP before HIPC debt relief to 19.9% after HIPC debt relief, or a 22.1% increase (IMF and IDA 2000). However, if all of the flow of debt relief could have been used to increase social spending, it would have meant an average level of social spending (for 2001-2003) that was 29.9% higher.

As will be explained in greater detail later, the Nicaraguan Government estimates the financial requirements for implementing the strengthened poverty-reduction strategy to be US$1,136.7 million for 2001-2003 (US$378.9 million on average per year).[13] About half that portfolio has assured financing – from both domestic and foreign sources – and a large percentage of the remainder

---

11. Traditional debt-relief mechanisms include Paris Club debt-reduction operations on Naples terms and similar terms for commercial and non-Paris Club bilateral debt (but not multilateral debt).

12. Although debt-relief flows go beyond 2015, I limit the calculations to the period leading up to (and including) that year because of the significance of that year as a target date relating to major commitments by the international community, particularly that of halving world poverty (DAC 1996, Millennium Summit 2000).

13. The cost of the project and program portfolio to reduce poverty by 25% in the period 2000-2004, presented to the Consultative Group in May 2000, amounted to US$1,885.4 million. This was the figure presented in a previous draft of this paper.

Table 5. Nicaragua: external debt with commercial banks (US$ millions)

Year	Total	Arrears	Service
1990	1843.7	1387.7	0.5
1991	1711.8	1545.1	0.4
1992	1711.6	1547.0	19.8
1993	1739.9	1739.9	0.0
1994	1727.6	1727.6	0.4
1995	269.6	251.3	87.3
1996	272.4	250.1	4.7
1997	234.1	206.6	7.9
1998	246.3	199.1	44.4
1999	241.4	-	-

Source: *Banco Central de Nicaragua, Gerencia Internacional,* and Web site.

(about US$568 million) remains to be funded. Using these estimates, and the DSA estimates (IMF and IDA 2000), the expected budgetary savings of US$334.7 million over the three years – roughly 58.9% of the non-financed portion of the poverty-reduction plan – can come from debt relief. This still leaves an unfinanced portion (or financing gap) of roughly US$233.7 million, or an average of US$77.8 million annually. Given that the HIPC assistance will fall continuously after 2005, this gap will probably widen in the future.

IV. HIPC AND OTHER DEBT-RELIEF EXPERIENCES

In December 1995, the Nicaraguan government concluded a commercial debt buyback with private creditors at a 92% discount (i.e. debt was bought back at eight cents on the dollar). The outstanding amount was US$1,362.3 million, and the operation covered 81% of the creditors. The buyback, which meant a debt reduction of US$1,011.4 million, was financed through a grant provided by the IDA under its Debt Reduction Facility (US$40 million), a concessional loan from the IDB (US$40 million), and assistance from bilateral donors (US$30 million) (Nicaragua, *Ministerio de Cooperación Externa* 1996). However, the buyback did not release new resources to be invested within the country because most of the forgiven debt consisted of loans that were not being serviced (non-performing or impaired loans). In fact, the country remained in arrears to commercial creditors and still does not service all of its commercial debt (table 5). The DSA (IMF and IDA 2000) baseline scenario assumes another buyback of eligible commercial debt, discounted at 92%, as part of the "full use of traditional debt-relief mechanisms."

Because the commercial debt buyback had no net budgetary effect (in terms of reduced debt-service payments), no lessons can be extrapolated from the buyback in terms of the effect of debt relief on the budgetary allocations. However, a comparison of the amounts of nominal debt relief (relative to eligible debt) shows that the debt buyback offered a superior discount rate to that being offered by the HIPC Initiative. If, for example, the NPV of the projected outstanding stock of old debt (after traditional debt relief) in 2000 (US$4,502.3 million) was discounted by a factor of 0.92, it would imply debt relief of US$4,142.1 million, nearly one billion dollars more than is offered through the HIPC Initiative.

The same reasoning applies to the 1995 and 1996 debt relief provided by non-Paris Club bilateral creditors, also at 92% in NPV terms. Thus, all debt-reduction operations negotiated with non-Paris Club, bilateral, creditors were more generous than those being offered through the HIPC Initiative. Although the HIPC Initiative, because it includes multilateral creditors, has a broader coverage than the other debt-relief operations that Nicaragua has engaged in, it is not the most generous; debt operations with non-Paris club creditors and the commercial debt buyback were more generous.

V. DEBT RELIEF VIS-À-VIS OTHER FINANCIAL FLOWS

According to the figures published by the World Bank (WB 2000b), from 1990 to 1998, flows of grant aid to Nicaragua amounted to US$5,297 million, an average of US$588.6 million per year (equivalent to an average of 34.1% of GDP). By comparison, the average flow of debt relief in 2001-2015 will amount to US$194.2 million, or 5.8% of estimated GDP. Thus, the average annual flow of debt relief under the HIPC Initiative in 2001-2015, will add approximately 33% to the average aid level in terms of absolute quantities but only 17% when the GDP ratios are compared. Similarly, the estimated debt-relief dividend amounts to 19.4% of the average aid flow in the 1990-1998 period, but only 10% when the related GDP ratios are compared.

Debt service and aid flows have been closely related in Nicaragua because a significant proportion of the official aid flows Nicaragua received in the last decade was used to service external debt. This is particularly true of aid provided as balance of payments support. Thus, when debt obligations are reduced, the need for financing may be seen to be lower (i.e. Nicaragua will have a smaller financing gap) and aid flows may decrease. This would severely compromise any chance for significant poverty reduction because even a modest 10% decline in aid flows, when measured relative to Nicaragua's GDP,

Table 6.   Foreign direct investment in Nicaragua, 1970-1998

Period	FDI as % of GDP	FDI as % of ODA
1970-1979	0.92	37.98
1980-1989	0.00	0.00
1990-1998	3.61	13.12

would wipe out the net flow-reversal effect (dividend) from debt relief. In fact, the US$77.8 million funding gap for poverty reduction noted earlier, demands an increase rather than a decrease in aid.

Paradoxically, the least flexible types of aid (in terms of their local use) are most likely to survive potential aid cuts. Tied aid (aid conditional on the acquisition of goods and services produced by the donor country) and technical assistance (itself a form of tied aid) are always likely to be available because they provide distinct advantages to the donor country, yet they are both more expensive (in terms of the actual benefit per dollar spent) and concentrated at the high end of the technology scale, and thus unlikely to fit well in poverty-reduction programs that emphasize accessibility and basic services over rapid technological advancement. It also means that declines in aid that increase the concentration of these types of aid may further reduce the effectiveness of aid in reducing poverty.

Although it remains a small proportion of GDP, FDI increased significantly in the 1990s relative to earlier periods (during the 1980s foreign investment was virtually non-existent). Even though FDI flows remained only a small fraction of ODA flows in the 1990s (table 6), they have been increasing every year since 1990. In fact, FDI flows for 1998 (US$184 million) exceeded our estimate of the flow reversal from debt relief, or debt-relief dividend, of US$114.4 million. Thus the estimated HIPC debt-relief dividend will be (on average) significantly smaller than current flows of both ODA and FDI.

The Nicaraguan government anticipates that FDI flows will increase as debt relief becomes a reality. This is because the resources freed-up for investment in economic and social infrastructure and human development, with the associated improvement in productive conditions, will increase the return on investment in Nicaragua and make the country more attractive to foreign investors. However, this is expected to occur only over the medium- to long-term.

VI. LINKING POVERTY REDUCTION TO DEBT RELIEF:
RECENT EXPERIENCE

As part of the economic and social reform program, in January 1997, a poverty-reduction strategy was outlined and presented to the international community at the Consultative Group meetings in Geneva (March 1998), Washington (December 1998) and Stockholm (May 1999).

In 1998, the government promoted a dialogue on health sector reforms with citizens, unions, NGOs and donors. During that same year, the Government organized meetings throughout the country to get feedback on the reforms in the education sector. In November 1998, after Hurricane Mitch, the government created a presidential commission consisting of six consultative councils which met citizens and organizations to develop a plan for reconstruction and transformation, as well as policy recommendations, that were later presented at the Consultative Group meeting in Stockholm.[14]

In November 1999, the government began a revision process of the poverty-reduction strategy based on the results obtained from the most recent LSMS, and the experience accumulated since the beginning of this administration with the programs under implementation. The LSMS 1998 validated the poverty-reduction strategy followed in recent years, suggested new areas that require attention, and reinforced the need to complement some of the actions already taken. In August 2000, the country finished preparing the Interim PRSP, known as the Strengthened Poverty Reduction Strategy (SPRS).

The SPRS was announced as the result of a consultation process conducted at three levels:

- *inside the government* – joint meetings of the Economic and social cabinets, and with each ministry and the technical teams of each institution;
- *civil society* – through the *Consejo Nacional de Planificación Económica Social* (CONPES-National Council for Economic and Social Planning);[15]
- *donors, international organizations, and specialized agencies of the UN.*

Civil-society organizations, however, have complained about the lack of consultation on the PRSP, which, they say, the government did not even

---

14. The plan for reconstruction and transformation covered issues of physical infrastructure, social safety nets, environmental degradation, external aid, production growth and communication channels between the government and citizens.

15. Article 150 of the Political Constitution of Nicaragua empowered the president to create CONPES as a consultative body to support him in economic and social planning. CONPES was created by Decree 15-99 (February 1999). CONPES is composed of entrepreneurial, labor, and community organizations; NGOs, universities, political parties and government institutions.

present to the CONPES before sending it to Washington.[16] Economist Mario Arana, technical coordinator of the strategy at the Technical Secretariat of the Presidency, indicated that the SPRS consultation process will go forward at the local level throughout year 2001.[17]

The SPRS (Appendix A7) is guided by four main principles:
- Continued modernization of the state in order to increase the impact of social expenditures;
- Greater promotion of equity, with special attention to rural communities, women, indigenous groups and the inhabitants of the Atlantic Coast
- More transparency and accountability;
- Broader participation of society in defining, implementing, and following-up of the SPRS.

These principles guide four lines of action:
- Broad-based economic growth with an emphasis on generating productive employment and on rural development;
- Investment in human capital;
- Better protection for vulnerable populations;
- Strengthening institutions and good governance.

Three crosscutting themes overlay all lines of action:
- Reduction in environmental degradation and ecological vulnerability;
- Increase in equity;
- Further decentralization.

From the consultative process, nine specific national targets and a number of indicators for the SPRS were generated. A monitoring and evaluation system will provide measurable information on progress and will facilitate the timely adoption of corrective actions. The goals, targets and intermediate indicators selected are the result of a participatory consultation, analyses of relevant characteristics and needs of the poor, an assessment of public sector implementation capacity and budgetary constraints, and a review of country commitments in the context of United Nations international conferences. The long-term targets, which aim, at a minimum, to meet those set out as objectives by the OECD-DAC for the year 2015, are complemented by additional goals and targets that resulted from the consultations, and reflect country-specific characteristics (Appendix: table A7).

---

16. *El Nuevo Diario, En misterio compromisos con BID, FMI y BM, Negocian a espaldas de la sociedad civil,* 29 August 2000.

17. *Confidencial, Lista estrategia antipobreza,* No. 210, 24-30 September 2000.

Table 7. Nicaragua: SPRS investment portfolio (consolidated)

Program	2001-03	2001	2002	2003
Total (in US$ millions)	1136.7	360.7	378.1	397.9
Pillars	973.0	311.5	321.3	340.2
Broad-based economic growth	444.5	139.0	146.0	159.6
Better protection for vulnerable groups	170.1	50.6	57.7	61.7
Investment in human capital	355.6	119.8	117.1	118.7
Education	253.7	84.7	82.2	86.8
Health	92.6	32.3	32.2	28.0
Nutrition	3.5	0.8	1.2	1.5
Population	5.8	1.9	1.5	2.4
Governance	2.8	2.1	0.5	0.2
Cross-cutting themes	163.7	49.2	56.8	57.7
Environment and vulnerability	98.0	22.6	39.4	35.9
Decentralization	65.7	26.6	17.4	21.7

Source: Government of Nicaragua, *A strengthened poverty reduction strategy,* 2000, annex 3, p. 120.

The SPRS' investment estimates amount to US$1,136.7 million for 2001-2003 (US$380 million yearly, table 7).[18] Almost half of the portfolio has assured financing (both domestic and foreign), and an important part of the remainder (roughly US$600 million, or US$200 million annually) is being discussed with possible donors.

As conceived by the government, the SPRS is not only a series of project outlays but also a better-focussed framework for all investments directed toward the poor. The government has projected poverty-related expenditures to increase from 53% of the total expenditure (excluding interest payments) in 1999 to about 64% by 2003; and from below 17% of GDP to more than 21%. That is, by 2003, about one fifth of Nicaragua's GDP will be spent on poverty-focussed programs (in the order of US$115 per capita). As expressed in the DSA (IMF and IDA 2000), most of the increase in poverty-related public spending will be funded by reallocating resources, by using the proceeds of privatization, and from HIPC Initiative debt relief.

---

18. The previous projection was US$1885.4 million for 2000-2004.

VII. CONDITIONALITY: THE GOVERNMENT, THE PRIVATE
SECTOR AND CIVIL-SOCIETY VIEWS

A.   THE PRGF (PREVIOUSLY THE ESAF) AND THE HIPC INITIATIVE

Views on conditionality differ widely among government officials, private sector leaders and civil-society representatives. The range of views expressed and some of the reasoning behind those views are summarized below.

Most government officials view the conditions established in the PRGF as prerequisites for a healthy economy. Some private sector leaders, however, argue that the PRGF acts against private investment because it encourages fiscal measures that discourage investment and reduce competitiveness. For other entrepreneurs, the PRGF, and especially the PRSP, represent an opportunity to participate in the design of a medium- and long-term development strategy. They believe that the PRSP should not be seen as an additional condition that will put additional pressure on the country but as a welcome opportunity for participation.[19]

1.   The private sector's position

A leader from the *Unión de Productores Agropecuarios of Nicaragua* has urged developed countries to open up their markets for agricultural products because, for countries like Nicaragua, "…openness is more beneficial than any HIPC Initiative…"[20] For example, Nicaragua cannot export rice to Japan because it is subject to tariffs as high as 1000%. Also, with the current low international prices for sugar, Nicaragua's sugar cannot be exported to developed markets. Moreover, the US has enormous protectionist barriers for peanuts, but goods not produced by Nicaragua, like computers and cars, are freely traded. Then, "…if developed countries grant poor countries with debt relief through the HIPC, they should have the courtesy of allowing poor countries to sell freely in their markets."[21]

For one economist at RCA International, the division of countries between North and South implies the existence of winners and losers. "The North is protectionist with the agricultural sector but demands market openness. This is a reason for the fall in prices of southern goods, such as sugar, wool and

---

19. *Confidencial*, El ESAF como una oportunidad y no como condicionalidad, no. 167, 7-13 November 1999.

20. *La Tribuna*, "Se necesita mayor apertura de mercados," 31 May 2000.

21. Ibid.

coffee. The lack of a national economic policy suffocates agriculture and favours financial and high technology activities."[22]

The industrial sector is experiencing production problems too. The president of the *Cámara de Industria* affirms that although Nicaragua has the cheapest labour in Central America, the country cannot attract investment because of higher costs of basic services and the lack of commercial ports (the country has no port on the Atlantic coast), among other variables. As a result, some businesses have closed down operations in Nicaragua and moved to neighbouring countries, like Honduras (a relevant example is the tobacco company TANIC).[23]

The president of COSEP[24] referred to the Marshall Plan as decisive for reactivating Europe after World War II and argues that Nicaragua "…has not been given a similar opportunity. We propose the creation of a high-risk trust fund to promote investment, production, and development."[25] This business leader indicated "…with a fund like that, in a very short period of time Chihuahua became one of the three wealthiest Mexican states, with more economic capacity, after being the poorest and most retarded."[26]

2.   The civil-society's position

One influential independent economist shares the views presented above. In his words, "The HIPC Initiative is another theoretical experiment of the rich countries. Debt forgiveness is not a solution for poverty, which cannot be reduced unless rich countries give poor countries access to their markets."[27]

The Executive Director of the *Grupo Propositivo de Cabildeo e Incidencia* considers the structural reform embedded in the PRGF to be regressive – it supports neither economic development nor transformation, and does not allow countries to invest in sustainable human development. Why? To comply with the program, the country has to acquire new debt that it cannot pay, getting into a vicious circle of reform and indebtedness. The requirements related to governance and poverty reduction have made the situation more

---

22. *Confidencial*, ESAF deja "ganadores y perdedores," no. 199, 9-15 July 2000.

23. *Confidencial*, Cámara de Industria también sufre crisis, no. 199, 9-15 July 2000.

24. *Consejo Superior de la Empresa Privada* (highest council of the private sector).

25. *La Tribuna*, COSEP ante Grupo Consultivo. Mayor transparencia e incentivos para producir, 23 May 2000.

26. *El Nuevo Diario*, Terán aclara participación del COSEP en Washington, "Nuestro aval es para Nicaragua," 18 May 2000.

27. Interview, 23 May 2000; and *La Tribuna*, Condonar la deuda no resuelve el problema, 12 June 2000.

dramatic and difficult for Nicaragua, because the country has not invested in human development in the last 50 years.[28]

B.   THE POVERTY-REDUCTION STRATEGY PAPER

The private sector sees the poverty-reduction strategy as necessary and fully supports it, but it is not convinced that "those programs are sufficient to elim-inate the causes of poverty in general, and specially of extreme poverty."[29] For some civil-society organizations, the PRSP represents a "nice experiment." However, because the PRSP is a demand from the multilateral agencies that the Nicaraguan government had to comply with, it has profound weaknesses. It is a set of mending patches because it is not based on a structural analysis of the causes of poverty. The government is making the mistake of apparently preparing a strategy without giving serious consideration to the communities. Nonetheless, civil-society organizations support this approach because it opens a "window for human development," allows the country to assign at least 85% of debt relief to poverty reduction, education and health programs, contributing to increases in the country's human development index.

The president of COSEP (a private-sector organization), pointed out "…It is fine to implement programs to alleviate poverty. However, the country needs massive investment to increase production and generate a large quan-tity of jobs, not only to remedy poverty, but also to eliminate it forever."[30]

For the executive director of the *Grupo Propositivo de Cabildeo e Incidencia* (a civil-society organization), "the government is doing some mockery con-sultations which are not functional. It will not allow people to express their ideas about what should be the local action to alleviate or reduce poverty."[31] In his opinion, a poverty-reduction strategy is not a useful tool for fighting poverty. It is only a document the government has to prepare to fulfil a condition.

Only some sectors, mainly representing Managua, formally participated, through the *Coordinadora Civil para la Emergencia y la Reconstrucción* (CCER, civil-society organization), in the preparation of the PRSP. Nevertheless, the CCER maintains that they were only partially consulted and that they first knew about the PRSP through the IMF.[32] One economist from the CCER,

---

28. Interview, 20 May 2000.
29. *El Nuevo Diario*, Terán aclara participación del COSEP en Washington, "Nuestro aval es para Nicaragua," 18 May 2000.
30. *Ibid.*
31. Interview, 20 May 2000.
32. *Confidencial*, Lista estrategia antipobreza, no. 210, 24-30 September 2000.

describes the document as a "sum of good intentions without real support to make it viable, and lacking an effective counterpart in society."[33] He also stated, "It is in our interest that any poverty-reduction strategy be subjected to a wide debate in all territories and social sectors. At the same time, it should include the matrix of priorities, objectives, and principles approved in the Consultative Group meeting held in Stockholm in May 1999. We do not see the Stockholm follow-up process as different from the structuring of the poverty-reduction strategy."[34] Mario Arana, technical coordinator of the PRSP at the Technical Secretariat of the Presidency, in response to this comment, argued that "there has been a radical change in the way the country prepares a national strategy. ... I believe we have made a sincere effort to listen to what people have to say and to reflect on all that can be reflected on, after all proposals are in..."[35]

Collaboration between the private sector and civil-society organization was practically absent, in part because NGOs were initially created as solidarity organizations, which were later transformed into agencies that execute programs and projects. Also, donor coordination is weak. This goes against the PRSP process and the possibility that donors assume their responsibility in the allocation of resources. Moreover, donors need to unite their efforts in order to strengthen civil-society participation and expand it to the local level.

From the viewpoint of the journalist of IBIS-Denmark,[36] the PRSP should have been developed from the bottom-up (community → municipality → department → CONPES) instead of from the top-down, this approach should have applied throughout the process (planning, implementation, monitoring and follow-up). People from the communities have important contributions to make, and for the PRSP to be successful it must involve civil society at the local level early in the process. IBIS is working with four municipalities to prepare local PRSPs, which will be presented at the department-level forums, sent to the CONPES, and published in the press.

The director of *Grupo Fundemos* (civil-society organization) suggests that "... civil society's challenge is to transform the PRSP into a social development plan that benefits the less favoured citizens."[37] She also called for

33. *Confidencial*, Lista estrategia antipobreza, no. 210, 24-30 September 2000.

34. *Confidencial*, Sociedad civil desconoce documento, no. 210, 24-30 September 2000.

35. *Confidencial*, Lista estrategia antipobreza, no. 210, 24-30 September 2000.

36. An NGO that belongs to the Coordinadora Civil para la Emergencia y la Reconstrucción (CCER), a coordination body created after Hurricane Mitch. CCER is part of CONPES. Interview, 23 May 2000.

37. *La Prensa*, Sociedad civil exige seguimiento y control, 26 June 2000.

improving the consultation process with citizens: bring it to the farthest communities of the country through a permanent follow-up network. A representative of the CCER points out that the government policies (which are not enough to fight and eradicate poverty) and the civil-society proposals are incoherent.[38]

A former president of the central bank commented that the absence of a strategy to accelerate economic growth makes poverty reduction more difficult: "The usual recipes for poverty mitigation do not work in Nicaragua, because poverty is rooted and extreme poverty is very high... Moreover, there exists a vicious circle of intergenerational poverty... Then, the strength of the strategy to fight poverty is to consult with society, but that takes time..."[39]

In opposition to the previous views, the director of *Fundación Internacional para el Desafío Económico y Social* (a Nicaraguan think-tank) explained that the civil society "...has to make its proposals, and agree on the core issues for a national agenda. The idea is for the civil society to have its own vision of the country and, together with the political parties, achieve a consensus on the face that Nicaragua should have."[40]

One independent economist questions the increasing participation of civil society, basically because civil society does not have a position of its own. He argues "...how can it be tuned in with the government?"[41] He considers that the PRSP should be simple, include four to six very sensitive targets and be easy to manage. The specific targets could be reducing the illiteracy rate, reducing infant mortality, reducing maternal mortality, providing access to potable water for disperse rural communities, providing housing for low-income people, and improving the business climate to attract investment and create employment. In his opinion, the Interim PRSP will not be strategic, and the next administration will have to redraft it.

VIII. ALTERNATIVE POST DEBT-RELIEF REGIME

It is generally understood that Nicaragua needs to avoid another debt crisis. However, for the country to maintain its growth path and reduce poverty, it must rely on foreign resource inflows to some degree. If it is to avoid the debt

---

38. "Coordinadora Civil sale preocupada a Washington. Gobierno no lleva buenas cuentas," *El Nuevo Diario*, 18 May 2000.
39. "Ausencia de estrategia de desarrollo retrasa el ingreso a HIPC," *La Prensa*, 12 July 2000.
40. "Para un verdadero diálogo. Sociedad civil busca agenda nacional," *La Tribuna*, 17 May 2000.
41. Interview, 23 May 2000.

morass, a "national indebtedness policy" will need to be developed as one way to achieve a "vision of nation" that is agreed upon and implemented by all economic and social sectors of the country. Such a vision, hopefully based on a global conception of human development and the kind of country that Nicaraguans want to build, will establish the lines of action on issues such as governance, transparency, the rule of law, production and poverty.

The government, as a representative of the country's citizens, would be responsible for implementing the indebtedness policy and for contracting new debt. The government would inform the citizenry of the use and destination of funds, which would be directed at national priorities established in the nation's program. Negotiations with multilateral agencies and bilateral sources of funding would be public and transparent. Simultaneously, the government would work toward increased domestic saving capacity in the future.

The PRSP has the potential to represent that "vision of the nation" as the guiding light for the country's policies, programs, projects and actions – both domestically and externally. As expressed in the introduction of the report presented to the Consultative Group meeting, "…This report will serve as an additional mechanism to improve the coordination among the World Bank, the International Monetary Fund, bilateral donors, academics, the citizenry, and the Government of Nicaragua in our common fight against poverty."[42]

Some ideas put forward for consideration by opinion leaders for financing Nicaragua's development program while avoiding a future debt crisis include the following:

- Establishing a national fund for reconstruction to finance the development of public investment projects, strengthening the institutional capabilities of local governments, and developing civil-society projects.
- Setting up a high-risk trust fund (i.e. a private sector development fund) to foster private investment and growth at the levels required by Nicaragua to get out of its underdevelopment and poverty situation. The support of multilateral and bilateral agencies in the creation of the fund will be very important.
- Relying on grants and highly concessional loans. And, in order to establish an effective and efficient link between poverty and debt relief, a medium- and long-term government budget must be developed, based

---

42. Gobierno de Nicaragua, "Informe de avance sobre la lucha contra la pobreza: El papel del crecimiento económico, el capital humano y la protección social, Managua, Nicaragua," prepared for the Consultative Group Meeting. Washington, D.C., 23-24 May 2000, p. 4.

on extensive discussion and consultation between the government, civil society and congress.

One of Nicaragua's greatest challenges has been the need to foster growth in order to create employment, improve individual income, and have a better chance of reducing poverty, while avoiding future debt crises. A useful complementary effort to the debt-relief process already under way in Nicaragua will be the adoption of an Export-Led Poverty Reduction Program (EPRP) similar to those supported by the International Trade Centre (ITC). In the case of the ITC, the aim is "...to create new job and income opportunities, develop a basis for capital, technology, and skill accumulation within poor communities themselves, and, in turn, provide the foundations for fostering other dimensions of economic and social development in those communities."[43]

EPRPs are based on two main elements: harnessing the entrepreneurial capacity of the poor for export and linking that capacity to proven export-market opportunities. EPRPs involve some interesting elements:

- Export production does not need to focus only on the markets of a few highly developed Northern economies; there are growing opportunities to develop sub-regional and South-South export production.
- Exports from poor communities do not have to be limited to agricultural crops, and may include processed or semi-processed agricultural products, handicrafts, industrial goods, and services.
- Exports may come from organized rural or urban poor communities.

In relation to collaborative actions within the international community, EPRPs can play a significant role in the poverty-reduction strategy of the IMF and the World Bank, and the UNDP's poverty-alleviation strategy. Also, EPRPs are consistent with the World Bank's and IMF's work in the area of trade and private business development. In addition, EPRPs can contribute to advancing the goals of bilateral aid flows, often directed toward local efforts and policies aimed at promoting economic growth and employment. Finally, cooperation with business-oriented NGOs is viable, especially with those that promote the development of small enterprises in developing countries through exports.

Last, it is worth noting that, like any other country, Nicaragua cannot compete in all activities domestically or internationally. An important challenge is to focus efforts on developing the most promising productive sectors

---

43. International Trade Centre, ITC's export-led poverty reduction program (EPRP), Internal draft for discussion, April 2000, p. 1. Examples of successful EPRPs can be found in Ecuador, Israel, India, Sri Lanka, and Ghana.

of the country. Sector or cluster development implies the identification of emerging industries in which the country has potential and shows the distinctive elements necessary for becoming a world-class player. Some of these clusters have already been identified: Nicaraguan cigars are considered among the best in the world; sophisticated consumers appreciate gourmet coffee; and Nicaraguan crafts have won international competitions. Additional work is needed to develop the full potential of these and other sectors in which the country presents a competitive advantage.

CONCLUSION

Nicaragua's journey toward debt relief under the Enhanced HIPC Initiative has not been easy. Successive delays in achieving the decision point are explained by Nicaragua's difficulties in fulfilling some conditions included in the economic program agreed with the IMF, and concerns of the international community related to progress in improving governance, transparency and accountability in the management of public finances.

The research shows that the commercial debt buyback of December 1995, and the 1995 and 1996 non-Paris Club members' debt reduction, were superior (in terms of the degree of debt reduction) to the debt reduction offered under the Enhanced HIPC Initiative. Likewise, the annual estimated net saving from the Enhanced HIPC would be equivalent to additional aid flows of only 19.4% (relative to recent levels). It can thus be concluded that further reduction of debt is a priority. The country will not be able to take off completely unless it is freed of all its debt and invests heavily in human capital and in the creation of conditions to achieve high rates of economic growth.

Finally, a set of transferable lessons can be extracted from the present research, which could be useful in future debt-relief processes or for countries that are still struggling to fulfil the requirements of the multilateral institutions:

1. From the beginning, the development of the PRSP should adopt a bottom-up approach instead of a top-down approach, to be applied throughout the entire process (planning, implementation, monitoring and follow-up). Communities have important contributions to make, and for the PRSP to be successful, it must involve civil society at the local level early in the process.
2. Civil society must organize itself and develop a position of its own, before it is in tune with the government.

3. The national and international cooperation actions must be harmonized in order to mutually strengthen them, avoid duplication, and reduce operating costs.
4. To establish an effective and efficient link between poverty and debt relief, a medium- and long-term government budget, which results from a comprehensive analysis, discussion and consultation among government, private sector, political parties, civil society and congress must be developed.

REFERENCES

Banco Central de Nicaragua, *Informe Anual*, Managua, several years.

_____, *La política de manejo de la deuda externa de Nicaragua*, 1989.

Baumeister, E., *Estructura y reforma agraria en Nicaragua, 1979-1989*, Managua, Centro de Estudios para el Desarrollo Rural, 1998.

CEPAL, *Estudio económico de América Latina y el Caribe*, 1979, 1980, 1984.

CLACDS/INCAE and HIID, *Centroamérica en el Siglo XXI. Una agenda para la competitividad y el desarrollo sostenible*, 1999.

Confidencial, electronic edition, http://www.confidencial.com.ni, several issues.

El Nuevo Diario, electronic edition, http://www.elnuevodiario.com.ni, several issues.

Esquivel, G., F. B. Larraín and J. D. Sachs, "The External Debt Problem in Central America: Honduras, Nicaragua, and the HIPC Initiative," Development Discussion Paper No. 645, Harvard Institute for International Development, August 1998.

Grupo Propositivo de Cabildeo e Incidencia, *Cómo y dónde invertir los recursos de la condonación*, Managua, Editorial Ciencias Sociales-INIES, November, 1999.

_____, *Una ventana para el desarrollo*, Managua, Editorial Ciencias Sociales-INIES, July, 1999.

IDB, press releases, http://www.iadb.org/exr/prensa/2000.

IMF and IDA, *Nicaragua, Preliminary document on the Initiative for Heavily Indebted Poor Countries (HIPC)*, 23 August 1999.

_____, *Nicaragua, Decision Point Document for the Enhanced Heavily Indebted Poor Countries (HIPC) Initiative*, 7 December 2000.

Instituto Nicaragüense de Reforma Agraria, *Marco estratégico de la reforma agraria: versión resumida*, Managua, Organización de Estados Americanos, 1992.

International Trade Centre, "ITC's Export-Led Poverty Reduction Program (EPRP)," internal draft for discussion, April, 2000.

La Prensa, electronic edition, http://www.laprensa.com.ni, several issues.

La Tribuna, electronic edition, http://www.latribuna.com.ni, several issues.

Montiel, E. and T. Sandino, *Agenda para la competitividad de Nicaragua hacia el Siglo XXI*, 1999.

Nicaragua, Government of, "Así estamos reconstruyendo y transformando Nicaragua," prepared for the Consultative Group Meeting, Washington, D.C., 23-24 May 2000.

____, "Informe de avance sobre la lucha contra la pobreza: El papel del crecimiento económico, el capital humano y la protección social, Managua, Nicaragua," prepared for the Consultative Group Meeting, Washington, D.C., 23-24 May 2000.

____, "Una Nación, muchas voces: sociedad, gobierno, y economía en el nuevo milenio," Managua, Nicaragua, April 2000, prepared for the Consultative Group Meeting, Washington, D.C., 23-24 May 2000.

____, *A Strengthened Poverty Reduction Strategy*, August 2000.

Nicaragua, Ministerio de Cooperación Externa, *Negociaciones de deuda externa: 1990-1996*, Managua, 1996.

Nicaragua, Ministerio de Fomento, *Industria y Comercio, Globalización, liberalización y desarrollo humano sostenible en Nicaragua*, Managua, 2000.

Nicaragua, Secretaría Técnica de la Presidencia, *Estrategia de reducción de la pobreza, Primera parte: diagnóstico y lineamientos*, Managua, 21 January 2000.

Programa Latinoamericano y del Caribe del Centro Carter, *Las disputas de propiedad nicaragüense*, Atlanta, Georgia, 1995.

Sachs, J. D., "Helping the World's Poorest," *The Economist*, 14-20 August 1999.

____, "A New Global Consensus on Helping the Poorest of the Poor," Keynote address at the Annual Bank Conference on Development Economics, Washington, D.C., 19 April 2000.

Sachs, J. D. et al., *Implementing Debt Relief for the HIPCs*, Centre for International Development, Harvard University, August 1999.

The Economist, "Nicaragua Curious Chance," 3-9 June 2000.

United Nations, *Compendium of Social Statistics and Indicators 1988*, New York, UN, 1991.

UNDP, *Informe sobre desarrollo humano 2000*, Ediciones Mundi-Prensa, 2000.

World Bank, *Republic of Nicaragua. Poverty Assessment, Volume I: Main Report*, Report no. 14038-NI, June, 1995.

____, *World Development Indicators 1999*, CD-ROM, Washington, D.C., World Bank, 1999.

____, *HIPC Initiative: Status of Country Cases Considered Under the Initiative*, http://www.worldbank.org, 3 May 2000.

____, *World Development Indicators 2000*, CD-ROM, Washington, D.C., World Bank, 2000.

APPENDIX

Table A1.1. Economic Indicators, 1970-1979

Economic Indicators	1970	1971	1972	1973	1974	1975	1976	1977	1978	1979
GDP (US$ millions, 1980)	2008.6	2075.0	2121.1	2257.2	2577.5	2573.6	2707.7	2934.3	2704.2	1988.2
Rate of change	1.4	3.3	2.2	6.4	14.2	-0.2	5.2	8.4	-7.8	-26.5
GDP per capita (US$)	365.8	376.9	388.8	467.3	629.1	636.8	717.2	842.7	781.1	570.0
Rate of change	0.6	3.0	3.2	20.2	34.6	1.2	12.6	17.5	-7.3	-27.0
GDP per capita (US$, 1980)	946.2	946.2	936.3	964.5	1066.2	1030.6	1051.0	1104.0	986.1	702.8
Rate of change	-1.8	0.0	-1.0	3.0	10.5	-3.3	2.0	5.0	-10.7	-28.7
Inflation rate	–	–	–	–	–	1.9	6.2	10.2	4.3	70.3
Exports of goods (FOB, US$ millions)	178.6	187.2	249.4	277.8	380.9	375.1	542.0	636.8	646.0	567.0
Exports of goods (FOB, % of GDP)	23.0	22.6	28.3	25.4	25.0	23.6	29.3	28.4	30.2	35.2
Net foreign direct investment (US$ millions)	15.0	13.3	10.0	13.2	13.8	10.9	12.9	10.0	7.0	2.8
Net foreign direct investment (% of GDP)	1.9	1.6	1.1	1.2	0.9	0.7	0.7	0.4	0.3	0.2
ODA and official aid (US$ millions)	–	–	–	–	–	41.4	39.1	36.5	41.5	114.0
ODA and official aid (% of GDP)	–	–	–	–	–	2.6	2.1	1.6	1.9	7.1
Gross domestic investment (US$ millions)	142.9	150.0	114.3	264.3	478.6	340.4	319.1	567.4	262.4	-91.9
Gross domestic investment (% of GDP)	18.4	18.1	13.0	24.2	31.5	21.4	17.3	25.3	12.3	-5.7
Fixed gross domestic investment (US$ millions)	128.6	128.6	135.7	214.3	357.1	354.6	368.8	510.6	305.0	102.7
Fixed gross domestic investment (% of GDP)	16.6	15.6	15.4	19.6	23.5	22.3	20.0	22.8	14.2	6.4
Gross domestic savings (US$ millions)	121.4	128.6	164.3	157.1	271.4	198.6	340.4	446.8	326.2	124.3
Gross domestic savings (% of GDP)	15.6	15.6	18.7	14.4	17.8	12.5	18.4	19.9	15.2	7.7
Government expenditure										
Social and community services (US$ millions)	34.0	38.6	36.6	53.9	88.0	124.2	122.2	112.4	108.8	–
Social and community services (% of GDP)	4.4	4.7	4.2	4.9	5.8	7.8	6.6	5.0	5.1	–
Education (US$ millions)[1]	18.1	19.8	21.7	24.5	33.8	39.7	46.4	57.2	47.3	–
Education (% of GDP)	2.3	2.4	2.5	2.2	2.2	2.5	2.5	2.6	2.2	–
Health (US$ millions)[2]	13.1	16.0	11.2	12.6	21.8	34.3	36.6	38.1	36.2	–
Health (US$ millions)	1.7	1.9	1.3	1.2	1.4	2.2	2.0	1.7	1.7	–

Source: *Banco Central de Nicaragua*; World Bank, *World Development Indicators 1999*.
Notes: 1. Considers education and culture.
2. Includes public health, environmental higiene, and previsional and social assistance.

Table A1.2. Economic Indicators, 1980-1989

Economic Indicators	1980	1981	1982	1983	1984	1985	1986	1987	1988	1989
GDP (US$ millions, 1980)	2079.9	2191.4	2173.5	2273.8	2238.2	2146.8	2125.0	2110.0	1847.3	1815.9
Rate of change	4.6	5.4	-0.8	4.6	-1.6	-4.1	-1.0	-0.7	-12.5	-1.7
GDP per capita (US$)	712.6	813.6	878.6	785.0	842.3	737.8	633.1	626.0	397.2	388.0
Rate of change	25.0	14.2	8.0	-10.7	7.3	-12.4	-14.2	-1.1	-36.5	-2.3
GDP per capita (US$, 1980)	712.6	728.2	700.5	710.8	678.6	631.3	610.4	592.1	506.3	486.2
Rate of change	1.4	2.2	-3.8	1.5	-4.5	-7.0	-3.3	-3.0	-14.5	-4.0
Inflation rate	24.8	23.2	22.2	32.9	50.2	334.3	747.5	1,347.2	33,547.6	1,689.2
Exports of goods (FOB, US$ millions)	450.0	508.0	406.0	429.0	385.0	301.0	243.0	281.0	236.0	310.7
Exports of goods (FOB, % of GDP)	21.6	20.7	14.9	17.1	13.9	12.0	11.0	12.6	16.3	21.4
Net foreign direct investment (US$ millions)	0.0	0.0	0.0	0.0	0.0	0.0	0.0	0.0	0.0	0.0
Net foreign direct investment (% of GDP)	0.0	0.0	0.0	0.0	0.0	0.0	0.0	0.0	0.0	0.0
ODA and official aid (US$ millions)	220.8	144.9	120.8	120.3	198.0	221.8	352.4	261.8	280.3	449.5
ODA and official aid (% of GDP)	10.6	5.9	4.4	4.8	7.1	8.8	16.0	11.7	19.3	31.0
Gross domestic investment (US$ millions)	360.8	585.9	458.9	619.2	692.0	620.9	487.4	608.4	703.7	278.2
Gross domestic investment (% of GDP)	17.3	23.9	16.8	24.7	24.9	24.8	22.1	27.3	48.6	19.2
Fixed gross domestic investment (US$ millions)	314.4	530.3	406.9	535.6	605.5	555.8	399.3	507.7	739.0	283.6
Fixed gross domestic investment (% of GDP)	15.1	21.7	14.9	21.3	21.8	22.2	18.1	22.8	51.0	19.6
Gross domestic savings (US$ millions)	-46.4	106.1	212.1	326.4	287.2	431.4	255.0	531.8	-356.5	-52.6
Gross domestic savings (% of GDP)	-2.2	4.3	7.8	13.0	10.3	17.2	11.6	23.8	-24.6	-3.6
Government expenditure										
Social and community services (US$ millions)	–	249.9	261.0	286.0	363.9	326.6	272.4	246.7	121.0	75.2
Social and community services (% of GDP)	–	10.2	9.6	11.4	13.1	13.0	12.4	11.1	8.3	5.2
Education (US$ millions)	–	103.4	111.3	126.1	158.2	143.2	122.1	114.0	49.6	27.8
Education (% of GDP)	–	4.2	4.1	5.0	5.7	5.7	5.5	5.1	3.4	1.9
Health (US$ millions)	–	110.4	114.4	115.3	123.4	123.0	116.6	103.3	60.8	40.2
Health (% of GDP)	–	4.5	4.2	4.6	4.4	4.9	5.3	4.6	4.2	2.8

Source: Banco Central de Nicaragua; World Bank, *World Development Indicators 1999.*

Table A1.3. Economic Indicators, 1990-1999

Economic Indicators	1990	1991	1992	1993	1994	1995	1996	1997	1998	1999
GDP (US$ millions, 1980)	1814.2	1810.8	1817.8	1810.7	1871.1	1951.8	2045	2149.4	2236.8	2394.1
Rate of change	-0.1	-0.2	0.4	-0.4	3.3	4.3	4.8	5.1	4.1	7.0
GDP per capita (US$)	409.2	419.0	454.7	432.6	426.1	427.3	434.2	433.1	442.7	459.4
Rate of change	5.5	2.4	8.5	-4.9	-1.5	0.3	1.6	-0.3	2.2	3.8
GDP per capita (US$, 1980)	474.5	459.9	448.4	433.7	435.3	440.9	449.6	459.8	465.7	485.0
Rate of change	-2.4	-3.1	-2.5	-3.3	0.4	1.3	2.0	2.3	1.3	4.1
Inflation rate	13490.3	865.6	3.5	19.5	12.4	11.1	12.1	7.3	18.5	7.2
Exports of goods (FOB, US$ millions)	330.6	272.4	223.1	267.0	351.2	526.5	670.5	703.6	612.7	543.8
Exports of goods (FOB, % of GDP)	21.1	16.5	12.1	14.8	19.2	27.8	33.9	34.8	28.8	24.0
Net foreign direct investment (US$ millions)	0.0	0.0	15.0	39.0	40.0	70.0	97.0	173.1	–	–
Net foreign direct investment (% of GDP)	0.0	0.0	0.8	2.2	2.2	3.7	4.9	8.6	–	–
ODA and official aid (US$ millions)	332.4	837.0	656.2	319.2	596.9	651.7	931.3	410.1	562.2	–
ODA and official aid (% of GDP)	32.9	54.7	35.6	17.7	32.6	34.4	49.9	21.3	28.0	–
Gross domestic investment (US$ millions)	194.3	350.8	355.0	334.3	405.9	454.4	546.6	–	–	–
Gross domestic investment (% of GDP)	12.4	21.3	19.3	18.5	22.2	24.0	27.7	–	–	–
Fixed gross domestic investment (US$ millions)	205.8	318.2	359.6	343.4	407.2	453.3	557.3	–	–	–
Fixed gross domestic investment (% of GDP)	13.2	19.3	19.5	19.0	22.2	24.0	28.2	–	–	–
Gross domestic savings (US$ millions)	-21.7	-141.7	-256.1	-136.8	-97.6	18.2	55.8	–	–	–
Gross domestic savings (% of GDP)	-1.4	-8.6	-13.9	-7.6	-5.3	1.0	2.8	–	–	–
Government capital expenditure (US$ millions)	24.3	57.9	110.8	123.3	167.0	220.3	211.5	204.8	209.8	389.8
Government capital expenditure (% of GDP)	1.6	3.5	6.0	6.8	9.1	11.6	10.7	10.1	9.9	17.2
Government expenditure										
Social and community services (US$ millions)	177.0	170.4	190.2	196.3	221.3	241.0	245.6	221.1	239.0	389.0
Social and community services (% of GDP)	11.3	10.3	10.3	10.9	12.1	12.7	12.4	10.9	11.2	17.2
Education (US$ millions)	79.4	80.1	86.3	79.9	92.8	86.5	93.6	103.3	103.2	144.0
Education (% of GDP)	5.1	4.9	4.7	4.4	5.1	4.6	4.7	5.1	4.9	6.3
Health (US$ millions)	77.8	69.8	76.6	71.3	81.5	91.6	90.8	83.2	79.0	120.2
Health (% of GDP)	5.0	4.2	4.2	3.9	4.4	4.8	4.6	4.1	3.7	5.3

Source: Banco Central de Nicaragua; *World Bank, World Development Indicators 1999.*

Table A2. Nicaragua: Evolution of poverty and extreme poverty (% of total population)*

	Extreme poverty			Poverty**		
	1993	1998	Change	1993	1998	Change
National	19.4	17.3	-2.1	50.3	47.9	-2.4
Urban	7.3	7.6	0.3	31.9	30.5	-1.4
Rural	36.3	28.9	-7.4	76.1	68.5	-7.6
Managua	5.1	3.1	-2.0	29.9	18.5	-11.4
Pacific region						
Urban	6.4	9.8	3.5	28.1	39.6	11.5
Rural	31.6	24.1	-7.5	70.7	67.1	-3.6
Central region						
Urban	15.3	12.2	-3.1	49.2	39.4	-9.8
Rural	47.6	32.7	-14.9	84.7	74.0	-10.7
Atlantic region						
Urban	7.9	17.0	9.0	35.5	44.4	8.9
Rural	30.3	41.4	11.1	83.6	79.3	-4.3

Source: Government of Nicaragua, *A Strengthened Poverty Reduction Strategy*, August 2000.
Notes: *   Data from the Living Standards Measurement Surveys (LSMS) 1993 and 1998.
   ** According to the Compendium of Social Statistics and indicators 1988, published by the United Nations, the percentage of population in absolute poverty for the period 1977-1986 was: urban 21%, and rural 19%. Absolute poverty refers to the portion of population with household income below the poverty line, which is defined as the level below which a minimum nutritionally adequate diet plus essential non-food requirements are not affordable.

Table A3. Evolution of Nicaragua's debt, 1970-1999 (US$ millions on
December 31)

Year	Total debt (%)	Multilateral (%)	Bilateral (%)	Commercial (%)	Others (%)
1970	174.8	46.7	27.9	22.5	2.9
1971	212.9	47.2	26.3	24.4	2.2
1972	255.1	42.0	22.5	34.1	1.4
1973	346.7	33.0	17.9	48.3	0.7
1974	502.7	31.6	16.9	50.7	0.8
1975	644.0	30.5	14.3	54.7	0.5
1976	680.6	33.7	17.9	48.0	0.4
1977	873.8	31.2	22.9	44.3	1.7
1978	961.3	33.3	18.2	46.3	2.3
1979	1,561.8	27.9	32.2	37.4	2.6
1980	1,850.5	28.8	36.5	32.2	2.5
1981	2,537.2	26.4	38.4	33.1	2.1
1982	3,032.5	23.8	42.6	31.8	1.8
1983	3,989.6	21.5	47.8	27.9	2.8
1984	4,649.9	19.4	51.3	26.3	3.1
1985	5,522.3	16.6	56.8	24.0	2.7
1986	6,464.2	15.4	59.9	21.1	3.5
1987	8,044.5	13.2	61.2	21.7	3.9
1988	8,622.4	11.9	63.0	21.4	3.8
1989	9,597.1	12.0	65.8	18.8	3.4
1990	10,715.4	12.0	67.4	17.2	3.4
1991	10,312.5	10.5	69.8	16.6	3.0
1992	10,792.1	11.5	69.9	15.9	2.7
1993	10,987.3	11.8	70.3	15.8	2.1
1994	11,695.0	12.6	71.2	14.8	1.5
1995	10,248.4	15.5	80.7	2.6	1.2
1996	6,094.3	27.6	66.4	4.5	1.6
1997	6,001.0	27.6	67.1	3.9	1.4
1998	6,287.1	30.2	65.5	3.9	0.5
1999	6,498.9	33.4	62.5	3.7	0.4

Source: Banco Central de Nicaragua, Annual Report 1975,1977,1978; Gerencia Internacional Web site.

Table A4. External debt stock by creditor, 1990-1999 (US$ millions on December 31)

Concept	1990	1991	1992	1993	1994	1995	1996	1997	1998	1999
Multilateral	**1286.8**	**1087.6**	**1243.0**	**1291.2**	**1472.0**	**1587.2**	**1681.8**	**1657.1**	**1897.2**	**2168.9**
BID	433.5	406.9	464.7	474.7	554.0	644.1	706.0	737.1	826.8	895.0
BCIE	340.3	362.6	394.8	424.3	467.6	493.1	502.7	442.0	447.0	448.1
BIRF	304.0	79.1	68.7	56.1	45.4	36.0	27.6	16.2	14.7	9.4
IDA	61.9	110.9	184.0	207.9	255.0	272.8	323.0	362.3	487.9	596.7
OPEP	37.9	38.3	40.6	40.9	37.8	36.1	33.0	32.7	27.9	23.0
FIDA	23.7	25.0	24.8	19.8	20.2	20.5	18.7	18.5	21.1	21.9
Other	85.5	64.8	65.4	67.5	92.0	84.6	70.8	48.3	71.8	174.8
Bilateral	**7221.8**	**7199.6**	**7548.1**	**7726.9**	**8325.2**	**8271.8**	**4044.5**	**4027.0**	**4115.0**	**4063.2**
Paris Club	1,172.9	890.4	1,458.0	1,355.8	1,647.7	1,329.3	1,327.9	1,199.4	1,600.9	1,470.0
Central America	714.8	779.7	818.5	855.9	886.2	940.6	979.5	998.7	1,051.6	1,119.2
Ex-socialist countries	3,249.0	3,533.7	3,732.6	3,880.1	4,093.2	4,261.7	1,065.3	824.6	743.2	717.8
Latin America	1,435.2	1,291.0	1,327.2	1,390.2	1,444.9	1,451.4	387.1	469.5	428.4	375.2
Other	649.9	704.8	211.8	244.9	253.2	288.8	284.7	534.8	290.9	381.0
Commercial	**1843.7**	**1711.8**	**1711.6**	**1739.9**	**1727.6**	**269.5**	**272.4**	**234.1**	**246.3**	**241.4**
Banks (Categ. USA)	1,821.1	1,687.3	1,687.3	1,725.4	1,725.6	247.8	247.8	196.8	196.8	196.8
Banco de Santander	0.0	0.0	0.0	0.0	0.0	16.8	20.8	21.8	19.5	17.3
Banco Bilbao Vizcaya	0.0	0.0	0.0	0.0	0.0	2.6	1.5	1.0	0.5	0.5
Other	22.6	24.5	24.3	14.5	2.2	2.3	2.3	14.5	29.5	26.8
Providers and other	**363.1**	**313.5**	**289.4**	**229.3**	**170.2**	**119.9**	**95.6**	**82.8**	**28.6**	**25.4**
Rosario Minning	9.9	11.2	11.3	10.1	10.1	7.6	5.0	2.5	0.0	0.0
Neptune Minning	5.5	5.5	5.5	6.5	3.9	3.9	3.9	0.0	0.0	0.0
Esso Standar Oil	47.1	47.9	45.0	37.5	29.9	15.7	6.2	0.0	0.0	0.0
Lagoven	16.2	13.2	9.5	5.7	1.7	0.0	0.1	0.1	0.1	0.1
Other	284.4	235.7	218.1	169.5	124.6	92.7	80.4	80.2	28.5	25.3
TOTAL	**10,715.4**	**10,312.5**	**10,792.1**	**10,987.3**	**11,695.0**	**10,248.4**	**6,094.3**	**6,001.0**	**6,287.1**	**6,498.9**

Source: *Banco Central de Nicaragua, Gerencia Internacional* and Web site.

Table A5.   Debt service (actual payments in US$ millions)*

Year	Payments of principal	Interest	Total
1980	42.3	87.9	130.2
1981	70.7	120.9	191.6
1982	59.3	143.5	202.8
1983	120.9	33.2	154.1
1984	109.2	48.3	157.5
1985	97.8	43.7	141.5
1986	82.0	27.9	109.9
1987	100.3	16.5	116.8
1988	76.7	29.8	106.5
1989	52.8	13.3	66.1
1990	41.7	12.3	54.0
1991**	411.7	206.2	617.9
1992	116.4	55.9	172.3
1993	102.0	92.0	194.0
1994	124.5	117.6	242.1
1995	228.6	95.3	323.9
1996	159.4	69.5	228.9
1997	211.2	131.6	342.8
1998***	123.9	88.3	212.2
1999***	94.1	74.1	168.2

Source: *Banco Central de Nicaragua, Gerencia Internacional* and Web site.
Notes: *   Real service of the public sector. It does not include interest capitalization and payments with exports
(prefinancing).
** Includes interest payments to IADB and BIRF/IDA due in previous years for US$180.6 million.
*** Preliminary figures.

Table A6. Public external debt stock reductions by creditor (US$ millions)

INSTITUTION	1990	1991	1992	1993	1994	1995	1996	1997	1998	1999
Multilaterals	–	–	–	–	1.3	–	–	103.7	–	–
IADB	–	–	–	–	1.3	–	–	–	–	–
CABEI	–	–	–	–	–	–	–	103.7	–	–
Bilaterals	–	259.0	53.0	147.7	140.2	441.3	4,208.1	–	138.6	94.6
USAID	–	259.0	–	–	–	–	–	–	–	–
France	–	–	–	–	–	–	–	–	13.4	79.1
Netherlands	–	–	48.6	–	8.5	15.7	–	–	5.0	–
Cuba	–	–	4.4	34.6	–	6.2	5.6	–	4.6	4.2
Finland	–	–	–	94.6	–	–	–	–	50.1	–
Germany	–	–	–	18.5	114.6	415.8	–	–	–	–
Taiwan	–	–	–	–	17.1	–	–	–	8.5	–
Spain	–	–	–	–	–	2.7	–	–	–	–
Italy	–	–	–	–	–	–	–	–	8.4	5.8
Mexico	–	–	–	–	–	–	29.6	–	–	5.5
Norway	–	–	–	–	–	–	1,065.7	–	–	–
Russia	–	–	–	–	–	–	1.3	–	–	–
Czech Republic	–	–	–	–	–	–	3,099.9	–	–	–
Austria	–	–	–	–	–	–	6.0	–	–	–
Canada	–	–	–	–	–	–	–	–	39.1	–
United Kingdom	–	–	–	–	–	0.9	–	–	9.5	–
Commercial	–	–	–	–	–	1,011.4	–	–	–	–
Commercial banks (USA)	–	–	–	–	–	1,011.4	–	–	–	0.0
Total	**0.0**	**259.0**	**53.0**	**147.7**	**141.5**	**1,452.7**	**4,208.1**	**103.7**	**138.6**	**94.6**

Source: Banco Central de Nicaragua, Departamento de Programación Externa.

Table A7. Nicaragua's matrix of goals, targets, and intermediate indicators
for the Strengthened Poverty-Reduction Strategy (SPRS).

International targets 2015	National goals	National targets 2005	Intermediate indicators
Reduce extreme poverty by 50%	*Poverty reduction*	Reduce extreme poverty by 25%	Increase of government spending on poverty-related outlays from 53% of budget in year 2000 to 64% by year 2003
			Growth of real GDP
Universal access to primary education	*Raising access to primary education to 90%*	Increase net primary enrollment rate from 75% in 1999 to 85%	Annual increase of 1.7% in net primary enrolment rate
			Annual increase of 1% in promotion rate of 3rd graders in rural areas
			Annual increase of 2% in number of children who complete primary school in six years
			Academic achievement measuring systemic effect, and first evaluation in 2001 for 3rd and 6th graders
			Annual increase of 1% in the net pre-school enrolment rate
			Increase to 6th grade all rural multigrade schools by 2005
			600 classrooms constructed and replaced annually
			Increase of number of schools with double shifts
Reduce maternal mortality rate by 75%	*Reduction in maternal mortality rate*	Reduce maternal mortality rate from 148 per 100,000 in 1999 to 129 per 100,000	Increase of institutional births from 47% in 1999 to 55% (annual increase of 3,700 new institutional births)
			Increase of prenatal care from 71.6% in 1999 to 82.6% (annual increase of 5,870 prenatal controls)
			Increase of early prenatal care from 31.9% in 1999 to 39% (annual increase of 3,400 early prenatal care controls)
			Program on population in public schools and non-formal program introduced by 2002
Reduce infant and under five mortality rates by 65%	*Reduction in mortality rates of infants and children under 5*	Reduce infant mortality rate from 40‰ in 1998 to 32‰ Reduce mortality in children under 5 year-old from 50‰ in 1998 to 37‰	Increase in immunization for children under 1 year
			Increase in immunization for children under 5 years
			Diarrhea in children under 6 reduced from 19.6% in 1998 to 15% by 2002
			Acute respiratory infections in children under 6 reduced from 27.3% in 1998 to 23% by 2002

Table A7 (continued)

International targets 2015	National goals	National targets 2005	Intermediate indicators
Provide access to reproductive health for all individuals of appropriate age	*Access to reproductive health services*	Reduce the unsatisfied demand for family planning among women with partners in the 15-19 age group from 27.1% in 1998 to 25% by 2003	Increase of access to reproductive health services by women of childbearing age from 21% in 1999 to 25% by 2005 (annual increase of access by 14,000 women of childbearing age during the 2000-2005 period)
		Reduce the unsatisfied demand for family planning among women with partners in the 20-24 age group from 19.7% in 1998 to 17.9% by 2003	Program on population in public schools and non-formal program introduced by 2002
Have a sustainable development strategy implemented by year 2005	*Implement National Strategy for Sustainable Development*	National Strategy for Sustainable Development implemented by 2005	Policy and environmental plan published and implemented; Forestry and development law approved; Fisheries law approved; Biodiversity law approved
Reduce chronic malnutrition to 7%	*Reduce chronic malnutrition*	Reduce chronic malnutrition in children under 5 from 19.9% in 1998 to 13% in 2005	Chronic malnutrition in children under 5 reduced from 19.9% in 1998 to 17% in 2002
Increase to 100% national water coverage	*Increase access to water and sanitation*	Increase national coverage of water from 66.5% in 1999 to 75.5%	Annual increase of 1.5% in national coverage of water
Increase to 87% national access to sanitation		Increase access to safe water and sanitation in rural dispersed areas from 39% in 1999 to 54%	Annual increase of 2.5% in access to safe water in rural dispersed areas
		Increase national access to sanitation from 36% in 1999 to 50.2%	Annual increase of 2.4% in access to sanitation
		Increase access to sewage in urban areas from 33.6% in 1999 to 47.3%	Annual increase of 2.3% in access to sewage by the urban population
Decrease illiteracy rates to 10%	*Reduce illiteracy rate*	Reduce illiteracy rate from 19% in 1998 to 17% by 2002	Illiteracy decreased by 2% in 2002
			Increase of years of schooling among the 10-19 age group from 4.6 years in 1998 to 4.9 years in 2002

Source: Government of Nicaragua, *A strengthened poverty reduction strategy*, 2000, p. 19-21.

L'endettement des pays les plus pauvres : le cas du Mali[*]

Massa Coulibaly
Amadou Diarra
& Sikoro Keita

RÉSUMÉ

Le 6 septembre 2000, le Mali bénéficiait d'un allégement de sa dette extérieure d'un montant nominal de 870 millions de dollars dans le cadre de l'Initative PPTE, équivalent à un peu plus d'un tiers de sa dette en valeur nominale actuelle. Cette décision fut capitale pour le pays dont presque deux tiers de la population vit en-dessous du seuil de la pauvreté. Toutefois, des défis majeurs seront à relever avant le point d'achèvement de l'Initiative PTTE renforcée, surtout que l'approbation de la candidature du Mali par les institutions de Bretton Woods s'est faite avec des réserves importantes, parmi lesquelles, la faiblesse du Cadre stratégique de lutte contre la pauvreté (CSLP) intérimaire présenté par le Mali. Par ailleurs, du fait que l'allégement s'étend sur une période aussi longue que trente ans, l'Initiative PTTE à elle seule ne semble pas suffire pour éliminer définitivement la crise d'endettement au Mali. Un ensemble d'options serait à souhaiter, incluant en plus de l'Initiative PTTE, l'arrêt des fuites de capitaux, la lutte contre les fraudes fiscales, l'émission d'obligations publiques, et toutes les autres recettes traditionnelles de financement de l'endettement.

ABSTRACT

On September 6, 2000, Mali received US$870 million in foreign debt reduction under the HIPC Initiative. This amount is equivalent to just over one third of the country's foreign debt in current terms. This decision was a breakthrough for Mali, where at least two thirds of the population lives below the poverty line. However, some major challenges will have to be overcome before the Enhanced HIPC Initiative completion point is reached, particularly since the Bretton Woods institutions approved Mali's application with

* Les auteurs tiennent à remercier Yiagadeesen Samy pour ses précieux commentaires sur une version préalable de ce travail, ainsi que pour son aide durant la rédaction-révision.

serious reservations partly as a result of Mali's weak Interim Poverty Reduction Strategy Paper. In addition, largely because the reduction is spread out over a lengthy 30-year period, the HIPC Initiative alone seems insufficient to permanently eliminate Mali's debt crisis. A combination of measures in addition to the HIPC Inititiave would be the most effective, including halting capital flight, fighting tax fraud, issuing domestic public securities, and all the other traditional methods of financing debt.

INTRODUCTION

Au début des années 80, le Mali a connu une crise d'endettement se traduisant par son incapacité à honorer les échéances de paiement des intérêts et de remboursement du principal. Aussi s'est-il engagé dans des programmes d'ajustement structurel dès 1982 et dans des facilités renforcées depuis 1988. Plus spécifiquement, la nécessité de réduire le fardeau de sa dette l'a conduit à quatre passages devant le Club de Paris (1988, 1989, 1992 et 1996), des négociations avec la Russie en vue du traitement de la dette envers l'ex-URSS aux conditions du Club de Paris, des moratoires avec la Chine sur des prêts assortis d'intérêt nul, solliciter et obtenir des allégements de dette envers des créanciers bilatéraux comme l'Egypte, la Libye, le Maroc, le Qatar et la Yougoslavie, demander son éligibilité au bénéfice des facilités prévues dans l'initiative PPTE.

Vu la persistance de la crise d'endettement et compte tenu de l'évolution récente des relations extérieures, aux plans commercial et financier, il n'est pas inutile de tester la soutenabilité du niveau restant d'endettement du pays, de mesurer la viabilité de l'initiative PPTE, et de proposer des voies de sortie de crise, voire des stratégies de développement et de croissance durable.

La première partie de cette étude présente les principales caractéristiques de l'économie du Mali à travers les indicateurs macro-économiques et sociaux ainsi que de la balance des paiements. La deuxième porte sur la problématique de l'endettement en termes de politique d'endettement, de niveau du stock et de mesures de soutenabilité de la dette. La troisième partie analyse les mécanismes d'allégement de cette dette, qu'il s'agisse des mécanismes traditionnels ou de l'initiative PPTE. La quatrième partie établit le lien entre l'allégement de la dette et la réduction de la pauvreté, analyse l'évolution du processus du CSLP au Mali et rend compte du point de vue du secteur privé et de la société civile. La conclusion donne un aperçu des perspectives de l'après-PPTE au Mali, estime l'impact de l'initiative PPTE, et propose des solutions aux financements de la dette.

I. PRINCIPALES CARACTÉRISTIQUES DE L'ÉCONOMIE

Les principaux traits de l'économie malienne se révèlent à partir de l'évolution d'un certain nombre d'indicateurs macro-économiques les plus couramment utilisés. Ils sont complétés par les indicateurs sociaux pour faire relever l'amélioration ou la détérioration de la situation socio-économique de la population.

Tableau 1.   Évolution d'indicateurs économiques et sociaux (% annuel)

	1970-80	1980-90	1990-99	Ensemble période
PIB réel	4,0	2,0	3,7	3,3
PIB/ht	-	0,4	1,6	1,0
RNN réel*	-	3,7	4,8	4,2
RNN/ht*	-	1,9	2,6	2,2
Déficit balance paiements (BP)**	51,1	6,0	- 3,0	18,1
Déficit BP/PNB**	26,7	0,5	- 7,2	7,3

*   Il s'agit de la période 1980-98.
**   Il s'agit de la période 1970-97.
Source: DNSI, *Comptes économiques du Mali*, avril 1999.

A.   INDICATEURS MACRO-ÉCONOMIQUES

De 1970 à 1999, le PIB réel du Mali est passé de 360 milliards de francs CFA à 921 milliards de francs CFA, soit un taux annuel moyen de croissance de 3,3 %, toutefois irrégulière sur la période, 4 % pour la première décennie 1970-80 contre 2 % seulement pour la décennie 1980-90, et ensuite 3,7 % par an depuis 1990. La croissance pendant la période 1970-80 aurait pu être encore plus forte ne ce fut-il la sécheresse des années 1972-74 qui a entraîné une baisse du PIB de 3 %.

Les contre-performances du début des années 80 ont donné lieu a l'application des politiques d'ajustement structurel, qui ont eu pour effet une croissance régulière de 1982 à présent, excepté les années 1992-1993 où l'on observe une diminution du PIB, de 4 % ; d'où l'intérêt pour le Mali de l'ajustement monétaire à l'intérieur de l'Union économique et monétaire de l'Afrique de l'Ouest (UEMOA) c.-à-d. la dévaluation du franc CFA en janvier 1994. De 1994 à 1999, le taux de croissance du PIB a été de 5,5 % par an. Par rapport à la population, le PIB réel est passé de 78 000 francs CFA en 1980 à

94 000 francs CFA en 1999, soit un accroissement moyen de moins de 1 % par an. Depuis 1994, la croissance moyenne est de 3,5 %, ce qui est légèrement supérieure à l'accroissement naturel de la population estimé à 3 %.

La conséquence immédiate du faible taux de croissance, surtout du PIB, est la faiblesse de l'épargne locale et donc de l'investissement local, d'où le constat que le secteur privé ne répond pas toujours à la hauteur des espoirs fondés sur son rôle de moteur de la croissance, aux opportunités offertes par la libéralisation des marchés et la privatisation des entreprises publiques, et ceci bien que l'environnement macroéconomique soit de plus en plus assaini. Le taux d'épargne est passé de 7,7 % en 1980 à 25,3 % en 1996, avec le plus fort taux de 27 % en 1994 et un creux de 5 % en 1985 lorsque le cours du coton (principale matière première d'exportation) avait considérablement chuté. L'investissement direct étranger ne semble pas pallier l'insuffisance de l'effort interne pour l'accroissement des capacités intérieures de production et la modernisation du système productif. Au contraire, celui-ci n'a cessé de baisser depuis 1995, passant ainsi de 111 millions $ US à 30 millions $ US en 1998, soit une baisse moyenne de 35 % par an.

B.   INDICATEURS SOCIAUX

À des indicateurs macro-économiques faibles correspondent des niveaux faibles de satisfaction des besoins sociaux de la population. Le Mali est confronté à un grave problème de pauvreté touchant 72 % de la population c.-à-d. de personnes vivant avec moins de 1 $ US par jour. Le *Rapport du Programme des Nations Unies pour le développement* (PNUD 1999) établit, pour le Mali, l'indicateur de développement humain (IDH) à 0,375 (obtenu sur la base d'une espérance de vie de 53 ans, d'un PIB réel par habitant de 740 PPA équivalent à 271 $ US, d'un taux d'alphabétisation des adultes de 35,5 % et d'un taux brut de scolarisation de 25 %). Ce niveau d'IDH classe le Mali au 166e rang sur 174 pays.

En 1993, on comptait 4 médecins par 100 000 habitants contre la moyenne de 14 p. 100 000 dans les pays moins avancés (PMA) et 76 p. 100 000 dans les pays en développement. En 1996 encore, on dénombrait, pour 1000 habitants, 2 lignes téléphoniques, 11 téléviseurs et 0,3 ordinateurs. Enfin, en 1998, le rapport national sur le développement humain durable établissait à 48 % le déficit de conditions de vie, soit 54 % de la population est privée d'accès à l'eau potable, 60 % de la population est privée d'accès aux services de santé, et 30 % de la population est privée d'accès à une bonne alimentation.

Figure 1. La structure des importations

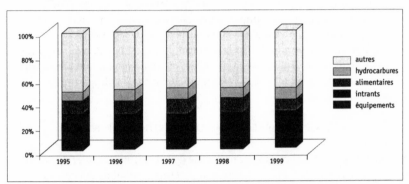

Figure 2. La structure des exportations

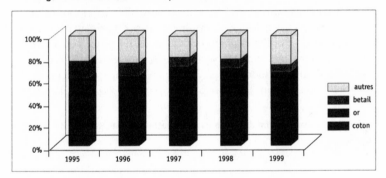

C.   BALANCE DES PAIEMENTS

Si la promotion des exportations, surtout des exportations de biens non traditionnels et de services, est nécessaire pour la croissance et le développement économique, le Mali a encore du chemin à faire vu le déficit structurel de sa balance des paiements depuis de nombreuses années. De 1970 à 1997, le solde de la balance des paiements s'est dégradé en moyenne de 18 % par an. Depuis l'entrée en application des programmes d'ajustement en 1982, la détérioration est revenue à 3 %, soit une amélioration de 1,8 point par an.

Par rapport au produit national brut (PNB), la balance des transactions courantes est restée déficitaire avec une aggravation annuelle moyenne de

9,6 %. La chute abrupte du prix du coton et de l'or dans la période de 1995 à 1998, a entraîné une baisse des recettes d'exportation bien que la facture des importations augmentait compte tenu de leur caractère relativement incompressible et de la dévaluation de la monnaie sous régionale.

Les exportations dominantes sont le coton, l'or et le bétail, trois produits qui, à eux seuls, représentent 73 % de la valeur totale tandis que les importations portent essentiellement sur les équipements, les hydrocarbures et les denrées alimentaires.

II. LA PROBLÉMATIQUE DE L'ENDETTEMENT

La faible intégration de l'économie nationale dans les échanges internationaux et la baisse des recettes d'exportation ont davantage affaibli les capacités de remboursement du pays. Depuis le début des années 80, la dette pèse lourdement sur les finances publiques, entraînant la non-satisfaction d'obligations contractuelles (76 millions $ US d'impayés en 1980), d'où l'accumulation d'arriérés de paiements (annexe A1). Face à ces difficultés, le remboursement a dû être plusieurs fois rééchelonné et certaines parties du principal annulées. De nouvelles propositions d'allégement ont été faites, telles que l'initiative en faveur des pays pauvres très endettés, sur la base de critères d'éligibilité que le Mali remplit. Pendant la période 1989-97, les arriérés d'impayés sont passés de 6 millions $ US à 582 millions $ US, avec en moyenne 90 % sur le principal.

Figure 3. La ventilation de l'encours de la dette selon les sources

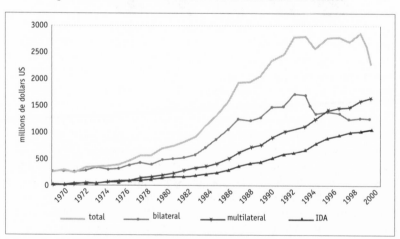

Tableau 2.   Les étapes de l'endettement du Mali

	1960-1970	1970-1976	1976-1982	1982-2000
Principales destinations	Création d'entreprises publiques	Projets d'infra-structures de base	Électrification	Prêts d'ajustement structurel pour le budget national
Principales sources	Chine et anciens pays socialistes	IDA	Fonds arabes	IFI - Bretton Woods
Types de prêts	Prêts clearing	Prêts concession-nels à long terme	Prêts concession-nels à moyen terme	Prêts financiers

Source : les auteurs.

A.   SOURCES DE L'ENDETTEMENT

L'allure de la courbe d'endettement du Mali est celle de source bilatérale. Celle-ci comprend principalement la dette vis-à-vis de la France, du Japon, de la Chine et de l'ex-URSS, et les fonds arabes. La modification de la structure de la dette, de bilatérale à multilatérale (annexe A1) s'expliquerait par l'évolution de la politique d'endettement du pays, mais aussi par les rééchelonnements et annulations de créances bilatérales, ainsi que les décaissements obtenus dans le cadre des politiques et réformes d'ajustement.

B.   POLITIQUES D'ENDETTEMENT

Comme indiqué dans le tableau 2, quatre politiques d'endettement bien distinctes se dégagent de l'évolution de l'endettement extérieur du Mali.

Les premières années après l'indépendance (1960-1970), sont caractérisées par un endettement extérieur, principalement, auprès des pays de l'ancien bloc socialiste, notamment l'ex-URSS et la Chine. Après 1970, l'industrialisation a été partiellement l'œuvre du secteur privé et l'État s'est surtout consacré à la mise en œuvre d'une politique de désenclavement du pays. Ainsi de 1970 à 1976, la politique d'endettement a été orientée vers le financement des projets d'infrastructure, de transport et de moyens de communication.

De 1976 à 1982, la politique d'endettement a été surtout marquée par la mobilisation des « pétrodollars » en quête de recyclage sous forme d'aide publique au développement. Les fonds arabes ainsi mobilisés ont été utilisés pour le désenclavement du nord du pays avec la construction de la route Sévaré-Gao ainsi que la réalisation des barrages hydroélectriques de Sélingué et de Manantali. Depuis 1982, la politique d'endettement se singularise par la fréquence des prêts d'ajustement structurel contractés dans le cadre de la mise en œuvre des programmes de réformes économiques soutenus par le FMI et la Banque mondiale. L'endettement est depuis lors limité aux seuls prêts concessionnels c.-à-d. aux prêts dont l'élément "don" est supérieur à 35 %.

C.   L'ÉVOLUTION DU STOCK DE LA DETTE

De 1970 à 1997, la dette extérieure du Mali a évolué au rythme annuel de 9,6 % soit environ 100 millions $ US par an. En 1997, le stock total de la dette était de 2 945 millions $ US (annexe A1) soit 314 $ US par habitant alors que le PNB est de 264 $ US par tête. Sur la même période, les nouveaux décaissements sont passés de 23 millions $ US en 1970 à 147 millions $ US en 1997 (annexe A3), soit une augmentation moyenne annuelle de 7 % seulement. Quant au service de la dette, le paiement est passé de 5 millions $ US en 1973 à 106 millions $ US en 1996.

Le stock total de la dette du Mali a commencé à être relativement important à la fin des années 70; les 500 millions $ US sont atteints en 1978 et l'accumulation va se poursuivre à partir de là pour atteindre le milliard de dollars en 1984. L'on n'assiste pas pour autant à une accélération de l'emprunt nouveau. En effet, à partir de 1984, l'écart se creuse entre l'encours de la dette et les décaissements nets en faveur du Mali, corrigé du différentiel de l'année 1970 de base.

La crise de remboursement survint à la fin des années 80 quand bien d'échéances étaient arrivées à terme et que les capitaux de prêt se faisaient rares suite à la crise (en terme d'incapacité durable de payer les intérêts de la dette) dans la plupart des pays en développement avec des moratoires aux plus endettés comme le Mexique, le Brésil ou l'Argentine. Comme dans la plupart des autres pays qui connaissent une crise d'endettement, celle-ci a pour causes:

- l'auto-entretien de l'endettement à travers la capitalisation des intérêts dus, phénomène d'autant plus amplifié que le taux d'intérêt aura été élevé ;
- le fait que l'endettement soit disproportionné par rapport aux ressources locales; cela n'est pourtant pas perceptible en ce qui concerne les nouveaux emprunts, qui dans le cas du Mali, représentent en moyenne 7 % du PNB ;
- le financement des importations, surtout de biens de consommation courante, sur endettement plutôt que le développement des infrastructures et équipements en vue de promouvoir le développement économique c.-à-d. le financement d'investissements dont le taux de rentabilité est au moins égal au service de la dette ;

- le processus cumulatif de l'endettement qui fait que de nouveaux prêts sont recherchés pour rembourser les échéances et payer les intérêts dus.

Pour finir, l'emprunt ne génère plus de ressources suffisantes pour garantir la solvabilité. Au contraire, le pays doit puiser dans ses propres ressources pour maintenir sa solvabilité. Le seuil d'insoutenabilité est atteint, la charge des intérêts nécessitant le recours à de nouveaux emprunts.

D.   ENCOURS ET SERVICES

L'encours à long terme de la dette extérieure du Mali (plus de 90 % du stock total) a connu un rythme de croissance quasi exponentiel de 1970 à 1999. De 238 millions $ US en 1970, il est passé à 2 246 millions $ US en 1999, soit une hausse annuelle moyenne de 8 %. L'examen de la structure de l'encours révèle aussi que la dette extérieure du Mali est surtout une dette publique, la dette commerciale (ou dette privée) représentant rarement plus de 5 % de l'encours total. Ainsi, le rythme de croissance de la dette extérieure du Mali résulte de la progression de la dette publique qui se décompose en dette multilatérale et dette bilatérale.

Très faible en 1970, car ne représentant que 2,5 % de l'encours total, la part de la dette multilatérale a régulièrement progressé et prédomine à partir de 1995 alors que celle de la dette bilatérale régressait de façon régulière à partir de la même période. Cette évolution est due d'une part, aux annulations et rééchelonnements de dettes obtenus par le Mali auprès de ses créanciers bilatéraux membres du Club de Paris (surtout en 1994 après la dévaluation avec une réduction de l'encours bilatéral de 23 %); et, d'autre part, aux décaissements rapides effectués dans le cadre de l'exécution des programmes d'ajustement structurel ainsi que le recours de plus en plus fréquent aux ressources concessionnelles de l'Association internationale de développement (IDA) pour la réalisation de nombreux projets de développement.

Au 31 décembre 1999, l'encours se répartissait uniquement en dette publique multilatérale (72 %) et en dette publique bilatérale (28 %). À cette date, les principaux créanciers multilatéraux étaient l'IDA (37 %), la Banque africaine de développement (12 %) et le FMI (11 %); les principaux créanciers bilatéraux membres du Club de Paris comprenaient la France (9 %), le Japon (4 %) et les autres bilatéraux dont la Chine (5 %), l'ex-URSS (4,6 %) et les Fonds Arabes (4,2 %).

Comme l'encours, le service payé de la dette extérieure du Mali s'est aussi accru pendant les vingt dernières années, passant de 1 million $ US en 1970 à 73 millions $ US en 1998 (annexe A3).

E.   ARRIÉRÉS DE DETTE

Selon les sources gouvernementales, le Mali n'accumule pas d'arriéré extérieur depuis 1994, le service de la dette étant correctement réglé. Cependant, il convient de préciser qu'il s'agit là du règlement des échéances courantes. En effet, en dépit de la non-disponibilité de toutes les données, des arriérés de dette subsistent. Ces arriérés comprennent:
- la dette vis à vis de la Chine qui a toujours accordé au Mali des moratoires successifs de paiement ;
- la dette due à la Russie (ex-URSS) qui a aussi fait l'objet de plusieurs moratoires mais dont une réduction du stock de 80 % a été obtenu dans le cadre du Club de Paris ;
- la dette monétaire vis à vis de la France constituée du solde débiteur du compte d'opérations de l'ancienne Banque centrale du Mali au moment de sa liquidation en juin 1984 à la suite de l'intégration du Mali à l'UEMOA, et des avances consenties par le Trésor français au Trésor malien depuis 1970 et pour lesquelles aucune conditionnalité de remboursement n'a été précisée.

Le Mali a connu ses premiers arriérés de paiement en 1980 avec un total de 76 millions $ US dont 75 millions $ US sur le principal (annexe A1), quand la période de grâce de la première génération d'emprunts arrivait à terme. Les premiers programmes d'ajustement permettront d'alléger ces arriérés qui seront apurés en 1985. De 1985 à 1988, le pays n'accuse aucun arriéré de paiement. Au début des années 1990, les arriérés réapparaissent, passant de 72 millions $ US en 1990 à 582 millions $ US en 1997, soit une augmentation annuelle moyenne de 35 %. Rapporté au PNB, les arriérés d'impayés ont passé de 3 % en 1990 à 24 % en 1997.

F.   POIDS DE LA DETTE

Trois principaux indicateurs permettent d'apprécier le poids réel de la dette sur une économie, à savoir les ratios d'endettement, les indices de vulnérabilité et la valeur actualisée nette de la dette. En examinant certains ratios caractéristiques de la dette extérieure, on relève les évolutions suivantes:
- le rapport de la dette extérieure au PNB est passé de 71 % en 1970 à 109 % en 1997, soit un niveau d'endettement extérieur à l'échelle de l'activité économique supérieur à la valeur critique de 50 %;
- le rapport de la dette extérieure sur les exportations s'est réduit de 425 % à 335 % sur la même période mais reste supérieur au seuil de tolérance de 275 %;

• le ratio du service de la dette sur les exportations a augmenté de 2 % à 13 % et demeure inférieur au seuil critique de 20 %.

Au vu de ces données, on remarque que la dette extérieure du Mali se caractérise de nouveau par son évolution rapide. Ces données révèlent en outre une inadéquation entre cette progression et les grands agrégats macro-économiques surtout en 1985 et 1994, deux années au cours desquelles les mauvaises pluies ont lourdement pesé sur l'activité économique.

Le poids de l'endettement, mesuré par le ratio de l'encours au PNB, a régulièrement baissé sur la période 1970-80, à l'exception de la sous-période 1973-74 qui correspond à celle de la grande sécheresse du Sahel. L'accroissement est ensuite régulier jusqu'en 1985 et le ratio devient quasi stationnaire de 1986 à 1989. Enfin, suite à la dévaluation de 1994, le ratio augmente fortement pour s'établir à 141 % avant de commencer à diminuer progressivement depuis cette date. Evalué par rapport aux recettes d'exportation, le poids de la dette a presque toujours été lourd sur la période d'analyse.

Le ratio semble avoir fortement augmenté au cours de la période 1980-94, au taux moyen de 6 % par an. Depuis 1994, le poids a baissé de 10 % par an, mais demeure élevé face à la faiblesse des recettes d'exportation du Mali et surtout face à la faiblesse de cette structure des exportations, dominée par trois produits seulement, le coton, l'or et le bétail. En plus des ratios d'endettement, le poids de la dette extérieure s'apprécie aussi à partir de la vulnérabilité de l'économie nationale. Deux indices sont à cet effet révélateurs. Il s'agit de la sécheresse cyclique et de la structure des exportations.

Comme les autres pays sahéliens, le Mali est confronté également à une sécheresse cyclique qui entraîne des baisses très importantes de la production agricole et des exportations de coton et de bétail. Les deux grandes sécheresses de 1972 à 1975 et de 1983 à 1985 ont entraîné une chute des exportations de bétail respectivement de 75 % et 60 %, et une baisse de la production de coton de 20 % à chaque période. On assiste donc à la fois à une diminution du PNB et à une baisse des exportations. Les ratios d'endettement se détériorent donc plus rapidement: de 1982 à 1985 le rapport dette extérieure/PNB a cru de 65 % à 126 %, celui de la dette aux exportations de 349 % à 432 %.

La vulnérabilité générale de l'économie malienne à chaque sécheresse est exacerbée par sa dépendance d'une gamme limitée d'exportations de produits primaires. En 1999, les exportations présentaient la structure suivante: coton (34 %), or (32 %), bétail (7 %) et autres (27 %). Ainsi, environ deux tiers des exportations du Mali sont concentrées sur deux produits, le coton et l'or, dont les cours sont susceptibles de fluctuations considérables avec des impacts sur les recettes d'exportations. Toute baisse des cours du coton et de l'or sur le marché international peut conduire à un alourdissement du poids de la dette.

En plus des ratios d'endettement et des indices de vulnérabilité, la valeur actualisée nette est aussi utilisée pour évaluer le poids de la dette. L'utilisation de la valeur actualisée au lieu de la valeur nominale se justifie par le fait que la valeur actualisée tient compte des conditions et de la concessionnalité du portefeuille de prêts et traduit ainsi avec précision les coûts de la dette en devise courante. La valeur actualisée de la dette (VAN) représente donc le mouvement de futurs paiements de service de la dette corrigé de la valeur temps de l'argent (t) – t étant soit le taux d'escompte, soit à défaut le taux d'intérêt commercial de référence (TICR) publié par l'OCDE. Ainsi :

$$VAN = \frac{SD_1}{\left(1+t\right)} + \frac{SD_2}{\left(1+t\right)^2} + \cdots + \frac{SD_n}{\left(1+t\right)^n}$$

En valeur actualisée, l'encours de la dette extérieure a cru de 1996 à 1999 de 1,265 milliard \$ US à 1,403 milliard \$ US, soit une hausse de 111 %. La part de la dette multilatérale demeure plus importante que celle de la dette bilatérale et les plus grands créanciers sont l'IDA (35 %) et les bilatéraux membres du Club de Paris (19 %). Quant au ratio de la valeur actualisée sur les exportations, il a diminué de 259 % en 1996 à 211 % en 1999. Cependant, il demeure supérieur au seuil de 200 % retenu par le FMI et la Banque mondiale comme soutenable dans le cas précis du Mali.

III. MÉCANISMES D'ALLÉGEMENT DE LA DETTE

Les mécanismes d'allégement de la dette font suite à la crise de rembourse-ment ou simplement à la précaution de faire en sorte que le remboursement des intérêts ne se fasse au détriment du niveau de vie et de l'investissement dans les pays débiteurs. Quels que soient les mécanismes, la stratégie de sortie de la crise d'endettement repose sur trois fondements :

• les accords de rééchelonnement consistant à différer les remboursements du principal arrivés à échéance ;
• la mise en œuvre de réformes d'ajustement structurel tendant à réduire les importations et à stimuler les exportations pour dégager des ressour-ces en vue de payer les intérêts de la dette ;
• l'octroi de nouveaux prêts de la part des structures financières interna-tionales et des banques en vue de la croissance et des paiements des intérêts.

Tableau 3. Évolution de la valeur actualisée de la dette (VAN) du Mali (millions de $US)

Année	(VAN)	Ancienne dette						Nouvelle dette
		Totale	Bilatérale		Multilatérale			
			Totale	Club de Paris	Totale	FMI	IDA	
1997	1239	1239	378	246	861	133	423	0
1998	1325	1316	386	250	930	146	453	9
1999	1403	1384	391	253	993	161	485	19
2000	1474	1452	395	255	1057	171	522	22
2001	1534	1511	399	258	1112	177	558	23
2002	1559	1530	400	259	1130	159	590	29
2003	1582	1517	396	258	1121	138	617	65
2004	1609	1498	393	258	1105	115	637	111
2005	1641	1471	390	257	1081	93	650	170
2006	1672	1435	385	254	1050	71	658	237
2007	1712	1391	378	249	1013	49	660	321
2008	1760	1353	372	245	28981	30	680	407
2009	1815	1312	367	241	945	15	656	503
2010	1890	1274	359	233	915	5	650	616

Source : IMF, *Mali Net Present Value of Debt after Rescheduling, 1997-2017*, 1999.

A. MÉCANISMES TRADITIONNELS

Les techniques d'allégement de la dette extérieure peuvent être regroupées en trois catégories :
- les techniques de réaménagement consacrées à la dette extérieure vis-à-vis des créanciers publics ;
- les techniques utilisées pour le réaménagement de la dette extérieure due aux créanciers privés ;
- les annulations de dettes.

Selon la nature des créanciers (publics ou privés), les mécanismes consacrés au réaménagement de la dette sont ceux proposés aux pays débiteurs dans le cadre du Club de Paris pour les créances publiques et dans le cadre du Club de Londres pour les créances privées (généralement dues aux banques commerciales)[1].

Au-delà des techniques du Club de Paris et du Club de Londres, les annulations pures et simples de la dette constituent aussi des mécanismes d'allégement. Jusqu'à la mise en place de l'initiative PPTE, elles étaient consenties uniquement par les créanciers bilatéraux. L'annulation de créances se fait dans

---

1. Voir annexe A6 pour de plus amples détails sur les mécanismes de fonctionnement des Clubs de Paris et de Londres.

le cadre des dettes contractées auprès des pouvoirs publics, sinon dans le cas des banques, l'annulation prend la forme de décotes pour lesquelles des provisions sont faites dans les limites fiscalement tolérables.

B.   L'ALLÉGEMENT OBTENU

D'abord, il faut dire que le Mali n'a pas obtenu d'annulation de dette du Club de Londres. Les allégements obtenus ne concernent donc que les créances publiques des pays membres ou non du Club de Paris.

Les allégements de dette accordés par les pays membres du Club de Paris ont été obtenus à l'issue de quatre passages devant ledit Club ainsi qu'à la faveur de la dévaluation du franc CFA de 50 % en janvier 1994 (annexe A2). Les passages successifs du Mali devant le Club de Paris ont permis d'obtenir un allégement total de dette à hauteur de 230 millions $ US :

- 65 millions aux conditions de Toronto (1988)
- 54 millions aux conditions de Londres (1989)
- 76 millions aux conditions de Toronto renforcé (1992)
- 35 millions aux conditions de Naples (1996), soit 67 % de réduction de la VAN auprès de trois de ses créanciers (France, Pays Bas, Royaume-Uni) et le rééchelonnement au taux du marché sur 23 ans dont 6 de différé. L'Italie a accordé un rééchelonnement sur 33 ans dont 3 ans de grâce au taux d'intérêt concessionnel.

Au-delà de ces allégements, les pays membres du Club de Paris ont aussi accordé au Mali une annulation de dette de 413 millions $ US en 1996, soit 123 % des flux nets et 138 % des transferts nets reçus pour atténuer les effets de la dévaluation. À elle seule, cette annulation représente plus de 71 % de l'ensemble des allégements obtenus par le Mali de 1988 à 1996 et élève ainsi la moyenne des allégements à 22 % des flux nets et à 25 % des transferts nets. Sans cette annulation exceptionnelle de dette, lesdites moyennes se situeraient respectivement à 6 % et 7 %.

Les allégements des pays non membres du Club de Paris peuvent être regroupés en deux catégories :

- les moratoires successifs accordés par la Chine et l'ex-URSS. Il convient toutefois de préciser que les négociations avec la Russie sur la dette de l'ex-URSS ont abouti en août 1998 au principe de l'annulation de 80 % de ladite dette et du rééchelonnement des 20 % restants selon l'option B de Naples c.-à-d. sur 33 ans sans différé ou 25 ans avec un différé de 6 ans si la réduction obtenue en valeur actualisée nette est réduite à moitié. Cependant, l'accord bilatéral à conclure dans ce cadre n'est toujours pas signé.

- les différentes annulations de dette accordées par le Maroc (274 millions FCFA), l'ex-Yougoslavie (170 millions FCFA) l'Allemagne et le Qatar (3,3 milliards FCFA) et d'autre part de l'allégement consenti par la Côte d'Ivoire en 1997 selon les termes de Naples, soit une réduction de 67 % du stock de la dette et le rééchelonnement du reliquat sur 23 ans avec 6 ans de différé et au taux d'intérêt de 6 % par an.

C. LIMITES

La principale limite des mécanismes traditionnels d'allégement de dette résulte de l'exclusion totale de la dette multilatérale de leur champ d'application en dépit de sa part sans cesse croissante dans l'encours total.

Aussi, avant les termes de Naples, l'assiette de réaménagement dans le cadre du Club de Paris ne comprenait que les échéances impayées et celles arrivant à maturité pendant la période couverte par un programme d'ajustement structurel avec le FMI. Ainsi les rééchelonnements accordés à la suite des trois premiers Club de Paris ne concernaient que des échéances arrivant à maturité pendant des périodes relativement courtes, soit un an et demi pour 1988, deux ans pour 1989 et trois ans pour 1992. N'abordant pas le long terme et ne portant pas sur l'encours, les premiers mécanismes d'allégement de dette ont tout au plus permis de différer à court terme le problème de trésorerie.

Il semble que le rééchelonnement au Club de Paris a donné peu de résultats satisfaisants. En effet, à la fin des années 80, seulement 10 % des pays lourdement endettés sont parvenus à une situation de solvabilité. Deux critiques sont généralement adressées à ce mécanisme. Premièrement, il faut attendre que le débiteur soit incapable de rembourser pour engager le mécanisme, soit une absence d'anticipation des difficultés à venir. Deuxièmement, l'intervention du FMI pour mettre en œuvre une politique susceptible d'enrayer les causes des difficultés de remboursement, enlève au débiteur toute souveraineté de décision et donc toute obligation morale d'endosser les échecs futurs de la politique d'ajustement en tant que condition d'éligibilité au rééchelonnement.

De façon plus générale, il faut dire que le rééchelonnement fait différer le remboursement du capital emprunté, laissant subsister le problème du paiement des intérêts. La réduction des intérêts serait difficile dans le cas de la dette concessionnelle dont le taux est déjà jugé très bas (moins de 1 %). Elle le serait également dans le cas des banques de développement qui se seraient refinancées à leur tour sur le marché international des capitaux à des taux auxquels elles ont souscrit à moins de bénéficier de subventions des pays industrialisés. Le palliatif est resté jusqu'ici le recours par le Club de Paris aux mécanismes de rééchelonnement avec délais de grâce des paiements dus par les pays débiteurs.

D.   L'INITIATIVE PPTE: OBJECTIFS ET CRITÈRES D'ÉLIGIBILITÉ

L'initiative PPTE est une combinaison de deux mesures qui se renforcent réciproquement, à savoir le mécanisme de rééchelonnement de dette et les politiques d'ajustement structurel, avec pour objectif général «ramener à des niveaux soutenables la charge de la dette», et donc sortir du cycle infernal des rééchelonnements. La soutenabilité de la dette est décidée au regard du niveau de deux ratios, celui de la VAN et celui du service de la dette: le ratio VAN/exportations doit être compris entre 200 % et 250 % selon le pays, et le ratio service/exportations doit être de l'ordre de 20 % à 25 %. Ne pas être dans ces fourchettes ne signifie pas que le pays est condamné surtout que les deux ratios peuvent paraître contradictoires s'ils ne sont pas contenus l'un dans l'autre. Il est ainsi admis que le ratio de la VAN puisse être inférieur à 200 % dès lors que le ratio exportation/PIB est supérieur à 40 %, et le ratio recettes budgétaires/PIB est au moins égal à 20 %.

Dans ces conditions, le ratio VAN/exportations est remplacé par VAN/recettes budgétaires dont le niveau doit être au plus, égal à 280 %. Dans tous les cas, les deux ratios peuvent être utilement pris en compte en même temps qu'un certain nombre d'indicateurs dont le niveau renseigne sur la santé de l'économie et les chances de sortie de la crise d'endettement, notamment la concentration des exportations, la charge budgétaire du service de la dette extérieure, le ratio dette/PIB, et la couverture des réserves internationales.

Dans le cas spécifique du Mali, son éligibilité à l'initiative PPTE s'appuie sur le lourd fardeau de sa dette extérieure, sa vulnérabilité aux chocs externes, ses bons antécédents sur une assez longue période, son éligibilité à la facilité d'ajustement structurel renforcée (FASR), et son caractère exclusivement IDA. Le Mali a été déclaré éligible en septembre 1998. Sa dette s'élevait à près de 3 milliards $ US dont 53,7 % de dette multilatérale, et il présentait 3 ans de bons antécédents. Il ne pouvait plus obtenir de rééchelonnement de sa dette à travers les mécanismes traditionnels, ayant bénéficié en mai 1996 d'allégement aux conditions de Naples. À l'époque, les indicateurs de soutenabilité de sa dette se situaient à :

- 254 % le ratio de la VAN de la dette sur les exportations ;
- 12 % le ratio du service de la dette sur les exportations ;
- 17 % le service de la dette en pourcentage des recettes publiques hors dons ;

- 13 % les recettes fiscales en pourcentage du PIB ;
- 48 % la VAN de la dette en pourcentage du PIB ;
- 21 % la concentration ou la variabilité des exportations définie comme étant l'écart type des exportations sur la période 1986-95, en pourcentage de la moyenne.

L'initiative PPTE fixait le ratio VAN/exportations à 200 % et celui du service de la dette/exportation à 20 %. L'assistance attendue à la fin du processus (décembre 1999) était de 128 millions $ US dont 44 millions de la Banque mondiale, 14 millions du FMI, 37 millions des bilatéraux et 32 millions des multilatéraux autres que le FMI et la Banque. Cette assistance correspondrait à une réduction de dette de 10 % et à une remise du service de la dette d'environ 250 millions. Toutefois, le point d'achèvement de l'initiative PPTE n'a pu être atteint faute de satisfaction des conditions :

- de mise en œuvre, dans les délais requis, des réformes structurelles dans les secteurs du coton, de l'énergie, des télécommunications et des banques :
  - la finalisation de l'audit technique de la filière coton et l'élaboration d'un plan d'action conforme aux conclusions dudit audit ;
  - l'ouverture des secteurs de l'énergie et des télécommunications à la compétition et lancement des appels d'offres pour la privatisation des entreprises publiques, EDM (Énergie du Mali) et SOTELMA (Société des Télécommunications du Mali) ;
  - la finalisation du plan d'action du secteur financier et le lancement des appels d'offres pour la privatisation de la BMCD (Banque malienne de crédits et de dépôts) et de la BIM (Banque internationale pour le Mali).
- de réalisation des progrès dans les programmes avec la Banque mondiale et relatifs à l'éducation et à la santé :
  - la préparation d'un plan de financement du secteur de l'éducation dans le cadre du Programme décennal de l'éducation (PRODEC) actualisé qui clarifiera les mesures envisagées permettant d'améliorer l'efficacité des ressources publiques au niveau de l'enseignement secondaire et supérieur ;
  - la mise en œuvre des procédures de gestion du Programme de développement socio-sanitaire (PRODESS) et la mobilisation des ressources de ce programme.
- de préparation du document cadre stratégique de lutte contre la pauvreté (CSLP) à partir du plan d'actions de lutte contre la pauvreté mis en place depuis 1998 pour une éligibilité à l'initiative PPTE renforcée.

En septembre 2000, le Mali a de nouveau été déclaré éligible, bénéficiant d'un allégement de sa dette extérieure de 870 millions $ US en valeur nominale sur une période de 30 ans. Cet allégement fait suite, selon la Banque mondiale et le FMI, aux progrès que le Mali a accompli sur le plan des réformes macroéconomiques et structurelles, atteignant ainsi le point d'achèvement de l'initiative initiale en faveur des PPTE et le point de décision par rapport à l'initiative PPTE renforcée.

IV. L'ALLÉGEMENT DE LA DETTE ET LA RÉDUCTION DE LA PAUVRETÉ

Après l'approbation en septembre 2000 de son CSLP intérimaire, le Mali est maintenant en pleine phase d'élaboration de son CSLP final. La durée de cette phase étant généralement d'une année, on s'attend à ce qu'elle s'achève le plus vite possible pour que le pays retrouve rapidement une esquisse définitive de sa politique globale de développement. Parmi les critiques adressées au dossier Mali dans le cadre de sa candidature à l'initiative PPTE, il ressort des faiblesses au niveau du CSLP intérimaire. Ces faiblesses sont rapidemment passées en revue dans cette section après une présentation de l'état de pauvreté au Mali.

A. INDICATEURS DE PAUVRETÉ ET RÉALITÉ MALIENNE

Les principaux indicateurs ici retenus sont :
1. le seuil de pauvreté (SP) ou le niveau minimum de consommation qu'il faut à un individu pour subsister;
2. le taux ou l'incidence de la pauvreté (P0) ou encore la proportion de pauvres dans l'ensemble de la population;
3. la profondeur de la pauvreté (P1) ou l'indice volumétrique de pauvreté mesurant le déficit de revenu des pauvres par rapport au seuil de pauvreté;
4. l'indice de pauvreté humaine (IPH) en tant que combinaison de trois variables que sont :
   · le risque de décéder à un âge précoce;
   · le taux d'analphabétisme des adultes;
   · les mauvaises conditions de vie mesurées par le manque d'accès aux services de santé et à l'eau potable et le taux de malnutrition chez les enfants de moins de 5 ans.
5. l'indice de développement humain (IDH), en tant que moyenne arithmétique simple de trois indicateurs relatifs respectivement à l'espérance de vie à la naissance, au niveau d'éducation (combinant alphabétisation et scolarisation) et au revenu par habitant.

Au regard de ces indicateurs de pauvreté, il apparaît clairement que la pauvreté reste un problème préoccupant au Mali. Le PIB par habitant est de

Tableau 4.   Les indicateurs de pauvreté au Mali

	1994	1996	1998
1. Seuil de pauvreté (SP, en FCFA)	77204	102971	103130
2. Taux de pauvreté (P0)	68.8%	71.6%	69.0%
3. Profondeur de la pauvreté (P1)	46.9%	48.4%	31.0%
4. Indice de pauvreté humaine (IPH)	–	58%	55%
Taux brut de scolarisation	36.4%	42.3%	50.0%
Taux d'alphabétisation des adultes	17.1%	21.3%	31.0%
Probabilité de décéder avant 40 ans			33.6%*
Accès à l'eau de robinet	9.3%	10.2%	
Accès à la santé		27.9%	
5. Indice de développement humain (IDH)	0.251	0.309	0.333
Espérance de vie (nombre d'années)	56.8	56.8	
PIB/habitant (en FCFA)	79571	85337	

* Donnée de 1997 de PNUD, *Rapport mondial sur le développement humain*, 1999.
Source : ODH-LCP, *Rapports annuels sur le développement humain durable au Mali*, 1998, 1999.

seulement 270 $ US soit 740 en parité de pouvoir d'achat (PPA) contre 990 en moyenne dans l'ensemble des PMA.

B.   STRATÉGIE NATIONALE DE LUTTE CONTRE LA PAUVRETÉ (SNLP)

La SNLP est un programme national développé par le gouvernement malien et le PNUD de 1996 à 1998. Elle s'appuie sur la nécessité d'assainir l'environnement macroéconomique et financier dans le cadre des politiques d'ajustement structurel afin d'asseoir les conditions favorables à la croissance économique et au développement, permettant ainsi d'améliorer les conditions de vie de la population. Évidemment il ne s'agit pas d'ajouter de nouvelles conditionalités de réduction de la pauvreté mais de les inscrire dans les conditionalités existantes de l'ajustement ou de l'initiative PPTE.

Sur une période de 5 ans, la SNLP prévoit un budget de 373 millions $ US (environ 75 millions $ US par an) répartis entre 8 axes stratégiques (annexe A5). Le budget annuel de la SNLP est supérieur à l'allégement annuel de dette attendu de l'initiative PPTE, et moins que la moyenne annuelle de paiement de service de la dette, 87 millions $ US, sur la période de 1994 à 1996. Autant dire que beaucoup reste à faire en matière de réduction de la pauvreté et de développement économique.

C.   DU CSLP INTÉRIMAIRE AU CSLP FINAL

Plusieurs faiblesses ont été décelées dans le document intérimaire du CSLP soumis par le gouvernement malien dans le cadre de sa candidature à l'initiative

PPTE. Au nombre de celles-ci, figurent le manque de détails sur l'utilisation des revenus de l'allégement de la dette, le manque d'articulation cohérente entre les causes de la pauvreté et les actions de politiques économiques proposées, la non-adéquation de la SNLP comme base du CSLP, et l'absence d'un plan de participation des différents acteurs clés du développement.

En ce qui concerne le détail de l'utilisation des fonds provenant de l'initiative PPTE, aucune information n'a en effet été réellement fournie dans le document intérimaire. Puisqu'une utilisation stratégique des fonds dans des secteurs prioritaires est un gage de l'engagement des autorités, l'absence d'une telle information aurait pu mettre les décideurs dans une position inconfortable vis-à-vis de la bonne foi du gouvernement malien. L'indication de secteurs prioritaires d'intervention comme la santé, l'éducation, mais aussi le développement rural et le renforcement du secteur privé, est en effet une nécéssité pour le succès de l'opération. Dans le cas du Mali cependant, une répartition détaillée de l'enveloppe par rapport à des secteurs définis s'avérait difficile étant donné qu'on ne semblait pas avoir une idée précise du montant total de l'allégement.

La SNLP ne pouvait, dans sa version originelle, prétendre couvrir ni tous les secteurs de développement du pays, ni toute la population malienne. Et pourtant, des statistiques officielles indiquent que plus de 70 % de la population malienne vit au-dessous du seuil de pauvreté. D'où la préférence pour un programme unique et global de développement national intégrant la SNLP, surtout dans un pays où la rareté des ressources ne saurait permettre l'existence de deux programmes similaires. Voilà donc une des critiques importantes qui a été adressée et qui met en cause l'adéquation de la SNLP comme programme de référence pour le développement global du Mali.

Au contraire, le CSLP se veut un cadre conceptuel plus global et plus cohérent, en ce sens qu'il devrait toucher toute la population du pays, tous les secteurs de développement, et avec une articulation logique entre les différents axes de l'activité socioéconomique. Après avoir présenté le CSLP intérimaire en septembre 2000, le Mali est actuellement en plein processus d'élaboration du CSLP final. Pour y parvenir cependant, des efforts importants devront être déployés.

En effet, la SNLP étant le socle du CSLP intérimaire, il sera, avant tout, nécessaire d'en élargir le cadre, en y intégrant les branches d'activités manquantes. Par exemple, comment imbriquer efficacement la politique de décentralisation dans l'ensemble de la stratégie? Comment articuler la politique d'intégration régionale afin que les entreprises maliennes soient en mesure de supporter la concurrence avec leurs homologues de la Côte d'Ivoire et du Sénégal? Quelles politiques macroéconomiques adopter pour soutenir une croissance économique vigoureuse à long terme?

Voilà des questions qu'il conviendrait de se poser au moment précis où l'on entame le CSLP final, afin que la stratégie soit plus robuste et moins vulnérable aux chocs extérieurs. Il faut noter que l'UEMOA est actuellement en phase d'application depuis l'adoption d'une politique douanière commune en janvier 2000, et que la CEDEAO (Communauté des États de l'Afrique de l'ouest), qui regroupe 15 États de l'Afrique de l'Ouest, a franchi des étapes cruciales sur le plan politique au cours de l'an 2000.

Par ailleurs, la nécéssité de renforcer le volet des politiques macroéconomiques est incontestable car un accent particulier doit être mis sur les mécanismes de création des richesses. Dans Keita (2000), il est démontré que pour passer du revenu actuel de 250 $ US que connaît le pays, à celui de 500 $ US par habitant, par an pendant dix ans, un taux de croissance annuel du PIB réel de 9,5 % est nécessaire. En d'autres termes, l'objectif actuel du gouvernement d'un rythme de croissance annuel de 5 % du PIB réel n'est pas suffisant pour combattre la pauvreté au Mali. Une accélération de la création de richesses est absolument indispensable.

Au chapitre de la participation des différents acteurs de développement, il est clair que c'est une exigence cruciale puisque le CSLP devient le cadre unique de référence pour toutes les interventions de développement dans le pays. La pleine participation de tous les acteurs aussi bien dans la phase de conception, de mise en oeuvre, que de suivi du CSLP est un réel impératif pour garantir le succès. Les programmes de développement des différents bailleurs de fonds ou partenaires au développement doivent être synchronisés et harmonisés avec ceux du gouvernement et des collectivités décentralisées. Le succès du CSLP dépendra également du degré d'implication des populations, pour une large appropriation des réalisations. A cet égard, le désir du gouvernement à rechercher une large participation de tous les acteurs ne fait aucun doute.

Le Mali a en effet acquis une solide tradition de larges consultations depuis les événements de mars 1991. Cependant, le CSLP intérimaire ne contient pas de détails sur le processus de participation. L'élaboration d'un plan précis de participation a souffert du manque de temps, comme d'autres aspects du document intérimaire. Le gouvernement l'a d'ailleurs reconnu et a déjà amorcé le processus de consultations pour pallier à cette lacune. Après avoir tenu une rencontre avec les bailleurs de fonds, puis avec la société civile et enfin avec les différents départements ministériels, le 1er février 2001, le Ministère de l'économie et des finances (chargé de coordonner l'ensemble du processus) a organisé un séminaire-atelier sur le processus participatif du CSLP. Un cadre institutionnel couvrant l'ensemble des activités du processus a été adopté à cette occasion.

En ce qui concerne l'articulation entre les causes de la pauvreté et les politiques économiques, la non disponibilité de données socioéconomiques actualisées a constitué un handicap majeur pour une évaluation précise du profil de la pauvreté au Mali. Les enquêtes les plus récentes dans le pays datent de cinq ans au moins. Ce sont, plus particulièrement, les Enquêtes démographiques et de santé (EDS), dont la dernière édition est celle de 1995-1996, l'Enquête budget consommation (EBC) pour l'évaluation des revenus et de la consommation alimentaire de 1988/1989, et l'Enquête nationale sur les activités économiques des ménages ou Enquête secteur informel (ESI) de 1989.

Il était par conséquent devenu indispensable de disposer rapidement de données plus récentes afin d'aboutir à des politiques économiques et sociales plus adaptées au contexte national et plus à même de conduire à des résultats concrets. À cet égard, le gouvernement a entrepris de conduire des enquêtes d'envergure nationale pour générer des données socioéconomiques et démographiques plus appropriées, à savoir, l'Enquête malienne d'évaluation de la pauvreté (EMEP), prévue du 15 janvier au 31 décembre 2001 (avec des résultats préliminaires en avril 2001), l'EDS prévue du 2 janvier à la fin avril 2001 (avec des résultats préliminaires en mi-mai 2001) et la publication en avril 2001 des résultats définitifs du recensement général de la population effectué en 1998. L'ensemble de ces données devrait permettre de bâtir des programmes et des politiques de développement plus adaptés et plus efficaces.

Pour la suite dans le calendrier des activités d'élaboration du CSLP final, un cadre unique de référence des politiques et stratégies au Mali devrait être disponible en décembre 2001.

D. POINT DE VUE DE LA SOCIÉTÉ CIVILE

Dans le cadre des mécanismes traditionnels, la société civile s'est appesantie sur l'option rachat en proposant deux schémas de conversion de dette publique détenue par les créanciers du Club de Paris (40 % de la dette du Mali).

Le premier est celui des ONG, et consiste en l'annulation avec affectation des ressources libérées au financement de projets de développement. A cet effet, un partenariat est à conclure entre l'État et une agence nationale de développement, à créer, regroupant toutes les ONG locales. Conformément à ce partenariat, les produits de l'annulation seront affectés, au prorata du service annuel à payer, à l'Agence qui financera des projets présentés par les ONG au regard des priorités du gouvernement, telles que les projets de construction d'écoles et de centres de santé, etc. L'annulation est consacrée par la remise par les créanciers membres du Club de Paris des titres de créances à l'Agence internationale de développement durable et de l'environnement (AIDE), titres ensuite rétrocédés à l'agence locale qui ainsi se retrouve créancière de l'État.

Le second schéma de rachat, *Direct Expatriate National Investment* (DENI) est celui de l'*US-Africa Business Council* (US-ABC), consiste à négocier avec un expatrié malien une partie de la dette avec une décote de 90 % contre une reconnaissance de dette échangeable au Mali, selon trois options :

- *Central Bank Accounting* : se faire rembourser en monnaie locale au prorata de la valeur faciale de la créance, dans le cadre de l'apurement de la dette intérieure;
- *Méthode de la privatisation à 100 %* : utiliser la créance rachetée pour acquérir des actions de sociétés d'État en cours de privatisation, conformément au schéma respectif de privatisation;
- *Growth-oriented method* : créer au Mali des entreprises grâce aux créances rachetées ; US-ABC peut faciliter, dans ce cas, les joints ventures.

Par rapport à l'initiative PPTE, la seule réaction jusqu'à ce jour enregistrée est celle de la Coalition nationale Jubilé 2000 du Mali qui soutient que cette initiative ne peut pas alléger la dette des pays concernés, encore moins lutter contre la pauvreté. Elle rappelle que sous sa première version, l'initiative n'a finalement concerné que 7 pays sur 41 et sous des conditionalités inappropriées. En dépit des promesses faites lors du sommet du G7 de Cologne d'alléger 100 milliards $ US de dette, seulement 4 milliards ont été annulés à la date du 1er trimestre 2000, et Jubilé 2000 du Mali en déduit que les pays du G7 n'ont aucune volonté politique à alléger la dette du tiers-monde.

La Coalition soutient également que les montants d'annulation prévus (70 milliards $ US) sont dérisoires et que l'initiative PPTE n'est donc pas « une solution à la dette du Tiers Monde », encore moins un moyen adéquat de lutte contre la pauvreté. La position de principe de Jubilé 2000 demeure une annulation totale et inconditionnelle de la dette, car le Nord doit au Sud, entre autres :

- les dettes liées à la traite des noirs, à l'esclavage, à la conquête coloniale, à la colonisation, à la libération de l'Europe des griffes du fascisme et du nazisme, à la mise en valeur et à l'exploitation coloniale ;
- le retour des biens culturels volés à l'Afrique ;

• le rapatriement des immenses capitaux volés à l'Afrique par des élites corrompues et qui sommeillent dans les banques du Nord.

Du côté des ONG, on ne s'estime pas avoir été associé à l'élaboration des documents de base de la lutte contre la pauvreté, encore moins son expérience de terrain valorisée. Le rapport intérimaire du CSLP semble s'appuyer exclusivement sur des documents officiels comme :

• le document cadre de politique économique et financière ;
• les documents de politiques sectorielles (éducation, santé, justice, etc.) ;
• les rapports annuels de l'Observatoire du développement humain durable ;
• les schémas d'aménagement du territoire.

Selon le Comité de coordination des actions des organisations non gouvernementales (CCA-ONG), qui regroupe 22 ONG exerçant leurs activités au Mali, puisque la pauvreté reflète la non satisfaction des besoins essentiels pour vivre décemment (alimentation, santé, habillement, logement) suite à des conditions économiques défavorables et à une mauvaise intégration sociale, la lutte doit passer nécessairement par le financement d'activités rémunératrices, de projets de santé et d'éducation en faveur des démunis. A ces volets largement partagés, certaines ONG ajoutent des dispositifs d'appui technique (information, formation, alphabétisation, appui organisationnel) et de défense des droits fondamentaux de l'homme (lutte contre les injustices sociales, promotion du genre, etc.).

Quant au Conseil économique, social et culturel (1998), il a fait de l'éducation et de la formation les deux facteurs essentiels de réduction de la pauvreté et de promotion d'un développement humain durable au Mali. Cette conviction repose sur la relation entre ces deux facteurs et l'accroissement de la productivité et du revenu, d'où la nécessité de réaliser un taux brut de scolarisation d'au moins 50 % pour espérer amorcer le décollage économique.

V. CONJECTURES SUR L'APRÈS-PPTE AU MALI

Quelles peuvent être les faiblesses du programme PPTE au Mali? Le programme permettra-t-il d'enrayer la pauvreté dans le pays? Y a-t-il des solutions de rechange à l'endettement extérieur?

A. QUELQUES CRITIQUES DU PROGRAMME PPTE AU MALI

L'Initiative PPTE est sans aucun doute une grande opportunité pour les pays pauvres très endettés. Elle leur permet de redevenir solvables tout en leur ouvrant des perspectives de croissance économique à long terme. C'est une véritable bouffée d'oxygène financière pour ces pays, qui arrive à un moment crucial de leur situation économique. Pour les pays débiteurs, il s'agit de retrouver de meilleures conditions de remboursements de la dette extérieure et la possibilité d'une meilleure articulation de l'appareil économique. Quant aux pays créditeurs, c'est avant tout le sentiment de contribuer à une amélioration des conditions de vie des moins nantis de la planète et le retour d'un meilleur climat de confiance pour des remboursements futurs. Par ailleurs, contrairement à l'époque où les programmes d'ajustement structurel étaient simplement « parachutés » de Washington, les pays bénéficiaires ont aujourd'hui la latitude de concevoir eux-mêmes leurs programmes de réduction de la pauvreté et de croissance économique. Le rôle des institutions de Bretton Woods est pratiquement réduit à la supervision ou à une simple coordination de l'ensemble du processus.

Ce nouveau paysage relationnel entre les PPTE et les institutions financières internationales n'est cependant pas libre de toute critique. Bien au contraire, en particulier dans le cas du Mali, il reste encore de nombreuses questions portant sur (1) les possibilités réelles du pays à développer un CSLP final de qualité ; (2) la durée du programme ; (3) le débit des injections financières ; et (4) les secteurs bénéficiaires des ressources PPTE.

Au chapitre de la qualité du CSLP final, il ne fait aucun doute qu'un grand pas vient d'être franchi en permettant aux PPTE d'être les propres architectes de leurs programmes de développement. Ceci constitue une avancée majeure dans l'adéquation des programmes aux contextes économiques réels des pays concernés. En permettant en effet aux PPTE de s'approprier la stratégie de développement de leur pays, on augmente incontestablement les chances de réussite du programme. Toutefois, il va sans dire que les PPTE devront porter une plus grande responsabilité du succès ou de l'échec de l'ensemble des opérations.

De plus, la qualité des CSLP sera fortement tributaire d'une part, de la disponibilité des ressources humaines impliquées dans le processus et, d'autre part, du temps imparti à sa mise en oeuvre. Or, malgré tout l'engagement des autorités des pays en développement, les ressources humaines qualifiées restent bien souvent limitées pour mettre en place, et en des temps records, des stratégies de développement aussi complexes que les CSLP. Le fait que les ressources du programme PPTE soient liées à la mise en place des CSLP ne contribuera pas nécessairement à la qualité des documents qui seront produits, même si l'on y gagne en rapidité dans l'exécution du travail. Or, la réussite des programmes en termes de réduction de la pauvreté et de croissance économique dépend avant tout de la qualité des documents CSLP.

La durée du programme, quant à elle, peut aussi constituer un handicap pour le succès des CSLP. Dans le cas du Mali, certes 870 millions de dollars sont importants, mais le fait que cette somme soit étalée sur 30 ans atténuera certainement son impact. Par ailleurs, s'il est vrai que les PPTE sont désormais les maîtres d'oeuvre pour la conception des CSLP, il demeure que cela se fera nécessairement suivant certaines lignes théoriques ou idéologiques de principe des institutions de Bretton Woods. Or, on en conviendra, toutes les politiques économiques du FMI et de la Banque mondiale ne sont pas toujours et dans tous les cas libres de toute critique. Ainsi, certaines d'entre elles peuvent même constituer des sortes de blocage au développement.

Prenons, par exemple, la politique sur les dépenses publiques pour les PPTE caractérisée par une forte aversion pour toute augmentation. Il est clair qu'on ne saurait rejeter la nécessité d'un contrôle stricte et rigoureux sur les accroissements de dépenses publiques dans les PPTE compte tenu de leur situation financière et économique actuelle. Pour éviter de nouvelles crises financières, économiques ou monétaires, une telle ligne de conduite est indispensable. En revanche, ceci ne doit pas empêcher une certaine souplesse dans ce domaine, surtout lorsqu'il est possible que cette forte rigidité des dépenses publiques conduise à l'échec du programme lui-même. C'est un peu le cas de la situation salariale des fonctionnaires au Mali. En clair, la situation des salaires au Mali, si elle perdure à son niveau actuel[2], ne saurait conduire ni à une amélioration de la productivité des travailleurs, ni à une diminution du niveau de corruption dans le pays. Le marché de travail au Mali souffre en effet de deux maux principaux : la quasi interdiction de tout licenciement de tra- vailleurs et la situation des rémunérations guère motivante. Ces deux faiblesses expliquent largement le niveau très bas de productivité dans le pays et la forte incitation à la corruption. Une très longue période de rigidité salariale au Mali pourrait donc conduire à une inefficacité des programmes de développement.

Aussi, le niveau annuel des injections financières a naturellement une incidence sur le rythme d'évolution de la performance économique. Dans des simulations récentes du FMI pour le Mali, il est prévu une réduction du ratio

---

2. Le niveau des salaires des fonctionnaires maliens est très faible en comparaison du coût de la vie. Seuls les fonctionnaires de la catégorie A vivent au-dessus du seuil de pauvreté défini dans le pays à 103 310 FCFA, quel que soit le niveau d'ancienneté. Par contre, pour les autres catégories, par exemple pour le B2, B1 et C, il faut avoir atteint des anciennetés respectives de 5, 10 et 20 ans avant de bénéficier d'un revenu supérieur au seuil de pauvreté. (Source : Rapport national sur le Développement Humain Durable, Mali 1999 ; Observatoire du développement humain durable, Banque mondiale et PNUD).

actuel service de la dette/exportations de 15 % à environ 7 % en 2019, en utilisant un taux de croissance annuel du PIB réel de l'ordre de 5 %. La question qui se pose est la suivante : ce rythme de croissance sera-t-il suffisant pour enrayer la pauvreté dans le pays? La réponse est évidemment non, selon ce qui a été mentionné antérieurement, et surtout qu'il n'est pas tenu compte des risques exogènes tels que la chute à long terme des cours de matières premières sur le marché international. Une injection financière plus importante annuellement (en ramenant, par exemple, la durée à 15 ans au lieu de 30) devrait conduire à un rythme de croissance plus élevé et une action plus rapide sur l'élimination de la pauvreté dans le pays, pour une capacité d'absorption nationale améliorée.

Enfin, par rapport au choix des secteurs pouvant bénéficier des ressources issues du PPTE, un partage judicieux des ressources doit être opéré entre le volet création de richesses et celui de la réduction de la pauvreté. Ce qu'il faut craindre surtout, c'est une allocation trop importante des ressources au secteur social (éducation et santé), au détriment de la croissance (développement rural et renforcement du secteur privé). Pour pérenniser l'amélioration des conditions de vie des populations, il est indispensable qu'un accent important soit mis sur la création de richesses dans le CSLP final.

B.   ESTIMATION DE L'IMPACT PPTE

Nous cherchons à évaluer, pour les années à venir, le ratio aide/PIB équivalent à l'allégement de dette. Pour ce faire, nous supposons que la croissance moyenne annuelle du PIB réel est de 4,8 % pour 1999 (équivalent à la moyenne annuelle de croissance sur la période 1994-98) ; 4,5 % pour 2000, 5.25 % pour 2001 et 2002, et 5 % pour les années suivantes (en nous basant sur les estimations du FMI et de IDA). Le PIB de l'an 1998 est de l'ordre de 2 694,7 millions $ US et en prenant cette année comme année de base, nous calculons le PIB pour les années futures.

Nous sommes ainsi en mesure de calculer la moyenne de l'allégement obtenu dans le cadre de l'initiative PPTE par rapport au PIB pour la période 2001-2015, et qui est donc égale à 1,06 % (cf. col. 5, tbl. 5). La moyenne d'aide/PIB pour la période 1989-1998 est par contre de l'ordre de 18,54 %, chiffre obtenu à partir des données du World Development Indicators de la Banque mondiale. L'allégement obtenu dans le cadre de l'initiative PPTE correspond donc à seulement 5,7 % de l'aide que le pays a reçu.

Le service de la dette pour la période 2001-2015 est estimé à 1 843,5 million $ US, ce qui représente une moyenne de 122,9 millions $ US (cf. col. 4, tbl. 5), alors que le service de la dette pour la période 1989-1998 a été de 772,5 millions $ US

Tableau 5.   L'impact de l'allégement de dette dans le temps
(millions de $ US et %)

Année	Allègement PPTE (millions $US)*	PIB (millions $US)*	Service de la dette (millions $US)*	Allègement PPTE/PIB
2001	42	3106.06	105.30	1.35%
2002	49	3269.13	113.30	1.50%
2003	50	3432.59	115.40	1.46%
2004	51	3604.22	117.70	1.42%
2005	51	3784.43	117.00	1.35%
2006	50	3973.65	119.30	1.26%
2007	49	4172.33	121.80	1.17%
2008	45	4380.95	121.50	1.03%
2009	43	4599.99	118.60	0.93%
2010	44	4829.99	120.10	0.91%
2011	47	5071.49	126.30	0.93%
2012	42	5325.07	127.30	0.79%
2013	42	5591.32	128.90	0.75%
2014	34	5870.89	140.10	0.58%
2015	26	6164.43	150.90	0.42%
Moyenne	**44.33**		**122.90**	**1.06%**

Source : * IDA et FMI, Document pour le point d'achèvement PPTE, *Debt Sustainability Analysis*, 2000.

(moyenne annuelle de 77,25 millions $ US). Le dividende sur la dette est donc de l'ordre de –45,65 millions $ US, i.e. 77,25-122,9. Si nous comparons les moyennes pour les périodes 2001-2005 et 1994-1998, on obtient un dividende de l'ordre de –22,52 millions $ US.

C.   CONJECTURES SUR DES SOLUTIONS DE FINANCEMENT DE LA DETTE

La dette, on le sait bien, est un frein au développement, parfois même un blocage. Cependant, il est à noter que le processus d'endettement dans les pays pauvres aura tendance à se poursuivre malgré l'existence des programmes PPTE. Aussi, le risque de nouvelles crises financières ou d'endettement dans le futur ne peut être écarté si certaines dispositions courageuses ne sont pas prises. On le sait, plusieurs solutions existent en théorie et en pratique pour faire face à la crise d'endettement, partant des annulations aux allégements, en passant par les rééchelonnements, les rachats de dettes, la conversion de la dette en capital-actions, ou toutes autres formes de conversion de l'endettement. En réalité, la solution du problème d'endettement des pays pauvres ne doit pas être uni-directionnelle. Il faut nécessairement envisager une combinaison de plusieurs options.

Pour bien cerner le problème, il importerait de revenir très brièvement sur l'origine de la crise. Il est bien connu maintenant que la crise de l'endettement dans les pays du tiers-monde a pour origine les gaspillages dont on fait l'objet des emprunts lourds contractés par des dirigeants de ces pays dans les années 80 et après suite aux chocs pétroliers des années 70. Les fonds ont été dilapidés soit dans des projets improductifs, soit à travers des détournements de fonds effectués par les élites mêmes de ces pays. Comble d'ironie, les fonds ainsi détournés se retrouvaient dans les banques des pays du Nord qui avaient émis les prêts.

L'ancien Président de la République française, François Mitterand, dans son allocution au Sommet de la francophonie à Dakar en 1989, disait : « ...malgré le volume important de l'aide internationale en direction des pays du Sud, il y a plus de flux monétaires et financiers du Sud vers le Nord que du Nord vers le Sud... ». Cette phrase met en évidence une des causes profondes du problème d'endettement des pays africains: les fonds continuent d'être détournés pour alimenter des comptes personnels dans des banques des pays du Nord. Ce phénomène est aussi connu sous le nom de fuite de capitaux.

Selon des données récentes de la Commission économique pour l'Afrique, les fuites de capitaux pour l'Afrique sont estimées à 22 milliards $ US pour la période 1982-1991. Il est temps de trouver des mécanismes pour que ces fonds « détournés »[3] soient tout au moins réinvestis dans les économies de ces pays, pour les redynamiser, générer des emplois et augmenter les recettes fiscales.

En dehors de cette importante piste, il y a aussi la possibilité pour les gouvernements de ces pays (plus particulièrement du Mali) de chercher à diversifier ses sources d'emprunts, par exemple en explorant les marchés financiers nationaux et régionaux à travers des émissions d'obligations ou d'autres actifs financiers. Plusieurs pays de la Région comme la Côte d'Ivoire, le Bénin, la Guinée ou le Sénégal ont déjà tenté l'expérience. Il s'agira pour le gouvernement malien de s'en inspirer, surtout que depuis septembre 1998, la bourse régionale des valeurs mobilières (BRVM), mise en place par les pays de l'UEMOA, tente de développer un marché financier régional. Son objectif étant de mobiliser l'épargne au niveau de la région ainsi que les investissements directs étrangers, afin de rendre les capitaux à long terme accessibles aux entreprises locales et aux gouvernements. Il y a aussi l'expertise des bailleurs de fonds à rechercher.

---

3. On dénombrerait plusieurs milliardaires dans ces pays en dehors des commerçants et des hommes d'affaires, malgré les niveaux dérisoires des salaires des fonctionnaires.

Les recettes traditionnelles, en particulier les échanges dette/capital et les annulations de dettes, peuvent également être utilisées ou explorées, d'autant que le Mali est en plein processus de privatisation de certaines entreprises et qu'à y regarder de plus près, il y aurait certainement encore de la place pour l'annulation de certaines dettes extérieures. Enfin, on ne saurait le passer sous silence : la durée de 30 ans pour le programme PPTE au Mali est trop contraignante pour l'économie du pays. Dans un tel contexte, il y a peu de place à terme pour des initiatives novatrices.

CONCLUSIONS

De bilatérale, au début de son indépendance, la dette publique du Mali est à dominance multilatérale depuis 1995. Le pays a pu bénéficier des mécanismes traditionnels d'allégement de sa dette jusqu'en 1996, sans que le niveau d'endettement soit pour autant soutenable. L'initiative PPTE est justement supposée conduire à cette soutenabilité et mieux participer à la réduction de la pauvreté qui demeure un problème des plus préoccupants au Mali.

Depuis l'approbation de son CSLP intérimaire en septembre 2000, les autorités maliennes sont pleinement engagés dans l'élaboration du CSLP final. De nombreux défis devront être relevés à cette fin, notamment l'élargissement du cadre de la SNLP (base du CSLP au Mali) à l'ensemble des activités de développement, l'implication effective de tous les acteurs dans le processus et la répartition judicieuse des ressources du PPTE à l'amélioration des conditions sociales et à la création de richesses dans le pays.

L'engagement du gouvernement pour le plein succès du programme ne fait aucun doute. Toutefois, certaines faiblesses (la durée trop longue de la stratégie, le faible niveau des injections financières annuel et la forte pression dans la préparation du CSLP final) combinées à certaines distorsions de l'économie (rigidité du marché de travail, corruption et exportation de capitaux) peuvent substantiellement atténuer l'impact recherché dans le programme et entamer l'espoir d'un après-PPTE viable.

Des dispositions correctives ainsi qu'une combinaison d'options différentes telles que l'arrêt des fuites de capitaux, la lutte contre la corruption et les fraudes fiscales, l'émission d'obligations publiques, et d'autres approches traditionnelles de financement de la dette publique seront souhaitables pour éliminer définitivement le spectre de la crise d'endettement au Mali.

RÉFÉRENCES

Agence pour le développement social, « La question du développement social », communication présentée au Salon du développement social de Bamako, 27-29 octobre 1999, *Les Cahiers de l'ADS*, 1999.

Auverny-Bennnetot, Ph., *La dette du tiers monde*, la Documentation française, 1991.

BCEAO, *Balance des paiements du Mali, 1997-98.*

Boote, R. et K. Thugge, « Allégement de la dette des pays à faible revenu – l'initiative en faveur des pays pauvres très endettés », série des brochures FMI n° 51F, 1997.

Brunner, K. et H. Meltzer, « Aggregative Theory for a Closed Economy », in J. Stein, *Monetarism*, Amsterdam, 1976, p. 69.

Buchanan, J. M., *Public principles of public debt: A defense and restatement*, Homewod, Illinois, 1958, p. 17.

CCFD, *L'initiative PPTE au-delà des effets d'annonce – Le point sur les allégements de dette en cours*, Campagne dette 2000, mars 2000.

Chenery, H. B. et A. M. Strout, « Foreign assistance and economic development », *American Economic Review*, 66, 1976, p. 132.

Diallo, A. A., « Les innovations en matière de traitement de dette publique : recommandations pour le Mali », mémoire de fin de cycle, COFEB/BCEAO, juin 1994.

DNSI, *Comptes économiques du Mali*, Bamako, avril 1999.

Domar, E. D., « The "Burden of Debt" and the National Income », *American Economic Review*, 34, 1944, p. 816.

Dudley, L. et C. Montmarquette, « Model of the Supply of Bilateral Foreign Aid », *American Economic Review*, 66, 1976, p.132.

Eurodad, « Debt Relief and Poverty Eradication: Mechanisms and Policies », report of seminar, 2-3 november 1999, The Hague, Eurodad, 1999.

FMI/IDA, *Cadre stratégique de lutte contre la pauvreté : Questions d'ordre opérationnel*, décembre 1999.

_____, Document final du point de décision relatif à l'initiative en faveur des PPTE, août 1998.

Foster, M., J. Healey, M. Martin et H. White, *Linking HIPC II Debt Relief with Poverty Reduction and Wider Aid Issues: Some Reflections and Suggestions*, London, ODI, 1999.

Gosselin, C. et B. Touré, « Cohérence des politiques et interventions canadiennes et pauvreté : Le cas du Mali », 20 mars 2000.

IDA and IMF, *Heavily Indebted Poor Countries (HIPC) Initiative – Update on Costing the Enhanced HIPC Initiative*, 1999.

IMF, « Mali: Enhanced Structural Adjustment Facility Medium-term Policy », framework paper, 12 July 2000.

IMF, WB and BIS, *Modifications to Heavily Indebted Poor Countries (HIPC) Initiative*, 23 July 1999.

IMF and OECD, *World Bank Statistics on External Debt.*

Keita, S., « Can Mali Get Out of Poverty? », Economic Report Series, USAID/Mali, 2000.

Mali, Coalition nationale Jubilé 2000, « Déclaration de la Coalition nationale Jubilé 2000 du Mali », *Info-Matin*, n° 647, 18 septembre 2000, p. 2.

Mali, Commissariat au Plan, *Manuel de procédures de la coopération au développement du Mali*, 1995.

Mali, Conseil économique, social et culturel, « Éducation et lutte contre la pauvreté », note introductive, mai 1998.

Mali, Ministère des finances, « Stratégie d'allégement de la dette publique du Mali dans le cadre de l'initiative PTTE », atelier national du Mali sur la formation d'une stratégie de la dette, Bamako, 25 mars - 3 avril 1999.

Martin, M. et A. Johnson, « Mise en œuvre de l'initiative PPLE : Questions clés pour les gouvernements des PPLE », document de base pour l'atelier national du Mali sur la formulation d'une stratégie de la dette, Bamako, 25 mars-3 avri 1999.

Mckinnon, R.J., « Foreign Exchange Constraints in Economic Development and Efficient Aid Allocation », *The Economic Journal*, 74, 1964, p. 388.

OCDE/PNUD, *Revue du système international de l'aide au Mali: Synthèse et analyse*, janvier 1995.

Papanek, F., « The Effect of Aid and other Ressources Transfers on Sawings and Growth in Less Developed Countries », *Economic Journal*, 82, 1972.

Phelps, E. S. et K. Shell, « Public Debt, Taxation and Capital Intensiveness », *Journal of Economic Theory*, 1(3), 1969, p. 330.

Ricardo, D., *On the Principles of Political Economy and Taxation*, vol. 1, Cambridge, 1951, p. 244-247.

Serieux, J. E., *Reducing the Debt of the Poorest : Challenges and Opportunities*, Ottawa, North-South Institute, 1999a.

_____, *Debt of the Poorest : A Brief Look at Some Issues*, Ottawa, North-South Institute, 1999b.

Togola, S., « La cohésion par la communication », *L'Essor*, 14275, 11 août 2000, p. 8.

Tolkemitt, G., *Zur Theorie der langfristigen Wirkungen öffentlicher Verschuldung*, Tübingen, 1975, p. 12.

United Nations, *Economic Report on Africa 1999 : The Challenges of Poverty Reduction and Sustainability*, Economic Commission for Africa, 1999.

Von Stein, L., *Lehrbuch der Finanzwissenschaft*, Auflage 4, B. 2, Leipzig, 1978.

World Bank, « External Debt of Developing Countries 1987-90 », Country tables, *in World Debt Tables*, Vol. 2, Washington, D.C., World Bank, 1990.

____, *World Tables, Sources and Methods*, Washington, D.C., World Bank, 1995.

____, Country tables, *in Global Development Finance 1999*, Washington, D.C., World Bank, 1999.

____, External debt management, *in World Development Indicators 2000*, Washington, D.C., World Bank, 2000.

____, Internal Guidance Note, *Poverty Reduction Strategy Papers*, Washington, D.C., World Bank, January 2000.

Annexe A1. Encours de la dette extérieure publique et arriéré de paiements (millions de $ US)

	Stock	Dette à long terme					Arriéré de paiements		
	Dette	Totale	Bilatérale	Multi-latérale	(IDA)	Commer-ciale	Total	Principal	Intérêt
1970	246	238	226	6	6	6	0	0	0
1971	269	261	244	11	10	6	0	0	0
1972	266	256	233	16	15	7	0	0	0
1973	299	290	253	30	22	7	0	0	0
1974	342	334	297	29	28	8	0	0	0
1975	351	338	277	43	41	18	0	0	0
1976	366	373	308	57	54	8	0	0	0
1977	460	450	359	83	67	8	0	0	0
1978	550	547	412	115	82	20	0	0	0
1979	556	552	371	159	102	22	0	0	0
1980	733	670	461	174	121	35	76	75	1
1981	835	730	476	224	140	30	2	0	2
1982	879	802	508	265	154	29	2	0	2
1983	993	903	538	318	172	47	2	0	2
1984	1249	1096	704	346	191	46	10	0	10
1985	1472	1306	856	400	224	50	0	0	0
1986	1764	1583	1023	504	277	56	0	0	0
1987	2092	1913	1220	632	340	61	0	0	0
1988	2067	1928	1195	706	390	27	0	0	0
1989	2126	2025	1260	746	432	19	6	1	5
1990	2466	2336	1424	896	498	16	72	9	63
1991	2595	2461	1451	998	569	12	193	25	168
1992	2897	2777	1711	1060	611	6	292	26	266
1993	2902	2785	1678	1103	656	4	227	18	209
1994	2694	2545	1293	1250	770	2	294	21	273
1995	2958	2739	1340	1397	863	2	370	28	342
1996	3020	2776	1314	1462	915	0	448	33	415
1997	2945	2687	1234	1453		0	582	43	539
1998		2827	1259	1568	1009	0			
1999		2246		1617		0			

Sources : World Bank, *Global development – Country tables,* 1999.
World Bank, *World debt tables, External debt of developing countries, volume II, Country tables,* 1987-90, 2000.
BIS-IMF-OECD, *World Bank statistics on external debt.*

Annexe A2. Allégement de dette obtenu (millions de $ US)

	1988	1989	1990	1991	1992	1993	1994	1995	1996
Rééchelonnement	62	21	12	10	28	29	0	0	19
Annulation	3	8	2	1	16	3	413	0	16
Total allégement	65	29	14	11	44	32	413	0	35

Sources : World Bank, *Global development – Country tables,* 1999.
World Bank, *World debt tables, External debt of developing countries, volume II, Country tables,* 1987-90, 2000.
BIS-IMF-OECD, *World Bank statistics on external debt.*

**Annexe A3. Décaissement sur prêts contractés et service de la dette
(millions de $US)**

	Décaissements sur prêts			Service de la dette				
	Total	IDA	Bilatéral	Total	Multilatéral	Bilatéral	Commercial	(%intérêt)
1970	3	1	22	1.0	0%	0	1	0
1971	6	3	3	1.0	0%	0.0	1	0
1972	18	5	9	1.0	100%	0.1	0.9	0
1973	20	4	11	5.0	20%	--	--	-
1974	33	7	25	2.2	33%	0.3	1.9	0
1975	31	13	14	3.2	33%	0.3	2.9	0
1976	33	13	18	3.7	25%	0.3	3.4	0
1977	59	13	32	6.6	29%	1.0	5.5	0.1
1978	65	15	24	8.7	43%	3.1	5	0.6
1979	78	21	34	8.8	38%	1.5	6.5	0.8
1980	95	19	50	9.5	33%	1.7	4.5	3.3
1981	112	19	55	9.6	33%	2.1	5.4	2.1
1982	117	14	68	9.1	67%	3.8	3.7	1.6
1983	156	19	72	14.4	50%	5.1	7.1	2.2
1984	119	21	71	19.9	44%	8.7	6.4	4.8
1985	107	29	58	38.2	37%	19.1	15.2	3.9
1986	179	45	87	35.2	42%	17.9	13.3	4.0
1987	136	44	52	28.0	46%	10.0	15.0	3.0
1988	154	61	37	47.0	32%	30.0	14.0	3.0
1989	174	48	89	38.0	37%	20.0	17.0	1.0
1990	167	44	52	42.0	40%	23.0	18.0	1.0
1991	144	69	42	30.0	40%	15.0	14.0	1.0
1992	166	62	76	50.0	31%	26.0	21.0	3.0
1993	87	47	21	67.0	60%	25.0	41.0	1.0
1994	122	93	2	77.0	31%	38.0	38.0	1.0
1995	192	86	47	77.0	29%	34.0	42.0	1.0
1996	164	84	35	106.0	55%	41.0	65.0	0.0
1997	147	75	3	68.0		41.0	27.0	0.0
1998				73.0				

Sources : World Bank, *Global development – Country tables,* 1999.
World Bank, *World debt tables, External debt of developing countries,* volume II,
Country tables, 1987-90, 2000.
BIS-IMF-OECD, *World Bank statistics on external debt.*

A4. Valeur actualisée nette (VAN) de la dette extérieure publique (millions de $ US)

	1997	1998	1999	2000	2001	2002	2003	2004	2005	2006	2007	2008	2009	2010
VAN totale	1239	1325	1403	1474	1534	1559	1582	1609	1641	1672	1712	1760	1815	1890
Ancienne dette	1239	1316	1384	1452	1511	1530	1517	1498	1471	1435	1391	1353	1312	1274
Bilatérale	378	386	391	395	399	400	396	393	390	385	378	372	367	359
Club de Paris	246	250	253	255	258	259	258	258	257	254	249	245	241	233
Multilatérale	861	930	993	1057	1112	1130	1121	1105	1081	1050	1013	981	945	915
FMI	133	146	161	171	177	159	138	115	93	71	49	30	15	5
IDA	423	453	485	522	558	590	617	637	650	658	660	680	656	65
Nouvelle dette	0	9	19	22	23	29	65	111	170	237	321	407	503	616

Source : World Bank, Mali Net Present Value (NPV) of Debt After Rescheduling (1997-2017), 1999.

A5. Budget du Programme d'action de la stratégie nationale de lutte contre la pauvreté (milliers de $ US)

Axes stratégiques	Etudes	Formation	Ressouces humaines	Investissement/ équipement	Fonction- nement	Total	(%)
1. Améliorer l'environnement économique, politique, juridique et social	2450	3290	3750	3700	1600	14790	4.0
2. Promouvoir les activités génératrices de revenus et l'auto-emploi	6500	4780	7885	111302	3050	133517	35.8
3. Améliorer l'accès aux services financiers et autres facteurs de production	2385	6110	1870	1720	950	13035	3.5
4. Promouvoir les filières agroalimentaires	2800	3475	4520	41010	2050	53855	14.4
5. Améliorer l'accès à l'éducation de base et à la formation	4050	6200	3780	74100	7000	95130	25.5
6. Promouvoir l'accès à la santé, nutrition, eau potable et assainissement	3800	6800	3250	15410	6000	35260	9.5
7. Améliorer les conditions d'habitat	3200	1700	1225	7300	1350	14775	4.0
8. Assurer une coordination efficace de la SNLP	3300	2100	2920	1800	2300	12420	3.3
Total	28485	34455	29200	256342	24300	372782	
(%)	7.6	9.2	7.8	68.8	6.5		100.0

Source : Observatoire du développement humain durable et de la lutte contre la pauvreté (1998), Stratégie nationale de lutte contre la pauvreté.

ANNEXE A6.
LES MÉCANISMES DE FONCTIONNEMENT DES CLUBS DE PARIS ET DE LONDRES

CLUB DE PARIS

Les différentes variantes proposées au Club de Paris sont:

a) le rééchelonnement simple qui consiste à rééchelonner, mais toutefois sans annuler, la dette sur une période de dix (10) ans avec un délai de grâce pouvant aller jusqu'à cinq (5) ans;

b) le traitement dit de Venise (pour les pays les plus pauvres) ou traitement de Houston (pour les pays à revenu intermédiaire) rallonge la période du rééchelonnement simple à vingt (20) ans dont dix (10) ans de différé pour les prêts APD (Aide Publique au Développement) et à quinze (15) ans dont huit (8) ans de différé pour les crédits commerciaux à garantie publique;

c) le menu à options de Toronto qui a été en vigueur de 1988 à 1991 offrait:

- pour les prêts APD une durée de remboursement de vingt cinq (25) ans dont quatorze (14) ans de différé à des taux d'intérêt concessionnels qui ne pouvaient dépasser les taux initiaux.

- pour les prêts non APD mais à garantie publique trois (3) options possibles:

- *l'option A* se composait de l'annulation d'un tiers des échéances couvertes par le réaménagement, et la consolidation des deux tiers restants au taux du marché sur une durée de quatorze (14) ans dont huit (8) ans de différé

- *l'option B* rallongeait la durée du réaménagement à 25 ans dont 14 ans de différé;

- *l'option C* maintenait la durée à 14 ans dont 8 ans de différé mais accordait cependant un taux d'intérêt plus concessionnel qui était égal au taux du marché réduit de 3,5 points ou de moitié s'il était inférieur à 7%.

d) le traitement dit de Londres ou encore appelé "Toronto amélioré" ou "Toronto renforcé", en vigueur depuis 1991, propose les variantes suivantes:

- pour les prêts APD la durée d'amortissement est prolongée de 25 ans à 30 ans mais le différé réduit de 14 ans à 12 ans.

- pour les prêts non-APD, les trois options sont modifiées comme suit:

- option A : annulation de 50% des échéances arrivant à terme au cours de la période de consolidation et rééchelonnement du solde au taux du marché sur une durée de 23 ans dont 6 ans de différé;

- option B : consolidation à des taux concessionnels de manière à réduire de 50% la VAN des paiements dus pendant 23 ans mais sans différé;
- option C : combinaison de la réduction du taux d'intérêt et du paiement partiel des intérêts et rééchelonnement de la dette sur 25 ans avec 5 ans de différé.

e) le traitement dit de Naples a succédé en 1994 aux conditions de Londres avec les offres suivantes:

- pour les prêts APD : réduction de la VAN de 67% et rééchelonnement du reliquat aux taux d'intérêts concessionnels initiaux sur 40 ans avec un différé de 16 ans ou réduction de la VAN de la dette de 50% et rééchelonnement du reliquat sur 30 ans avec un différé de 12 ans. Six pays (Béni, Bolivie, Burkina, Guyane, Mali, Ouganda) peuvent obtenir du Club de Paris des réductions du stock de leur dette. Le traitement du stock de dette du Mali est subordonné à la décision (non encore prise), le déclarant admissible à recevoir une aide au titre de l'initiative PPTE.
- pour les prêts non APD il y a trois options:
- Option A : réduction de la VAN de 67% et remboursement du reliquat sur 23 ans avec 6 ans de différé;
- Option B : réduction du service de la dette en vertu de laquelle la réduction en valeur actualisée nette est obtenue au moyen de taux d'intérêt concessionnels et rééchelonnement du reliquat sur 33 ans sans différé, période qui se réduit à 25 ans avec un différé de 6 ans si la réduction obtenue en valeur actualisée nette est de 50%;
- Option C, appelée aussi option commerciale qui n'est assortie d'aucune réduction en VAN et étale le remboursement sur 40 ans dont 20 ans de différé;

f) les termes de Lyon portent le taux de réduction de la VAN de 67% à 80% et remboursement du reliquat sur 23 ans dont 6 ans de différé;

g) les termes de Cologne améliorent le taux de réduction de la VAN de 80% à 90%.

CLUB DE LONDRES

Ses variantes les plus connues sont:

i) la proposition de Bailey qui consiste à échanger les dettes contre des exportations de biens et services;

ii) le plan Baker préconise le rééchelonnement des anciennes dettes et l'octroi de nouveaux prêts bancaires aux pays les plus endettés adoptant des programmes d'ajustement structurel.

iii) le plan Brady, qui s'articule autour du plan Baker, propose les options suivantes:
- réduction du principal;
- réduction des intérêts;
- octroi de nouveau prêts;

iv) le plan Miyazawa ou plan japonais comporte deux volets :
- l'octroi de prêts supplémentaires à des taux préférentiels aux pays qui acceptent un programme d'ajustement appuyé par le FMI;
- l'octroi d'une garantie de paiement des intérêts dus aux banques sur la partie de leurs créances transformées en obligations sans décote, en contrepartie d'un rééchelonnement du solde.

v) les rachats de dette avec décote et les conversions de dette :
- les conversions en obligations, lesquelles obligations sont échangées, sur la base de décote, contre un titre libellé en devise
- le rachat conversion en actifs réels. Un investisseur achète, avec décote e.g. la dette à 50% de sa valeur faciale, une créance à une banque (créancière du pays endetté) ; se fait rembourser la créance, avec une autre décote moindre, e.g. la dette à 60% de sa valeur faciale, par l'emprunteur ; enfin achète avec ce remboursement (fait en monnaie locale et non plus en devise), des actions dans des sociétés publiques locales telles que dans le cadre des opérations de privatisation ou procède à de nouveaux investissements productifs. La dette des créanciers privés a pu être rachetée par les pays pauvres sur le marché secondaire, avec de fortes décotes, grâce au concours de partenaires au développement bilatéraux et du Fonds de désendettement des pays IDA.
- le rachat conversion en exportation. A la différence du rachat conversion en actifs réels, ici le remboursement est utilisé pour payer les achats de produits destinés à l'exportation vers le pays de celui qui a racheté la créance.

Uganda's External Debt and the HIPC Initiative

Peter B. Mijumbi

ABSTRACT

This paper examines Uganda's experience with external debt and debt relief measures, in particular, the country's experience with the HIPC Initiatives (the original and the Enhanced one), and their relevance to poverty reduction. The Ugandan government's attempt to improve its record on social development has led to the country's first Poverty Eradication Action Plan (PEAP) in 1997, the second installment of which in 2000 has become Uganda's Poverty Reduction Strategy Paper (PRSP). Though Uganda's PEAP is not without its weaknesses, continued adherence to its main principles should ensure sustained progress in poverty reduction. The HIPC assistance is expected to free significant budgetary resources for Uganda's poverty reduction strategy, thus allowing the country to implement the development goals set out in its PRSP. In fact, average budgetary savings over the period 2000-2015 due to HIPC assistance is estimated to amount to as much as US$55.5 million per annum.

RÉSUMÉ

Cet article examine l'expérience de l'Ouganda par rapport à sa dette extérieure et les mesures d'allégement de cette dette, portant surtout sur l'expérience de ce pays par rapport aux Initiatives PPTE – originale et renforcée – ainsi que la contribution de ces Initiatives à la réduction de la pauvreté. La tentative du gouvernement ougandais d'apporter des améliorations sur le plan social a donné lieu au Plan d'Action pour Éradiquer la Pauvreté (PAEP 1997), dont la deuxième version (PAEP 2000) est devenue le document Cadre Stratégique de Lutte contre la Pauvreté (CSLP) pour l'Ouganda. Même si le PAEP pour l'Ouganda comporte des faiblesses, une adhésion à ses principes de base devrait assurer des progrès continus en ce qui concerne la réduction de la pauvreté. L'aide provenant de l'Initiative PPTE devrait libérer d'importantes ressources budgétaires pour appuyer la stratégie de réduction de la pauvreté en Ouganda, permettant ainsi au pays d'accomplir les objectifs reliés au développement établis dans son CSLP. En fait, les gains budgétaires moyens pour la période 2001-2015 provenant de l'Initiative PPTE sont estimés à plus de 55.5 millions de dollars US par année.

INTRODUCTION

Uganda's debt burden remains extremely high, especially for a country with one of the lowest per capita incomes in the world. The country's debt stock stood at US$3.68 billion at the end of June 2000 (Uganda 2000b). The liquidity effects of debt are depriving the budget of badly needed resources for investment in infrastructure to support the private sector as an engine of future growth, and for human capital development to ensure higher productivity. The debt overhang, although decreasing, continues to deter major foreign investors and is a major barrier to accelerated per capita growth rates and to poverty reduction in the rural areas.

Large annual debt payments limit foreign exchange reserve buildup and contribute to the balance-of-payments financing gap while placing significant pressure on the budget. The high debt-service burden reduces funding that would go to priority sectors (primary education, primary health care, water and sanitation, agricultural extension and rural roads) outlined by Uganda's Poverty Eradication Action Plan (PEAP).

The September 1996 decision of the World Bank and the IMF, to grant debt relief to heavily indebted poor countries (HIPCs) such as Uganda, provided a new lease on life through its aim of reducing indebtedness to a sustainable level while ensuring that the resulting debt relief is channelled into poverty-reducing priority social sectors. Uganda was the first country to qualify for HIPC debt relief under the original framework. It committed itself to channelling the debt-relief funds into a common fund, the Poverty Action Fund (PAF), to be used in poverty-reducing social sectors.

This paper examines Uganda's experience with external debt and debt-relief measures. Special emphasis is placed on the country's experience with the HIPC I (the original HIPC) and HIPC II (the Enhanced HIPC) initiatives, and their relevance to poverty reduction. Section I retraces Uganda's debt problems and gives a chronological overview of its debt-relief experiences. Section II examines the magnitude and importance of HIPC debt relief. Section III looks at the country's experience in linking poverty reduction to debt relief. Sections IV and V address conditionality views and the national post-debt regime strategy, respectively.

I. UGANDA'S EXTERNAL DEBT AND DEBT-RELIEF EXPERIENCE

This section examines the evolution of Uganda's external debt and the factors that generated it. It also gives a chronological description of Uganda's debt-relief experiences and ends with an assessment of the economic effects of debt reduction.

A. DEBT STOCK AND ARREARS

Between 1986 and 1994, Uganda's external debt (including arrears) rose by 121% (from US$1.4 billion to US$3.2 billion). This corresponded to an average increase of 10.4% a year. The sharpest increases occurred in 1987, 1989 and 1990 and were mainly due to new disbursements. However, the rise in external debt has been less pronounced since 1992, when the country embarked on a debt-reducing strategy. Uganda's inability to meet its debt-servicing obligations in full stretches back to the late 1970s (Uganda 1995). Total debt stock increased by 16% to 17% annually toward the end of the 1980s (Holmgren et al. 1999).

Over the years, Uganda's external debt increased as a result of:
- the oil shocks of the 1970s, which led to huge increases in oil prices;
- heavy borrowing from 1981 to 1985 and after 1987 for economic recovery and stabilization programs (the loans were managed poorly, and large sums were borrowed on unfavourable terms) (Edoku 2000);
- deteriorating terms of trade (1985-1992);
- a decline in coffee export earnings (1985-1993), which reduced foreign exchange earning capacity and thus limited Uganda's ability to service its debts;
- a highly expansionary fiscal policy (Mbire and Atingi 1997).

Uganda's debt burden rose from US$172 million in 1970 to US$3.6 billion in 1996-1997 and was estimated at US$3.2 billion by the end of June 1999 (World Debt Tables 1996; IMF and IDA 2000). In 1997, Uganda spent US$3 per person on health compared to US$9 per person on debt service annually (Debt Bulletin 1997). Debt as a percentage of GDP increased from 11.8% in 1971 to 66.1% in 1995 (Hayuni 1995). Debt service as a percentage of exports increased from 4% in 1980 to 23% in 1996 despite the fact that not all debt was being adequately serviced.

Uganda's debt has historically been medium and long term because short-term credits virtually ceased in the late 1970s, when political turmoil set in. As figure 1 shows, short-term debt as a proportion of total debt fell steadily from 1986. The fall was further accelerated by the commercial debt buyback in

Figure 1. Composition of Uganda's debt

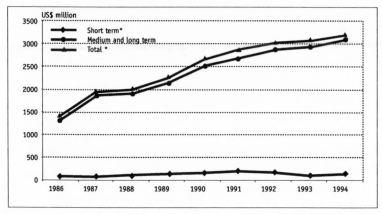

* Including interest arrears.

1993. By the end of 1994, short-term debt as a proportion of total debt had fallen to less than 2%.

The proportion of concessional debt to total debt rose steadily in the 1980s and 1990s, and exceeded 70% by the end of 1994. This was a reflection of adherence to new borrowing guidelines of the Government of Uganda, which required contracting only loans with a grant element exceeding 78%. Under these guidelines, the government contracted large multilateral concessional loans, which averaged US$200 million a year from 1989 to 1994, and turned down many commercial loans. Some multilateral and bilateral creditors continued to lend non-concessionally, with an ensuing rise in total and bilateral non-concessional debt.

The total external debt owed to multilateral creditors rose from 54% to 72% between 1989 and 1994. By the end of June 1996, it reached 76% and it rose further to 81% at the end of June 2000. The rise stemmed from extensive new fast-disbursing loans to support adjustment. Debt owed to commercial creditors fell sharply in 1992-1993 as a result of commercial debt buyback operations funded by the IDA and other donors. It accounted for 3% of total external debt at the end of June 1996 and by the end of June 2000 had fallen to 1.5%. Bilateral creditor debt, until it was reduced in 1994, rose due to capitalization of interest on debt rescheduled with the Paris Club and non-OECD governments.

Figure 2. Trend in Uganda's debt by creditor type, 1986-1994

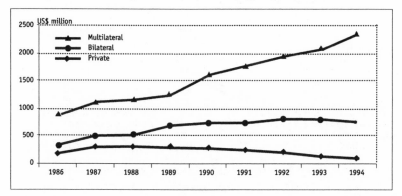

Before 1992, Uganda's capacity to service its debt fell steadily to about one third of programmed levels due to a shortage of foreign exchange. This led to a rise in arrears during the 1980s. In the early 1990s, thanks to Uganda's debt and adjustment strategies, donors stepped in and provided funds for multilateral debt service and commercial debt buyback. The bilateral arrears rose again sharply in 1997 and remain high, but the multilateral arrears have been eliminated by the HIPC initiatives.

Of total debt service paid from 1986 to 1993, between 60% and 70% was paid to multilateral creditors. This emphasis reflected their weight in the debt stock, the short nature of some (especially IMF) credits, and the lack of relief available for multilateral debt. Strenuous efforts have also been made since 1992 to keep current with the servicing of the Paris Club debt, which as it stands, is seen as ineligible for further relief. Non-OECD bilateral and commercial creditors have, however, received no payments, except where they have been funding essential projects or in the context of the commercial debt buyback.

B.   DEBT-RELIEF "RESCHEDULINGS"

Uganda has benefited from generous amounts of debt relief from the international community since the mid-1980s. This stems from the country's consistency in implementing structural adjustment programs (SAPs) since 1986 and also because it is considered a severely indebted low income country (SILIC). Uganda engaged in debt negotiations with the Paris Club six times between 1981 and 1995. It received debt relief under the Toronto terms in 1989, and

Table 2. Uganda's debt relief experiences

	Year	Terms of debt relief
Paris Club		
Toronto terms	1989	37%*
London terms	1992	50%*
Naples terms	1995	67%*
Lyon terms	1998	80%*
Cologne terms	1999	90%*
International Development Association	1992	88% on commercial debt stock
Multilateral debt fund (Uganda)	1993-1995	US$ 40 million per year
HIPC	1998	US$ 40 million per year
Enhanced HIPC	2000	US$ 45 million per year

Note: * The percentages show the proportion of the debt service falling due during the consolidation period that
could be written off.
Source: Government of Uganda, Ministry of Finance; Planning and Economic Development; Macroeconomic
Department.

Table 3.   Debt relief from 1991-92 to 1996-97 (in US$ millions)

	1991-92	1992-93	1993-94	1994-95	1995-96	1996-97
Multilateral (EEC)	3	2	–	–	–	–
Bilateral	12.90	12.93	36.35	41.20	50.20	53.31
Multilateral Debt Fund	37.84	48.33	–	–	–	–
Total debt relief	12.90	12.93	39.35	41.20	90.04	101.64
Total debt	2647.50	2637.20	2999.30	3386.90	3515.80	3660.20
Debt relief as % of total debt	0.50	0.50	1.30	1.20	2.60	2.60

Source: Bank of Uganda.

under the London terms in 1992. In February 1995, it qualified for an "exit rescheduling" under the Naples terms which translated into a stock reduction of 67% of eligible debt.[1] Table 2 shows Uganda's debt-relief negotiations in chronological order starting with the Toronto terms in 1989 and ending with the most recent Enhanced HIPC, whose implementation began in 2000.

Table 3 shows the amount of debt relief Uganda received from different creditors from 1992 to 1997. There was both a gradual increase in debt relief from bilateral sources and in debt relief going toward the multilateral debt-relief fund set by the government. Multilateral debt attracted very little relief

---

1. "Eligible debt" refers to debt incurred before a set cutoff date, with service falling due during a designated consolidation period. Debt relief is provided only on the service falling due during the consolidation period. This criteria generally limits the "eligible debt" to a small fraction of the total debt stock.

in this period but this changed dramatically in 1998, when the country began benefiting from HIPC I debt-relief flows. Debt relief, as a percentage of total debt, accounted for only 0.5% in fiscal year 1991-1992 and 1992-1993. It rose steadily to 2.8% by fiscal year 1996-1997 as a result of donor support for the Multilateral Debt Fund (MDF).

In 1997, Uganda owed US$3.7 billion in nominal terms to international creditors. Under the first HIPC Initiative, it received debt cancellation amounting to US$650 million in nominal terms. The Enhanced HIPC, agreed to at the G8 IMF/World Bank meetings in September 1999, saw an additional debt cancellation of US$1.3 billion. Considering that Uganda owed a total of US$3.2 billion (nominal) in June 1999, the debt relief from the two HIPCs amounted to 40% of this amount – a significant improvement over the early 1990s, when debt relief represented only 0.5% of total debt stock.

Looking back at the 1990s, these debt-relief operations reduced Uganda's overall debt to some extent, but the relief was limited because only a small portion of the country's debt was owed to the Paris Club and commercial creditors. Also, only a small proportion of Paris-Club debt was being considered in each operation.

Efforts have been made since 1992 to reschedule bilateral debt to non-OECD governments on comparable terms with Paris-Club debt. By 1995, three governments had concluded negotiations with the Ugandan government but on non-concessional terms and with no debt reduction. A reduction in debt owed to the Soviet Union was achieved through a debt buyback at 12% on the dollar from a private company that had purchased it. Failure to service most non-OECD debt led Uganda to reopen discussions on the prospect of converting such debt into local currency or a buyback at a heavy discount. These options were, however, greatly limited by Uganda's lack of hard currency from third parties to make these operations feasible with minimal inflationary implications.

The IDA, through its Commercial Debt Reduction Facility, gave Uganda the most generous reduction in February 1993. This eliminated 89% (US$153 million) of a total US$172 million in commercial debt principal at 12% of its original face value. The Netherlands, Switzerland, the European Union and Germany joined the IDA in contributing funds to this facility. Similar buybacks have been attempted and concluded with other residual creditors on comparable terms, but there are some holdouts.

Some pre-HIPC debt-relief assistance came for Uganda from multilateral creditors in the form of new money to help meet debt-service payments. For instance, the World Bank provided funds from its Fifth Dimension to help pay interest on International Bank for Reconstruction and Development (IBRD) loans.

C.   EFFECTS OF THE REDUCED BURDEN OF DEBT PAYMENT

A study by Kamanyire (1999) concluded that Uganda's large debt burden constrained investment and growth. Resources used to service debt were shown to contribute to the crowding out of public investment and the discouragement of private investment, as well as to the restriction of the flow of imports. Debt variables were found to reduce and render insignificant the coefficient of the aid variable, suggesting that the debt burden cancels out some of the positive effects of aid inflows (Kamanyire 1999). The results of the study suggest that the HIPC debt relief should significantly rejuvenate investor confidence and stimulate growth.

To put it differently, the assistance provided under the Enhanced HIPC Initiative is expected to free up significant budget resources for Uganda's poverty-reduction strategy and thus provide greater momentum toward achieving the development goals set out in Uganda's Poverty Reduction Strategy Paper (PRSP), the PEAP. The amount of resources made available under HIPC II in the first three years will, on average, be equivalent to about 0.7% of GDP and 10% of currently projected social expenditures (IMF and IDA 2000).

Debt relief arising from the HIPC Initiative has been channelled directly to the PAF, to be allocated to priority poverty-reducing expenditure programs (rural-feeder roads, agricultural extension, primary education, water and sanitation, and primary health care). As a result, spending under these programs has risen sharply. Prior to debt relief in 1998-1999, spending on PEAP programs that directly benefited the poor accounted for 16% of the government's budget (excluding donor project financing), but in 2000-2001, these programs account for 32% of the budget.

Debt relief and donor budget support have, for instance, enabled a large part of the "essential minimum health care package" to be financed. Both the water and rural roads sectors have since received large shares of extra funding made available from the debt relief, and total funding to these two sectors has doubled in real terms.

II. MAGNITUDE AND IMPORTANCE OF HIPC DEBT RELIEF

This section evaluates the adequacy of HIPC debt relief and how it compares with other debt-relief experiences. It also compares debt-relief flows to existing aid levels.

A. ADEQUACY OF HIPC RELIEF FLOWS

Uganda met the conditions for its completion point under the Enhanced HIPC Initiative in May 2000. It had earlier met conditions for and benefited from the first HIPC Initiative in April 1998. The total debt relief under HIPC II, from all of Uganda's creditors, will be about US$1.3 billion (US$660 million in net present value (NPV) terms, equivalent to 40% of external debt). When the amount of relief provided under HIPC I (US$650 million) is factored in, the relief obtained totals about US$2 billion.

Donor countries and the Government of Uganda expect that the debt relief provided under the HIPC Initiative will reduce Uganda's debt-service obligations and create room for additional public expenditures on poverty-reduction programs.

To put these expectations into perspective, it is important to gauge the expected impact of the HIPC Initiative on Uganda's overall debt burden. One way of doing this is to look at the most recent Debt Sustainability Analysis (DSA) results for Uganda, prepared by the IMF and IDA (IMF and IDA 2000).

The DSA used four key debt-burden indicators:

- the NPV of debt-to-exports ratio;[2]
- the NPV of debt-to-revenue ratio;
- the NPV of debt-to-GDP ratio;
- the debt-service ratio and the debt service-to-revenue ratio.

The DSA shows that the NPV of Uganda's debt-to-exports ratio is expected to fall below 150% in about nine years under the original HIPC (see Appendix A). With the Enhanced HIPC, this ratio starts below 150% and would be at 55% at the end of the same period. Without the HIPC initiatives, the debt-to-export ratio would not fall below 150% until well after 2014-2015.

The fiscal burden of debt, as measured by the NPV of debt-to-revenues, is expected to fall from a high of 242% in 1998-1999 to less than half, at 109% in 2009-2010 under the original HIPC. With the additional Enhanced HIPC

---

2. The NPV of debt is determined by discounting future debt payments at market interest rates. It thus reflects the current commercial value equivalent of the debt. Thus, debt incurred on concessional terms would have a smaller NPV than their nominal value.

flows, the figure starts at 130% and falls to 52% in the same period. Without HIPC assistance, the NPV of debt-to-revenues would still be at 117% in 2014-2015.

The DSA also showed that the debt-service ratio would fall from about 15% in 1998-1999 to less than 8% in 2009-2010 under the original HIPC. Under the Enhanced HIPC, it would start at 11% in 1999-2000, fall to 5% in 2009-2010, and remain below 5% thereafter. Without HIPC assistance, the ratio would be expected to fall below 10% only after 2015-2016.

The debt service-to-revenue ratio drops below 10% by 2001-2002 under HIPC I and would do so in 2000-2001 under HIPC II. Without HIPC assistance, it would not drop to this level until 2007-2008.

The preceding scenarios underline the importance of the HIPC initiatives in reducing Uganda's external debt to sustainable levels and indeed suggest substantial dividends to Uganda under these programs. In fact, when assistance from the HIPC and Enhanced HIPC initiatives is added to other debt-relief agreements (Paris Club and others), Uganda will be relieved of two thirds and three quarters of its debt service in the coming years.

The actual dividends (or budgetary savings) from debt relief as a result of the HIPC initiatives can be gauged by comparing Uganda's post-HIPC debt payments with its past repayment history (see Appendix B). Uganda paid an average of US$150.9 million from 1994 to 1998. Over the next 15 years (2001-2015) it expects to pay an average of US$95.4 million, and over the coming five years (2001-2005), US$67.5 million. The amount of budgetary savings, as a result, will average US$55.5 million over the period 2001-2015. This debt dividend corresponds to 8.9% of social expenditure in 1999-2000 and 3% of total expenditure in the same year. Over the period 2001-2005, the debt dividend is as much as US$83.4 million, on average, and accounts for 13.3% of social expenditure, and 4.6% of total expenditure in 1999-2000. This means that the debt dividend is front-loaded (though debt relief itself is not), providing more benefit in the first five years.

B.   HIPC EXPERIENCES

Lack of coordination and follow through are major shortcomings of the HIPC Initiative. The funds arising from the Initiative are assumed to be available, but instead of remitting them to creditors, they are channelled to agreed-on, poverty-reducing, priority social sectors. This expectation is unrealistic if the creditor nations do not come up with these funds in the first place.

Delayed implementation of the HIPC initiatives by creditors who have, otherwise, signed on, in principle, tends to distort Uganda's budget. Uganda captures the amount of expected debt relief accruing from its participation in the HIPC in its spending plans. Disbursement of the intended relief, however, does not always coincide with these plans, and this creates a problem for domestic fiscal planning and implementation. For example, the African Development Bank (AFDB) included year 2000 in its disbursement schedule, yet no implementation procedures for disbursement were made. While the modalities were being worked out, they required Uganda to keep servicing its AFDB debts. This meant remitting funds to a creditor that would otherwise have gone immediately to poverty-reduction spending. This also means that the government often has to perform a financial juggling act to maintain budgetary integrity.

III. LINKING POVERTY REDUCTION TO DEBT RELIEF: UGANDA'S EXPERIENCE

This section reviews the country's experience of linking poverty reduction to debt relief under the HIPC framework. In this regard, it examines Uganda's PRSP, the PEAP, by looking at its main elements, its main institutional features, its strengths and weaknesses, its targets for poverty reduction and attendant costs, how it is viewed by Ugandans, and its usefulness as a PRSP in the poverty-reduction effort.

A.   BACKGROUND

Uganda became one of the world's poorest countries as a consequence of the prolonged period of economic and social collapse (1971-1985). The country remains extremely poor and is currently ranked 158th (out of 174 countries) on the UN Human Development Index. It has, however, enjoyed a sustained and remarkable recovery, with economic growth averaging 7% a year in the 1990s and inflation being contained to single figures. Also, the proportion of the population in severe poverty fell from 56% in 1992-1993 to 44% in 1997-1998 and, if preliminary figures are confirmed, this figure is currently at 35% in 1999-2000 (Appleton 2000).[3] Over the 1990s, living standards in urban areas rose by over a half and in rural areas by over a third. The main blot on performance has been continued increases in poverty in the conflict-affected north, which is the poorest region. With that exception, growth in rural areas

---

3. The poverty line is defined in terms of the cost of meeting calorie needs, plus some allowance for non-food consumption. Specific poverty lines involve a large element of judgement, but the finding that poverty has been substantially reduced is not sensitive to the choice of poverty line.

was evenly distributed, and both food crop and cash crop households benefited. These improvements are only now returning Ugandan per capita income
to the level achieved in 1970, an indication of the extent of the collapse suf-
fered in the Amin-Obote II period.

B.   THE HIPC INITIATIVES

The first HIPC Initiative was expected to have provided an "exit strategy" for
countries such as Uganda from the debt-rescheduling process, leaving them
with sustainable debt levels. The country would then be expected to service its
debt and still be able to direct sufficient resources to poverty reduction.
However, unforeseen circumstances made this unachievable. In the case of
Uganda, the El Niño weather phenomenon and changes in global interest rates
made it difficult to achieve post-HIPC sustainable levels.

These experiences prompted the revision of the original HIPC to what is
now referred to as the Enhanced HIPC Initiative (or HIPC II). Under the
Enhanced HIPC Initiative, more countries will benefit from deeper and more
quickly delivered debt relief. The key elements of the Enhanced HIPC
Initiative are:

- Lowering the debt-sustainability thresholds to provide a greater safety
  cushion and to increase prospects for a permanent exit from unsustainable debt. The required NPV-to-Exports ratio was lowered from 202% to
  a uniform 150%;
- Faster debt relief starting from decision points;
- Floating completion points;
- A strong link between debt relief and poverty reduction.

The last element is a key requirement for a country to qualify for HIPC II debt
relief. The country is expected to prepare a national PRSP. In this regard, the
recently revised PEAP 2000 has been accepted as Uganda's PRSP and on its
strength, Uganda has become the first country to benefit from the Enhanced
HIPC Initiative.

C.   EVOLUTION OF THE PEAP

When the current government came to power in early January 1986, it outlined a 10-point program that, among other things, included a commitment
to eradicating poverty. In the early reform years (from 1987 to 1992) however,
this commitment, was not treated as a government priority. Instead, the government became more preoccupied with programs that promoted macroeconomic stability and efficient use of national resources. These SAPs, supported

by the World Bank and the IMF, became the cornerstone of Uganda's economic recovery and management.

Poverty eradication has assumed an important place in public discourse since 1992. With most of the macroeconomic reforms in place by 1993, the government's attention turned to improving service delivery and reducing poverty. At that time, it was recognized that the SAPs were not benefiting some vulnerable groups in the short-run. This resulted in the creation of a special Program to Alleviate Poverty and the Social Costs of Adjustment (PAPSCA) to mitigate the social costs of the demand-management measures (particularly fiscal tightening) associated with the adjustment programs. The PAPSCA was first piloted in 12 districts.

In 1994, policy analysts at the Ministry of Planning and Economic Development (before it merged with the Ministry of Finance to form the Ministry of Finance, Planning and Economic Development [MFPED]) pushed for an explicit poverty action plan. Their efforts culminated in a Consultative Group Workshop in 1995 that was attended by Uganda's President. The underlying theme of the workshop was concern over persistent high levels of poverty in Uganda, despite positive economic growth rates and several attempts to address the debt burden. This led to the establishment of a task force in 1996 and the formulation of the first PEAP in 1997 through a consultative process involving major stakeholders. The PEAP focussed on the need to direct the use of public resources and actions to eradicate poverty in Uganda. However, without a significant reduction in external debt service, the required increase in social sector spending was at this point impossible.

The first HIPC debt-relief Initiative formally announced at the World Bank/IMF annual meeting in September 1996 provided a window of hope for Uganda, which became the first beneficiary, reaching the completion point in April 1998 (Edoku 2000).

The processes leading up to the PEAP 2000, unlike that of the PEAP 1997, involved much wider consultations with government, civil society and academia to ensure wider acceptability and ownership of the plan. In its revised form, which did not differ greatly from the original, the PEAP 2000 continues to stand on the four main thrusts of:

- Creating a framework for economic growth and transformation;
- Ensuring good governance and security;
- Directly increasing the ability of the poor to raise their incomes;
- Directly raising the quality of life of the poor.

The revised PEAP has benefited from lessons learned and actions taken since it was first launched in 1997. These include the development of sector-wide approaches (SWAPS), participatory research findings by the Uganda Participatory Poverty Assessment Project (UPPAP), constraints identified in the Poverty Status Report 1999, and the costing of public actions and monitorable indicators in key poverty-oriented programs (Uganda 2000a, p. 6-12).

The purpose of the PEAP is to present an overall framework and principles for government planning and budgeting to support poverty-eradication efforts. The priorities articulated in the PEAP are implemented through sectoral plans and financed through the annual budget. The implementation of the PEAP is envisaged to operate not as a separate exercise but through the actions of each sector and the annual budgeting exercise.

The overall strategy of the PEAP is guided by the following principles (Uganda 2000a):

- The public sector should only intervene in areas where markets function poorly or are likely to lead to very inequitable outcomes.
- Where the public sector intervenes, it should use the most cost-effective methods, including the use of non-governmental organizations (NGOs) for service delivery where appropriate.
- Poverty eradication is a partnership and should involve the closest possible integration of the efforts of government with its development partners.
- All government policies should reflect the importance of distributional considerations, of gender, of children's rights, and of environmental impacts.
- Each area of public action will be guided by the formulation of desired outcomes and the designs of inputs and outputs to promote them.

D.   HOW IT IS IMPLEMENTED

Implementation of the PEAP is through a sector-wide programming approach by which sector objectives, sector outputs and sector-expenditure outcomes are identified. The different levels of Uganda's poverty-reduction planning and implementation framework, underpinned by Vision 2025, in the long term, and the PEAP, in the medium term, are shown in table 4.

The PEAP has guided the preparation of detailed sector plans. Eventually, all sectors will be covered by up-to-date, resource-constrained sector plans and investment programs, that focus on achieving the goals of the PEAP.

In turn, the PEAP and the sector plans set the framework for the preparation of district plans (although these are still in the early stages of development). Under Uganda's decentralized system of governance, the local authorities determine the implementation plan for sector programs based on local priorities. Community involvement in the planning framework is also being strengthened.

Table 4.   A guide to Uganda's poverty reduction planning and implementation
framework

Plan	Description
Vision 2025	An overview of long-term goals and aspirations by the year 2025
The PEAP	The national planning framework within which to develop detailed sector strategies
Sector Planning	Technical specifications of sector priorities, disciplined by hard budget constraints
District Planning	Implementation plans for sector strategies based on local priorities/needs
Medium-term expenditure framework (MTEF)	Annual, rolling 3-year expenditure planning, setting out the medium term expenditure priorities and hard budget constraints against which sector plans can be developed and refined
District MTEF	Setting out the medium term expenditure priorities and hard budget constraints against which district plans can be developed and refined
Annual budget and district budgets	Annual implementation of the three-year planning framework
Donor, NGOs and private sector	Participating and sharing information/ideas in developing sector plans and budgets
Participatory processes	Bottom-up participation of districts in the planning and monitoring process, as well as participatory poverty assessments, providing essential feedback on progress towards poverty-eradication goals

The detailed SWAPS and investment programs are drawn up within an overall Medium-Term Expenditure Framework (MTEF). The PEAP's expenditure implications are translated into concrete spending decisions through the MTEF, which has been developed to provide a clear analysis of the links between inputs, outputs and outcomes while ensuring consistency of expenditure levels within overall resource constraints. Since 1992, the MFPED has been developing a MTEF, which is presented to Cabinet as part of the annual Budget Framework Paper (BFP), covering three fiscal years.

E.   POVERTY ACTION FUND

To highlight the poverty focus of the public expenditure program, and the dedication of HIPC (and other) resources toward poverty-reduction programs, the government established the PAF in 1997. The PAF raised the profile of the government's poverty-reduction program and further demonstrated its commitment to securing the funds for its implementation.

The PAF is a means of making poverty-reduction spending and the use of savings from debt relief more transparent. Expenditure programs targeted by

Table 5.   Summary of PAF budget (billions of Uganda shillings)

	Budget	Projections		
	1999-2000	2000-01	2001-02	2002-03
Directly increasing incomes of the poor	**52.9**	**50.1**	**53.8**	**59.4**
Rural roads	24.5	30.5	32.9	37.2
Land Act	3.0	3.0	3.3	3.7
Agricultural extension	6.1	6.3	6.8	7.7
Micro finance/restocking	19.3	10.3	10.8	10.8
Directly improving quality of life of the poor	**268.0**	**371.1**	**410.4**	**486.3**
Primary health care	28.2	51.1	70.1	92.1
Water and sanitation	17.4	37.6	39.5	44.6
Primary education	222.4	281.4	299.8	348.4
Adult literacy	0.0	1.0	1.0	1.2
Studies for implementation of PEAP	**0.0**	**1.0**	**1.1**	**1.2**
Other district grants	**2.0**	**12.0**	**13.0**	**14.4**
Accountability	**11.3**	**15.7**	**17.2**	**20.3**
Total budgeted expenditure	**334.2**	**449.9**	**495.5**	**581.6**

Source: Government of Uganda, PEAP, 2000.

the PAF include rural feeder roads, agricultural extension, primary education, primary health care, water and sanitation and equalization grants, whose purpose (as defined in the constitution) is to make the quality of service delivery more even across different districts. Within this group of services, water supply was made a higher priority as a direct result of the finding, from participatory work, that the poor themselves regard water supply as a high priority.

Through the PAF, the government makes information readily available to the public on poverty-reduction programs. This allows civil society and the parliament to follow up on allocations made to the identified sectors. All PAF resources are published in the media. Lower levels of government (districts, schools and health care centers) are required to display PAF allocations in public places. Quarterly meetings are convened to discuss independent assessments of PAF expenditures. Civil-society groups, local and central government officials, and the media attend these meetings.

The PAF budget (table 5) includes the highest-priority public expenditures from a poverty-eradication perspective. Inclusion of a particular sector or program in the PAF is justified by the high economic and/or social returns on that type of expenditure, and by the priority which participatory work has shown the poor themselves attach to that program or sector.

Progress in the implementation of the PEAP has benefited from an increased availability of funds from debt relief, which has enabled the government to double the resources available to PEAP programs. Although the original intention was to create a transparent mechanism for ensuring that the resources saved from the HIPC Initiative were channelled fully to poverty-eradication programs, the PAF has evolved into much more than this. It has attracted additional donor support for poverty-reduction programs over and above some donors' regular programs.

In terms of budgetary provisions, perhaps the most startling statistic is that prior to debt relief in 1998-1999, spending on PEAP programs that directly benefited the poor accounted for 16% of the government's total budget (excluding donor project financing). In 2000-2001, however, these programs account for 32% of the budget. This represents a remarkable shift in the composition of the budget by any country's standard, and demonstrates a real commitment to the PEAP by the government.

The government of Uganda has considerable incentive to make the PAF a success, because this will attract more donor resources in subsequent years. It has raised the profile of social-sector expenditures, providing a public forum (through the quarterly meetings) for discussing PAF issues and reviewing progress. The quarterly reports enable civil society to monitor budget performance against plans (ever since the PAF was created budget outturns have been at least 95% of original budget proposals).

F.   MAIN INSTITUTIONAL FEATURES OF THE PEAP

To ensure ownership for developing and implementing the detailed sector plans, this responsibility is increasingly decentralized to the line ministries and the districts. While the PEAP sets out the overall framework, the individual line ministries take the initiative to develop and design the detailed plans within each sector. Where a multisectoral approach is required – for example, in the Plan for the Modernization of Agriculture – steering committees representing each of the relevant line ministries have been established. These set the overall framework and establish the basic principles, but within that framework, there is clear line ministry responsibility for each component. For example, responsibility for extension services and research rests with the Ministry of Agriculture, while the Ministry of Energy and Minerals is responsible for the rural electrification component. Combatting HIV/AIDS also requires a multisectoral approach, but again particular components are the clear responsibility of individual institutions (for example, the Ministry of

Health works with the districts to ensure that the necessary drugs are available at local health centers).

In accordance with Uganda's decentralization system (formally established under the Local Government Act of 1997), district authorities are responsible for delivering services within the policy guidelines of the national and sectoral programs. This makes their participation in the development and implementation of these sector programs critical to their success. Donor support in strengthening district capacity in planning, management and accountability will be essential for improving the partnership process. A major program to strengthen district capacity in this area will be the Local Government Development Program.

Fiscal decentralization is already well advanced in Uganda. As mentioned earlier, responsibility for providing a large number of services has been devolved to district and urban authorities in order to increase people's participation in the decision-making process, and to make decisions more transparent and public officers more accountable. Central ministries provide technical expertise to district administrators in preparing their three-year expenditure planning frameworks consistent with resource availability.

The PAF is implemented according to guidelines established by the MFPED and the line ministries. All line ministries are supposed to produce quarterly progress reports to ascertain the extent to which the PAF is being implemented. In order for PAF resources to be used effectively, 5% are directed toward ensuring that the funds are used properly. The following government agencies are involved in the monitoring of these resources:
- Directorate of Accounts;
- Auditor General;
- Public Accounts Committee;
- Inspectorate Department under the Ministry of Local Government;
- Inspector General of Government (IGG).

G. PERCEIVED STRENGTHS AND WEAKNESSES OF THE PEAP

1. Strengths

- The revised PEAP 2000 went through a wide consultative process involving government officials, NGOs and civil society. As a result, the people of Uganda can claim ownership of the program.
- The PEAP is not an end in itself but rather a process that continues to accommodate input from, and is shaped by, information from National Household Surveys conducted by the Uganda Bureau of Statistics

(UBOS); from poverty participatory assessments by the UPPAP; from sector plans and from research findings by individuals or research institutions. These updates make sure the PEAP remains relevant to situations on the ground.

- The PEAP is a forward-looking plan (1997 to 2017) and provides a holistic approach to poverty reduction.
- The debt-relief funds arising from the HIPC Initiative are channelled to the PAF, where they are made available to key poverty reducing sectors. These funds, by agreement with donors, are protected from budget cuts and from diversion.

2. Weaknesses

- There are tremendous difficulties involved in attempting to cost the PEAP. The process of drawing up the PEAP did not involve careful consideration of resource constraints. Prioritizing will have to continue during the implementation process so that the actions taken fit within the resource constraints.
- The MTEF is intended to guide all public expenditure decisions, including the use of resources committed by donors. However, some donor project financing is still not fully incorporated into the MTEF process and is therefore not fully consistent with sector development strategies and the implied allocation of financial resources.

Table 6.   Long-term expenditure framework resource projections – low and high scenarios

Resource scenario	Low	High
GDP growth	5.0%	8.0%
Increase in tax/GDP ratio per year	0.2%	0.2%
Increase in aid (real US$) per year	2.5%	5.0%
Increase in resources (in billions of Uganda shillings)		
5 years	600	950
10 years	1400	2400
PEAP financing gap (in billions of Uganda shillings)		
5 years	1124	774
10 years	324	(676)
Memo		
Tax/GDP ratio after 5 years	12.8	12.8
Aid/GDP ratio after 5 years	10.6	10.4

Source: Government of Uganda, PEAP, 2000.

- All sectors have yet to come up with proper targets and monitorable indicators needed to evaluate their performance in terms of the achievement of PEAP goals.
- Trade issues were marginalized in drawing up the PEAP and yet are key to the country's future economic growth and the fight to reduce poverty.
- There is often a lack of action to implement stated policy objectives arising out of the PEAP and the revision process.
- Crosscutting issues such as gender, AIDS and the environment are acknowledged but are not well incorporated into the planning framework.
- Security and public administration continue to command large budgetary shares despite being non-priority areas.

The current PEAP, which serves as Uganda's PRSP, has a funding gap (between proposed expenditures and available financing) of 1,200 billion Ugandan shillings (US$706 million).[4] Table 6 shows that the PEAP is affordable in the long term but only with predictable grants from the donor community. The gap between costs and available resources will be reduced by:

- increasing the proportion of donor financing via the budget;
- improving tax administration;
- switching spending to areas more directly associated with poverty reduction;
- increasing the prospects for achieving the high case growth target by implementing the Medium-Term Competitiveness Strategy (MTCS) and the Plan for Modernization of Agriculture (PMA).

The eventual exit from aid dependence will be based on revenues generated as a result of economic growth, and the share of the budget funded by donors should decline steadily if growth is maintained. Nevertheless, for the foreseeable future, there will continue to be a case for increased levels of budget support to fund the PEAP. The commitment should be seen as one for the long term.

H.   PEAP TARGETS FOR POVERTY REDUCTION

Appendix C summarizes the main medium- and long-term output/outcome targets for each sector and assesses the implications of what would happen if funding for a particular program remained at the 2000-2001 budgeted level. The detailed figures are the result of extensive consultation with the relevant line ministries, and all the estimates were discussed with senior management teams of the relevant ministries (Uganda 2000a).

---

4. Using an exchange rate of 1,700 Ugandan shillings per $US.

IV. UGANDAN VIEWS ON CONDITIONALITY

This section discusses public and private sector views (and those of other entities) on the conditionality associated with the PRSP and the Poverty Reduction and Growth Facility (PRGF).

A. GOVERNMENT

Government officials claim that the decision of whether or not to reform is solely domestic. Conditionality can tip the balance in favour of a reform program but cannot by itself induce the reforms. When the government believes that conditions facilitate the objectives of a program, the conditionality can come to reflect a negotiated understanding between the government and the donors. The conditionality then becomes part of a consensus-building process where the government and the donors together design the reforms. Such consensus-oriented conditionality is characterizing the Uganda reform program more and more (Holmgren et al. 1999).

With secured government ownership, conditionality has tended to become less relevant. According to a key architect of Uganda's reform program, sound economic management should not be driven, or even constrained, by conditionalities attached to donor assistance (Tumusiime-Mutebile 1995). Conditionality could, however, have negative effects if loans and credits are overloaded with conditions.

B. NON-GOVERNMENTAL ORGANIZATIONS

Holmgren et al. (1999) found that several NGOs and private sector representatives believe that the Government of Uganda has had to accept conditionalities in order to receive financial aid. According to them, "The government owns the reform program but it is based on IMF/WB conditionality rather than local participation. The government adapts to the donors' priorities and there are still significant policy conditions" (Holmgren et al. 1999, p. 39). Some NGOs were, at the same time, grateful for the donor conditionality in cases like the social sector spending targets linked to the HIPC Initiative, but, they also criticized donors for not sticking to their conditions and for being too weak in punishing non-fulfilment of conditions.

The premier crusader against debt, the Uganda Debt Network (UDN),[5] carried out civil-society regional consultations on the PEAP revision in April

---

5. The UDN is an advocacy and lobbying coalition of NGOs, institutions and individuals formed in 1996. It was formed as a result of civil-society concerns that Uganda's debt burden had reached unsustainable levels, which had serious adverse implications for social development.

Table 7.   Regional views on debt management

Eastern Region (Iganga)	**Priority sectors for borrowed funds** Government should limit borrowing to poverty eradication programs such as agriculture research, irrigation and small-scale industries. **Government's role in debt management** Increase public awareness on debt to improve monitoring. Involve civil-society organizations (CSOs) in addition to statutory organs. **CSOs/NGOs' roles in debt management** Complement government efforts to educate the public about debt.
South Western Region (Mbarara)	**Priority sectors for borrowed funds** Government should borrow for strategic programs such as education and health. **Government's role in debt management** Ensure that the current debt levels are well managed. Involve all stakeholders, grassroots upward, in monitoring.
Southern Region (Masaka)	**Priority sectors for borrowed funds** Government should take loans that have no strings attached and use them for agricultural development, health, education and infrastructure development. **Government's role in debt management** Educate the country about its indebtedness. **The role of the community** Be involved in planning and monitoring the use of borrowed funds.
Northern Region (Soroti)	**Priority sectors for borrowed funds** Agricultural research, education, health and security, environment and infrastructure. **Government's role in debt management** Promote transparency and accountability in debt management. Legislate to control debt. Keep proper records, involve all stakeholders in monitoring debt.
Western Region (Kabarole)	**Priority sectors for borrowed funds** Agriculture, environment, mining, small-scale industries, education, health and defense sectors. **Government's role in debt management** Promote bottom-up monitoring. Take loan repayment seriously. Put these funds to proper use.
Central Region (Kampala)	**Priority sector** Health, water and sanitation, agriculture, social infrastructure, security, rural electrification and credit schemes.

Source: "Revision of the Poverty Eradication Action Plan (PEAP)," Civil Society Regional Consultations.

2000. Among other things, views were sought on the PEAP's primary goal – the creation of a framework for economic growth and transformation. Based on this goal, among other actions, the government undertook to exercise prudent debt management, focussing public expenditure on poverty eradication. In this regard, government aims are in line with the conditionality for a PRSP, which in Uganda's case, is the PEAP. The results from the regional consultations appear in table 7.

From table 7 one can conclude that, with regard to debt and borrowing, citizens agree that the government should borrow to finance essential sectors of the economy. They identify agriculture, health, education and infrastructure as the top priority for borrowed funds. Small-scale industries and security were also mentioned in at least two regions. However, people demand transparency, accountability and involvement (through their representatives) in contracting and use of borrowed funds. They cite corruption, embezzlement of borrowed/public resources, and fraud as the real problems behind the debt burden, and want to see them addressed with more resolve.

C.   KEY INFORMANTS

The author also undertook a limited survey of key informants from government, NGOs and academia to elicit their views on the conditionality of a PRSP in order to qualify for HIPC debt relief. The UDN was especially sought out because of its relevance to the debt issue. It has undertaken to publicize and educate average Ugandans about the relevance of the debt burden to their livelihood. In this campaign, special radio programs have been sponsored during which ordinary Ugandans are invited to call in and air their views on the topic of debt. The following are some results of the calling.

- Most callers expressed ignorance in this area and did not understand how the country got into this mess in the first place.
- Others wonder if any measures are being taken to rectify the situation and ensure that mistakes are not repeated.
- Many are not sure about the benefits that accrue from debt relief and are worried that the funds may get diverted.

A session with a key government official in the Macroeconomics Department of the MFPED also confirmed that many people (including those considered to be enlightened) do not understand how debt relief under the HIPC Initiative works. Some have anti-IMF sentiments and are quick to write off or oppose any program with the IMF. Others, such as the UDN, are more objective but do not seem to differentiate between bad debt accumulated in the past and what is being contracted now. That is, they do not differentiate

between debt that is cautiously acquired and desirable, and the careless borrowing of the 1980s.

Strong views were expressed with regard to which sectors the HIPC relief
should be applied to. It was argued that debt relief was necessary in the first
place because poor countries were unable to sustain debt-service payments,
likely due to poor export earnings. So, when relief is granted and the conditionality requires that it be channelled to social sectors instead of directly productive ones, it comes off as a contradiction.

V. UGANDA'S STRATEGY FOR FUTURE BORROWING

This section lays out the country's debt strategy, which is designed to avoid
overindebtedness in the future.

A.   GOVERNMENT DEBT STRATEGY

Uganda's debt strategy is presented as going well beyond requests for additional relief from creditors. It involves the implementation of a number of
strategic plans by government. These consist primarily of efforts to maintain
the implementation of economic reforms that have led to sustained growth in
recent years. These efforts are spelled out in policies relating to improved debt
management and monitoring, new borrowing strategies, improved management and fiscal sustainability.

B.   IMPROVED DEBT MANAGEMENT

Under the existing debt strategy, the government of Uganda has taken the following steps to improve the institutional arrangements for contracting,
recording and monitoring external debt:

- It reactivated and now maintains a complete computerized database of its
  external debt in the Bank of Uganda.
- It analyses its debt portfolio and profile in semi-annual reports.
- It has centralized negotiations on all new loans in the MFPED and
  requires its signature for the validation of new loan contracts. Under the
  new national constitution, adopted in 1995, external borrowing by government or guaranteed by government has to be authorized by parliament.
- It established what it regards as clear and uniformly applied procedures
  for approving and undertaking debt-service payments.
- It has defined clear priorities for service payments, focussing on key multilateral institutions and bilateral creditors, which are major donors providing

large net transfers and has steadfastly stuck to extracting Paris-Club comparable debt-rescheduling terms.

To implement these policies, the Government of Uganda has undertaken a major capacity-building program aimed at:

- ensuring more effective debt management and auditing by the government itself by moving the debt-recording function from the External Debt Management Office (EDMO) in the Bank of Uganda to the Treasury Office of Accounts (TOA);
- providing officials from the EDMO and TOA with extensive training and capacity building in loan recording, analysis and interpretation, and in debt strategy design and implementation;
- upgrading the BOU's monitoring of government-guaranteed debts lent to parastatals and private companies, and of other loans contracted by parastatals but guaranteed by government, during the transition period, in order to eventually transfer this capacity to TOA; and retain a residual role in monitoring foreign exchange debt contracted by the private sector, through returns from commercial banks, for prudential purposes;
- enhancing the coordination by the External Debt Strategy Committee of government agencies in strategy design and implementation;
- strengthening the newly established formal structures for consulting donors locally on debt issues, through quarterly meetings in Kampala with donors that provide debt-relief funds.

C.   NEW BORROWING STRATEGY

Under the existing debt strategy, Uganda has adopted what it considers a highly responsible new borrowing policy, of contracting only loans that have a grant element in excess of 78%. The only exception to this policy are the IMF's PRGF loans, and a US$10 million annual commercial borrowing limit for essential project or trade financing in order to guard against negative contingencies. In addition, it has substantially reduced new debt by scaling down its Public Investment Program to a realistic level, including only "core" priority projects.

Under the updated debt strategy, Uganda intends to go further, and avoid contracting all new loans where possible. This was spelled out in the budget speech of 15 June 1995, by the Minister of Finance and Economic Planning:

"In future, the Government should not incur any further debts unless every effort has been made to secure grant financing. The acceptability of a project will rest both on the project itself and on the quality of the proposed funding."

In addition, the government intends to continue reviewing existing loan-financed projects to identify those that are non-performing and non-disbursing, and to clarify the scope for cancelling, restructuring or scaling down projects (and, where possible, related outstanding debt), for mobilizing grant (rather than loan) financing, or for reallocating undisbursed loan balances to more practicable projects.

D.   ENHANCED RESERVES MANAGEMENT

The Ugandan government and the Bretton Woods institutions strongly feel that reserves worth at least six months of imports are needed to protect against the risk of future sudden negative external shocks. In order to accelerate reserves accumulation, the BOU is enhancing its reserves management strategy, through a three-pronged strategy:

- Minimizing risks by investing in highly regarded international institutions with a top credit rating, such as other central banks, and by matching the currency composition of assets and liabilities in order to minimize exchange risks.
- Maximizing liquidity to allow timely debt servicing by concentrating on short-term deposits such as six-month treasury bills and certificates of deposit (CDs), and using overnight facilities, for example in the U.S. Federal Reserve.
- Maximizing returns, once risk and liquidity requirements have been met.

The BOU, with the assistance of the World Bank and the Federal Reserve of New York, produced the new Reserves Management Strategy. The BOU is also building its own capacity in reserves management through extensive training and staff attachments to other regional and international central banks and financial institutions.

It is believed that debt relief will be an essential complement to this strategy. Every dollar by which debt service is reduced allows an additional dollar to be invested in a slightly less liquid form, earning a greater return; or makes an additional dollar available to guard against external shocks.

E.   ENHANCED FISCAL SUSTAINABILITY

In recent years, the government has improved fiscal sustainability by containing expenditure, while pursing real increases in spending on the social sectors and key infrastructure. It has also increased the mobilization of domestic revenue by broadening the tax base and reforming the tax collecting institutions. These steps have dramatically reduced the budget deficit, to the point where the government is able to make net payments to the banking system, thereby increasing the availability of credit to the private sector, and enhancing stabilization measures to offset the coffee boom.

However, budgetary balance continues to be excessively dependent on donor resources, which are optimistically expected to continue flowing at current levels.

The government is substantially accelerating its recent successes in external debt management, reducing external borrowing, and prudent fiscal sustainability. However, these steps are closely linked with (and are to a large degree, dependent on) enhanced debt-relief measures by the international community.

This dependency on the international community is illustrated by the experience in 1999-2000, when, because of the poor performance of exports and the delay in receiving savings from the Enhanced HIPC Initiative, debt-sustainability ratios worsened relative to the previous year. However, strong loan disbursements in the same year more than compensated for the increase in debt repayments and led to a further increase in the capital account surplus. The significant improvement in the capital account was largely responsible for the improvement in the overall balance of payments in 1999-2000. Official transfers, which were dominated by grants, rebounded strongly, mainly due to donor debt-relief support.

The dependency is also clearly evident in the government's expectation that although its level of expenditure will increase substantially as a result of increased donor support for PEAP programs, the resulting fiscal deficit is entirely consistent with its fiscal strategy (in line with its external debt strategy). This is because the increased deficit will be fully funded by increased inflows of donor grants, highly concessional loans, and additional debt relief made available under the Enhanced HIPC Initiative.

Under this scenario, there will be no recourse to borrowing from the banking system to finance the deficits. The increase in the deficit in the medium term will therefore not undermine macroeconomic stability or the long-term sustainability of public finances (Government of Uganda 2000b).

CONCLUSION

This paper set out to document and evaluate Uganda's debt and debt-relief experiences in light of the HIPC I and HIPC II initiatives. Uganda, while it remains heavily indebted, continues to benefit from generous amounts of debt relief from the international community, especially under the combined HIPC initiatives. This is as a result of Uganda's consistency in implementing structural adjustment programs.

The assistance provided under the original and Enhanced HIPC initiatives is expected to free up significant budget resources for Uganda's poverty-reduction strategy, and thus provide a greater momentum toward achieving the development goals set out in Uganda's PRSP, the PEAP. Average budgetary savings between 2001 and 2015 with HIPC assistance are expected to amount to as much as US$55.5 million a year.

The most recent DSA shows that the NPV of debt-export ratio (a measure of fiscal burden of debt) starts below the required 150% under the Enhanced HIPC Initiative. Without any HIPC assistance, that feat would not be achieved until well after 2015.

In Uganda's case, the conditionality for a PRSP before benefiting from HIPC relief only further strengthened the planning process, and has led to the creation of a special fund, the PAF, to ensure that debt-relief funds are protected and channelled to poverty-reducing priority sectors.

It is necessary to continue adhering to a strict policy concerning new borrowing, which is formalized in the national debt strategy. This will ensure that debt continues to be managed in a competent fashion. Realization of this goal will very much depend on the goodwill of the international community.

REFERENCES

Appleton, S., "Poverty in Uganda, 1999-2000: Preliminary Estimates from the UNHS," Center for the Study of African Economies, University of Oxford, Oxford, UK, 2000.

Edoku, V. E., "Increasing International Financial Cooperation for Development Through Debt: The Case of Uganda," Financing for Development – Hearings with Civil Society, 6-7 November 2000, United Nations, New York, 2000.

Hayuni, J., Trends and Effects of External Public Borrowing: Uganda 1971-1992, MS thesis, Institute of Statistic and Applied Economics, Makerere University, Kamapala, 1995.

Holmgren, T., L. Kasekende, M. Atingi-Ego and D. Ddamulira, "Aid and Reform in Uganda: Country Case Study," Economic Policy Research Center, Research Series No. 23, Makerere University, Kampala, 1999.

IMF and IDA, "Initiative for Heavily Indebted Poor Countries: Second Decision Point Document (Uganda)," International Monetary Fund and the International Development Association, Washington, D.C., 2000.

Kamanyire, M., "External Financing and Economic Performance: The Case of Uganda," Economic Policy Research Center, Research Series No. 14, Kampala, Uganda, 1999.

Mbire, B. and M. Atingi, "Growth and Foreign Debt: The Ugandan Experience," Research Paper 66, The African Economic Research Consortium, Nairobi, Kenya, 1997.

Nyamugasira, W., "Monitoring of the Poverty Eradication Action Plan (PEAP)," a presentation at the Consultative Workshop on the Revision of the PEAP and Public Expenditure Review, Kampala International Conference Center, May 15-16, 2000, p. 7.

Tumusiime-Mutebile, E., "Management of the Reform Program," in Langseth, P., J. Katabor, E. Brett and J. Munene, eds., *Uganda Landmarks in Rebuliding a Nation*, Kampala, Fountain Publishers, 1995.

Uganda, Government of, "A Strategy for Reducing the External Debt of Uganda," unpublished report by the government presented to the international community outlining the country's Enhanced External Debt Strategy, 1995.

_____, *Revised Volume I of the Poverty Eradication Action Plan (PEAP) Final Draft Poverty*, Ministry of Finance, Planning and Economic Development, Kampala, Uganda, 2000a.

_____, *Background to the Budget 2000-2001*, Ministry of Finance, Planning and Economic Development, 2000b.

_____, *Background to the Budget 1994-1995*, Ministry of Finance and Economic Planning, 1994.

Appendix A. Uganda's key public external debt/sustainability indicators, 1998/1999 to 2014/2015

	1998/99	1999/00	2000/01	2001/02	2002/03	2003/04	2004/05	2005/06	2006/07	2007/08	2008/09	2009/10	2010/11	2011/12	2012/13	2013/14	2014/15
NPV of debt-to-export ratio																	
Before HIPC Initiative assistance	248.9	308.3	291.8	278.0	262.3	248.6	232.2	225.0	218.7	211.7	204.2	196.3	188.3	180.6	173.0	165.4	157.7
After original assistance	240.1	261.3	244.8	230.4	214.3	198.4	184.8	173.1	164.3	156.4	149.3	143.0	136.7	130.8	125.0	119.5	113.9
After proposed enhanced assistance	-	138.0	127.9	116.6	108.8	102.0	96.1	90.5	84.4	78.4	72.7	67.6	63.0	59.2	55.8	52.4	49.0
NPV of debt-to-revenue ratio																	
Before HIPC Initiative assistance	286.6	290.6	264.3	240.8	220.1	201.3	188.8	180.9	173.1	164.7	156.0	149.8	143.5	137.0	130.5	123.7	116.8
After original assistance	241.5	246.3	221.7	199.6	179.9	160.7	149.6	139.2	130.0	121.6	1141	109.1	104.2	99.3	94.3	89.4	84.4
After proposed enhanced assistnce	-	16.2	15.0	13.6	12.8	12.0	11.5	10.9	10.2	9.5	8.7	8.1	7.6	7.1	6.6	6.2	5.7
Debt-service ratio 1																	
Before HIPC Initiative assistance	22.4	23.4	18.7	17.5	18.1	16.1	14.6	12.9	12.9	11.8	11.5	11.1	11.1	11.1	10.8	11.0	11.0
After original assistance	14.4	18.1	12.3	11.2	10.6	10.5	11.5	11.1	10.5	9.4	8.6	7.7	7.0	6.9	6.7	6.7	6.7
After proposed enhanced assistance	-	11.1	6.0	5.7	5.6	6.0	7.5	7.5	7.2	6.4	5.8	5.1	4.7	4.7	4.7	4.9	5.0
Debt service-to-revenue ratio																	
Before HIPC Initiative assistance	22.5	22.0	16.9	15.2	15.2	13.1	11.8	10.4	10.2	9.2	8.8	8.5	8.5	8.4	8.2	8.3	8.1
After original assistance	14.5	17.1	11.1	9.7	8.9	8.5	9.3	9.0	8.3	7.3	6.6	5.9	5.3	5.2	5.1	5.0	4.9
After proposed enhanced assistance	-	10.5	5.5	4.9	4.7	4.9	6.1	6.0	5.7	5.0	4.5	3.9	3.5	3.6	3.6	3.7	3.7

Source: IMF and IDA, "Initiative for Heavily Indebted Poor Countries: Second Decision Point Document (Uganda)," Washington, D.C., 2000.

Appendix B. Impact of the HIPC Initiatives on the Debt Service

	Scheduled debt service before HIPC I and II (US$ million)	Scheduled debt service after HIPC II (US$ million)	Total HIPC debt relief (US$ million)	HIPC debt relief (% GNP)	% decrease in scheduled debt service	Debt relief ratio relative to aid ratio (%)	Budgetary saving (debt dividend) (US$ million)	Dividend as a % of social expenditure (1999-2000)	Dividend as a % of total expenditure (1999-2000)
Average (2001-2005)	170.5	67.5	102.9	1.3	60.4	9.7	83.4	13.3	4.6
Average (2001-2015)	216.0	95.4	120.6	1.1	55.8	8.6	55.5	8.9	3.0

Source: Bank of Uganda; North-South Institute.

Appendix C.   Summary of sector targets and implication of remaining at 2000-01 level of activity/investment

Main sector target outputs/outcomes	Implications of remaining at 2000-01 levels of activity/investment*
Roads	
Ten-year main road program fully implemented	Only 90% achieved
Rural network fully rehabilitated and maintained within 5 years	Only 75% rehabilitated/maintained
Plan for modernization of agriculture	
Agricultural advisory service to reach 80% of all households	Only 10-20% of households benefit
Fully fund administrative structures required by Land Act	Implemented in only 6 districts
Reduce adult illiteracy from 48% to 15-20% within 5 years	No significant reduction
Output targets not yet available for rural electrification	
Water for production, environment, forestry, outputs	
Education	
Primary pupil: teacher ratio 40:1	Ratio remains at 50:1
Each primary class to have own classroom within 5 years	10-15 years to complete
Job Evaluation pay increase for primary teachers (72%)	No pay increase
One set of textbooks/pupil (Vol. I and Vol. II) within 5 years	More than 20 years
One government-aided secondary school per sub county	More than 20 years
Construction of 850 community polytechnics within 5 years	
Health	
Support every village health committee	Only 10% of villages
Health Center II in every parish within 5 years	50% without center
Health Center II fully staffed (1 nurse; 2 aides); full drug	Only 1 nurse & 1 aide
Job Evaluation pay increase for medical workers (44%)	No pay increase
Renovation/rehabilitation of hospitals; further upgrade of HC IVs	
Increase spending to $11/person (WHO target $12)	Only $6 per person
Water and sanitation	
100% rural/urban safe water coverage within 10 years	75% safe water coverage after 10 years
Justice/Law and Order	
Doubling police/prison numbers	No increase
Job Evaluation pay increase (83%)	No increase
More detailed output/outcome targets under preparation	
All other sectors in MTEF	
Defence spending remains at 2% of GDP	
Public administration grows in line with population	

* In the absence of any increase in funding or reallocation of existing funds or adoption of cheaper alternative approach, including user fees.

Source: Government of Uganda, *PEAP*, 2000.

The Enhanced HIPC Initiative and Poor Countries: Prospects for a Permanent Exit

John Serieux

Given that 22 of the 41 HIPCs had reached at least their decision point by the end of 2000 (and thus gained eligibility for debt relief worth approximately 50% of the NPV of their existing debt), it can be rightly claimed that the Enhanced HIPC Initiative has succeeded in providing broad access to substantial debt reduction for these countries. However, the question of whether that Initiative offers the framework and amount of debt relief necessary to provide these countries with long-term deliverance from the spectre of unsustainable debt burdens still remains open. Also, given that the Enhanced HIPC Initiative has specifically identified poverty reduction as one of its objectives, the provision of sufficient wherewithal for substantial poverty reduction is also a challenge it must address.

With particular reference to the 22 countries that have reached the decision point, this paper analyses the available data with a view to determining how the HIPC Initiative is meeting those challenges. First, the magnitude of budgetary savings (dividend) from debt relief is estimated, and the sufficiency of these savings for those countries' poverty reduction programs is assessed based on case studies. Second, the expected flow of debt relief is examined *vis-à-vis* the expectations for income and export growth, and the credibility of these expectations evaluated. Finally, the ability of the program to reduce or mitigate the risk factors that these countries face is examined. The paper concludes with an assessment of the program's strengths and limitations, as suggested by the evidence thus far, and some ideas for action beyond HIPC debt relief.

However, this paper abstracts from the issue of the sufficiency of debt relief for removing these countries' debt overhangs.[1] Though one can perhaps establish some benchmarks for determining what constitutes a debt overhang (Serieux 2001), there is no purely objective or unequivocal procedure for determining the size of the debt overhang a priori. Though these countries clearly could not possibly have repaid those debts at less than bruising developmental costs (if at all), any estimate of the size of the overhang would have to be preceded by a clear enunciation of what constitutes acceptable costs, as well as some estimation of the countries' willingness to undergo these costs – a task which is beyond the scope of this paper.

I. DEBT RELIEF AND POVERTY REDUCTION

The movement from the original HIPC Initiative of 1996 to the Enhanced HIPC Initiative did not only mean broader, deeper, and faster debt relief, it also instituted a more explicit link between debt relief and poverty reduction. The original HIPC Initiative of 1996 conditioned debt relief quite broadly on the debtor country's demonstration "through its track record [under adjustment], an ability to put to good use whatever debt relief would be provided" (Boote and Thugge 1999, p. 11). The Enhanced HIPC Initiative, however, requires debtor countries to have a poverty reduction strategy in place – articulated in a *Poverty Reduction Strategy Paper* (PRSP) – by the decision point of the Initiative, and to have made substantial progress in implementing that strategy by the completion point (Andrews et. al. 1999). But that commitment to poverty reduction is not limited to the debtor countries. Both creditor and debtor countries, through the OECD/DAC commitments of 1996 (OECD 1996, 2000) and the resolutions of the Millennium Summit (UN 2000) have also committed to global poverty reduction. In effect, the Enhanced HIPC Initiative has been made into an instrument for advancing this larger global objective of poverty reduction.

Implicit in this responsibility for advancing the poverty-reduction agenda was the presumption that:
- debt relief amounts would be substantial;
- all amounts not paid on debt servicing would be available for debt relief;

---

1. Strictly defined, a debt overhang is that part of a country's debt which is not expected to be repaid. In the context of poor countries, however, a more suitable definition might be that part of the debt which the country cannot reasonably be expected to repay without incurring a significant development cost.

- the resources thus released for poverty reduction would be close to the amounts necessary for meeting the international development goals.

As we show below, while the effect of debt relief on scheduled debt-service levels will be substantial, particularly over the next few years, the budgetary effect, in terms of the amount of new resources released as a result of lower debt-service payments, will be somewhat smaller. Further, the resource requirements for the rate of poverty reduction that gives countries a chance of meeting international targets appear to be well above that which can be provided by debt relief.

A.   THE DEBT DIVIDEND

As table 1 shows, for 19 of the 22 countries that have reached the decision point of the HIPC Initiative (i.e. their likely debt-reduction amounts have been determined, and they can receive interim debt relief), debt relief will imply a substantial reduction in debt-service levels.[2] On average, these countries' scheduled debt service payments will fall by 46.1% over the next 5 years (2001-2005) and 35.9% over the next 15 years (2001-2015). The microeconomy of São Tomé and Principe will experience the largest decline in scheduled debt-service payments, over both the next 5 years and the next 15 years (78.8% and 72.8%, respectively). Senegal will experience the smallest decline in its debt service payments over the next 5 years (22.5%), and Honduras the smallest over the next 15 years (18.5%).

As a proportion of GDP, debt-relief amounts will average 2.9% over the next 5 years and 2.2% over the next 15 years. Debt-relief amounts will be equivalent to more than 10% of the GDP of São Tomé and Principe over both the next 5 years and the next 15 years. It will, however, amount to less than 1% of GDP for Senagal when averaged over the next 5 years, and will be a similarly small proportion of GDP for eight of the 19 countries when averaged over the next 15 years (table 1).

While changes in the stock of debt, or changes in future debt-service requirements, are the variations that count when trying to determine how debt relief affects countries' debt-related obligations, these adjustments do not necessarily translate into budgetary savings for the debtor country. Despite the fact that HIPCs paid an average of 23.4% of their export proceeds in debt-service payments over the 1990s (versus an average of 17.3% for developing

---

2. The data in table 1 (and the other tables) cover only 19 of the 22 countries because the relevant data for three of these countries (Guinea, Guinea-Bissau and Rwanda) were not provided in their *Debt Sustainabililty Analyses* (DSAs).

Table 1. Debt indicators for 19 post-decision-point HIPC countries

Country	Benin	Bolivia	Burkina Faso	Cameroon	The Gambia	Guyana	Honduras	Madagascar	Malawi	Mali
Debt service (US$ millions)										
1994-1998	50.40	415.10	49.00	474.30	27.70	116.00	512.10	108.70	91.10	91.20
2001-2005	40.50	257.40	37.00	286.80	11.40	41.20	224.90	64.20	50.80	65.40
2001-2015	49.80	462.70	53.50	343.30	17.10	51.10	343.30	106.60	61.70	78.70
Debt relief under HIPC (US$ millions)										
2001-2005	24.40	158.80	37.80	97.60	8.60	60.20	165.80	53.40	47.90	48.60
2001-2015	22.10	113.90	29.70	81.90	6.20	48.20	78.00	60.10	50.10	44.30
Debt relief under HIPC/GDP (%)										
2001-2005	0.81	1.53	1.09	0.88	1.53	6.99	2.49	1.08	2.33	1.41
2001-2015	0.59	0.92	0.70	0.57	0.97	4.77	1.11	0.90	1.97	1.06
Debt dividend (US$ millions)										
2001-2005	9.90	157.70	12.00	187.50	16.30	74.80	287.20	44.50	40.30	25.80
2001-2015	0.60	-47.60	-4.50	131.00	10.60	64.90	168.80	2.10	29.40	12.50
Dividend/flow of debt relief (%)										
2001-2005	40.70	99.30	31.80	192.10	190.00	124.20	173.20	83.20	84.10	53.10
2001-2015	2.90	-41.70	-15.30	160.00	170.90	134.70	216.60	3.60	58.70	28.20
Debt dividend/GDP										
2001-2005	0.30	1.50	0.40	1.70	3.00	8.70	4.50	0.90	2.00	0.80
2001-2015	0.10	-0.10	0.00	1.00	1.70	6.20	2.30	0.20	1.30	0.40

Table 1. (continued)

Country	Mauritania	Mozambique	Nicaragua	Niger	Senegal	São Tome and Principe	Tanzania	Uganda	Zambia	AVERAGE
Country Debt service (US$ m)										
1994-1998	112.50	127.10	258.00	60.20	274.60	3.00	219.70	150.90	268.40	170.20
2001-2005	54.50	53.60	141.30	36.20	172.40	1.40	148.80	67.50	174.00	99.40
2001-2015	49.70	73.70	140.80	31.50	135.30	2.40	206.10	95.40	137.30	102.80
Debt relief under HIPC (US$ m)										
2001-2005	59.90	114.80	193.00	41.70	50.10	5.10	122.40	102.90	259.40	111.20
2001-2015	38.30	123.90	194.20	42.50	31.40	6.40	103.00	120.60	173.80	99.50
Debt relief under HIPC/GDP (%)										
2001-2005	4.76	2.17	7.20	1.72	0.83	10.36	1.19	1.10	6.33	3.90
2001-2015	2.59	1.77	5.79	1.45	0.46	10.48	0.79	0.98	3.57	3.20
Debt dividend (US$ m)										
2001-2005	58.00	73.50	116.70	24.00	102.20	1.60	70.90	83.40	94.40	70.80
2001-2015	62.80	53.40	117.20	28.70	139.30	0.60	13.60	55.50	131.10	67.40
Dividend/gross flows of debt relief (%)										
2001-2005	96.80	64.00	60.40	57.50	204.20	31.60	57.90	81.00	36.40	63.70
2001-2015	163.80	43.10	60.40	67.50	443.00	9.60	13.20	46.10	75.40	67.80
Debt dividend/GDP										
2001-2005	4.50	1.40	4.30	1.00	1.70	3.50	0.70	0.90	2.30	2.00
2001-2015	3.80	0.80	3.40	0.90	1.80	1.40	0.20	0.50	2.50	1.40

Source: World Bank, *World Development Indicators* (2000); *Global Development Finance* (2000); IDA and IMF, *Debt Sustainability Analyses for the 19 Countries.*

Table 2.   Aid and debt relief for 19 post-decision-point HIPC countries

Country	Aid per capita (US$) 1994-98	Debt relief per capita (US$)		Debt dividend per capita (US$)		Debt relief as a % of aid (both in per capita terms)		Debt dividend as a % of aid (both in per capita terms)	
		2001-2005	2001-2015	2001-2005	2001-2015	2001-2005	2001-2015	2001-2005	2001-2015
Benin	44.8	3.6	2.9	1.4	0.2	8.0	6.5	3.1	0.4
Bolivia	90.8	17.9	11.8	17.9	-3.1	19.7	13.0	19.7	-3.4
Burkina Faso	41.2	3.1	2.2	1.0	-0.2	7.5	5.3	2.4	-0.5
Cameroon	37.3	6.0	4.5	11.6	7.4	16.1	12.1	31.1	19.8
The Gambia	40.3	6.0	4.0	11.5	6.5	14.9	9.9	28.5	16.1
Guyana	157.8	68.3	53.4	84.9	70.9	43.3	33.8	53.8	44.9
Honduras	57.5	23.2	10.6	40.9	22.7	40.3	18.4	71.1	39.5
Madagascar	32.8	3.2	3.1	2.6	0.3	9.8	9.5	7.9	0.9
Malawi	43.5	4.0	3.7	3.4	2.3	9.2	8.5	7.8	5.3
Mali	129.2	4.0	3.2	2.1	1.0	3.1	2.5	1.6	0.8
Mauritania	99.2	20.7	12.2	19.9	19.0	20.9	12.3	20.1	19.2
Mozambique	63.6	6.1	5.8	3.9	2.6	9.6	9.1	6.1	4.1
Nicaragua	139.1	35.3	32.0	20.9	18.9	25.4	23.0	15.0	13.6
Niger	32.4	3.4	3.1	2.0	2.0	10.5	9.6	6.2	6.2
Senegal	66.1	4.8	2.8	9.9	11.7	7.3	4.2	15.0	17.7
Sao Tome and Principe	363.6	32.0	35.3	10.1	3.8	8.8	9.7	2.8	1.0
Tanzania	30.6	3.4	2.5	1.9	0.4	11.1	8.2	6.2	1.3
Uganda	36.1	4.3	4.3	3.5	2.1	11.9	11.9	9.7	5.8
Zambia	95.1	23.8	14.6	8.7	10.6	25.0	15.4	9.1	11.1
Average	**84.3**	**14.4**	**11.2**	**13.6**	**9.4**	**17.1**	**13.2**	**16.1**	**11.2**

Source: World Bank, *World Development Indicators* (2000); *Global Development Finance* (2000); IDA and IMF, *Debt Sustainability Analyses for the 19 Countries.*

countries generally), with few exceptions, they were unable to service all of their debts. In fact, Serieux (2000) estimates that they covered only 44.5% of debt service falling due over the period 1990-1994. Thus, a fall in debt-service obligations will translate into a fall in realized savings on debt-service payments only if it succeeds in reducing debt-service obligations to below actual repayment levels.[3] This saving, or debt-relief dividend, as it is often called, is estimated in table 1 by subtracting post-debt-relief obligations from average debt-service payments over the period 1994-1998.[4]

The estimated budgetary savings (dividends) after debt relief are, not surprisingly, smaller than actual debt-reduction amounts, and the proportion decreases over time. As table 1 indicates, the debt dividend is expected to average US$77.9 million, or 92.7% of debt-relief amounts, over the next 5 years, but only US$51.1 million or (70.9% of debt-relief amounts) over the next 15 years (2001-2015). In effect, over the next 15 years, assuming that countries meet all scheduled debt-service payments, the average reduction in debt-service payments, relative to debt-service levels over the 1994-1998 period, will be 30% smaller than the amount of debt relief received.[5] As a result, these countries can expect to save only 2% of (World Bank/IMF estimated) GDP over the next 5 years, and 1.4% over the next 15 years.

One can perhaps gain a better appreciation of the relative impact of the flow of HIPC debt relief by comparing it to the aid flows received by these countries. Table 2 presents the values of per capita aid flows from 1994-98 and compares these to expected debt-relief flows per capita. The numbers suggest that debt-relief flows will generally be only a modest fraction of the aid flows these countries received over the last few years. Over the next 5 years, the gross budgetary savings from debt relief will be as high as 53.8% of previous aid

---

3. Since that time (1990-94) there has been significant bilateral debt reduction (Paris Club and non-Paris Club) for most countries. Thus it would take less than a 55.6% average reduction in scheduled debt service under the HIPC Initiative to reduce scheduled debt service below actual amounts.

4. This method implicitly assumes the counterfactual (what would have occurred in the absence of debt relief) to be that these countries would have continued to pay approximately the same average amount in debt-service payments over the next few years. Though simplistic, this counterfactual is not far removed from observed behaviour – countries' debt-service levels have tended to be flat over the last few years. Though extending this over the next 15 years is a stretch, most other counterfactuals would require assumptions about growth, exports, payment ability etc. that would probably be no more credible when extended this far into the future.

5. Even this amount exaggerates the effect of HIPC debt reduction per se because the definition used includes savings from traditional debt relief and savings that would have occurred even without debt relief because of reductions in scheduled debt-service amounts over time, and these were sometimes substantial (as in the case of Senegal).

levels for Guyana, but as low as 2.4% for Burkina Faso. For the 19 (post decision point) countries in table 2, it will average only 16.1% over that period.
That average falls to 11.2% when the 15-year span (2001-2015) is considered
(with a high of 39.5% for Guyana and a low of −3.4% for Bolivia).[6]

What this implies generally, is that, with a few exceptions, debt relief represents only a modest increase in resource flows to these countries. If, as is often
feared, other resource flows are reduced as creditor countries and agencies
attempt to reduce the expansionary effect of debt relief on their budgets, the
resource-enhancing effect of debt reduction will be seriously compromised
and, for some countries, possibly negated. In fact, it will take only an 8%
reduction in aid flows (on average) over the next 5 years to cancel out half the
net-flow effect of debt relief.

B.   THE POVERTY REDUCTION DEFICIT

There is no necessary correlation between the resources needed to generate
the rate of poverty reduction that is required for meeting internationally
agreed targets (such as that of halving world poverty by 2015) and the poverty
reduction engendered by debt relief. It is the level and depth of poverty existing in each country that will determine the rate of improvement in material
circumstances necessary to pull half of the disadvantaged out of poverty,
whereas debt-relief levels are related to debt ratios that have little direct relation to poverty. In addition, as we have shown, debt-relief amounts tend to
overstate the resource implications of debt reduction. It is, therefore, not surprising that, for countries that have estimated their resource needs for poverty
reduction, the resource flows associated with debt relief are insufficient to
bridge the financing gap between traditionally available resources (domestic
budgetary resources and aid) and required resources. In short, a financing gap
continues to exist even after the dividend from debt relief is accounted for.

Andersen and Nina (2001), in this volume, describe how Bolivian municipalities have developed poverty reduction focused municipal development
plans in keeping with the country's PRSP. The costing of these plans, when
extrapolated for the whole country, project an annual financing requirement
of US$636 million (table 3). Traditional budgetary resources (municipalities
own income and traditional transfers from the central government) will only
cover 47% of these costs. The debt-relief dividend (in the form of additional
transfers from the central government) is expected to cover an additional

---

6. The negative number implies that over the period the average scheduled debt-service
level will exceed pre-HIPC levels.

Table 3.   Aggregate annual budget for the municipal development
             plans of Bolivia (2001-2005)

	US$ millions	% of costs
Annual costs of Municipal Development Plans (2001-2005)	636	100
Total funding for Municipal Development Plans	527	83
Debt relief	159	25
Municipalities' own income	94	15
Regular transfers (not including debt relief)	204	32
Natural gas royalties	70	11
Poverty Reduction Deficit	109	17

Source: Andersen and Nina (2001).
Note: Numbers are extrapolated to cover all municipalities.

25%. This leaves 28% of the poverty reduction budget to be financed from other sources. Luckily, Bolivia expects windfall gains from increased natural gas exports (derived from recently discovered deposits). This new income will cover an additional 11% of the cost of poverty reduction (if the income can be so directed). But this still leaves a financing gap of US$109 million, or 19% of the national poverty reduction budget (table 3). Given that Bolivia's debt-relief dividend will become negative after 2006 (debt-service payments are expected to exceed pre-debt-relief levels), this financing gap is expected to widen over time.

Nicaragua's PRSP estimates that the cost of planned poverty reduction initiatives over the next three years will be just over US$1.1 billion (Government of Nicaragua 2000), or an average of US$379 million a year. Even with the proceeds of debt relief, more than half of that portfolio does not have assured financing (Castro-Monge, 2001). In effect, poverty reduction needs are, thus far, well ahead of resource commitments.

Despite the fact that, in its Poverty-Reduction Fund, Uganda has a well-developed machinery for channelling both the savings from debt relief and other development assistance into poverty reduction, Mijumbi (2001) shows that, this country too, faces a poverty-reduction deficit. Budgeted spending on PEAP activities for the fiscal year 2000-2001 was US$1.25 billion.[7] This budget is fully funded by locally generated resources, debt-relief dividends, and foreign assistance. However, if all scheduled PEAP related activities had been implemented, the budget would have expanded to US$1.95 billion. Thus, in

---

7. Using an exchange rate of US$1 to 1700 Ugandan shillings.

the 2000-2001 budget, an additional US$700 million worth of poverty-reduc-
tion activities have essentially been delayed for lack of immediate funding
(Mijumbi 2001). The budget reflects, in effect, a funding gap equivalent to
36% of planned spending on poverty reduction. Further, this funding gap is
not limited to a single year but is expected to last several years into the future
even under the best-case scenario.

**Table 4.   Alternative resource mobilization scenarios for financing
poverty reduction in Uganda**

Condition	Low scenario	High scenario
GDP growth rate (%)	5.0	8.0
Annual increase in tax revenue as a percentage GDP	0.2	0.2
Rate of increase in (real US$) ODA (%)	2.5	5.0
Expected new resources (US$ million)		
in 5 years	353.0	559.0
in 10 years	824.0	1,412.0
Expected financing gap (US$ million)		
in 5 years	661.0	455.0
in 10 years	190.0	-398.0

Source: Mijumbi (2001).
Note: Exchange rate used is 1,700 Ugandan shillings per US$1.

Table 4 presents two scenarios (reflecting pessimistic and optimistic
assumptions) and their implications for the funding gap. The low scenario
(which assumes only modest GDP growth and the continuation of the current
rate of increase in ODA receipts) would leave Uganda with a poverty-reduction funding gap of US$661 million after 5 years and US$190 million after 10
years. The more optimistic scenario (which anticipates an increase in growth
levels and a doubling of the rate of growth in ODA) would still leave Uganda
with a funding gap after 5 years (of US$455 million) but a surplus of US$398
million after 10 years. Thus, even with an acceleration of growth in both per
capita income and ODA receipts, Uganda still does not expect to be able to
meet the annual expenditure requirements of its poverty reduction program
within 5 years. It hopes to do so in 10 years only if the most optimistic expectations are met.

Thus the experience of a sample of these countries suggests that HIPC debt
relief will only release a fraction of the resources necessary for the poverty
reduction envisaged by these countries' poverty reduction strategies. Yet,
these programs have poverty reduction targets that are at or below the internationally agreed target (of halving world poverty by 2015). Also, since the

dividend from debt relief will become smaller over time, that funding gap will widen.

II. MAINTAINING SUSTAINABLE DEBT LEVELS

Having defined a sustainable debt level as the ratio of debt to exports of 150% or less (or, alternatively, a debt-to-government revenue ratio of 250%), the Enhanced HIPC Initiatives determine debt-reduction amounts, and the timing of debt-relief flows, so as to keep countries' debt levels below that threshold into the foreseeable future. As figure 1 shows, based on their estimates of expected export and income growth in these countries (and, therefore, their expected accumulation of new debt), these countries are not only expected to stay below the sustainability threshold, they are expected to experience decreasing debt-export ratios well into the future.

**Figure 1. Average debt service/exports ratio for
19 post-decision-point HIPCs**

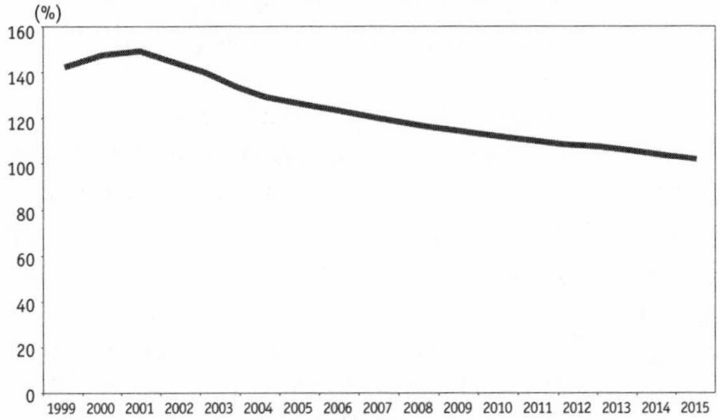

Source: IDA and IMF, *The Challenge of Maintaining Long-term External Debt Sustainability*, 2001.

If current projections materialise, the average debt-to-export ratio of the countries that had reached the decision point by the end of 2000 will be only 95% in 2015. However, as figures 2 and 3 suggest, fulfilling these projections would require truly exceptional all-round performances by these countries. They would have to grow at an overall average (annual) rate of at least 5.4% for the period 2001-2015, and average annual export growth would have to reach or exceed 7.9%. By comparison, these countries' average annual growth

Figure 2. Real and projected GDP growth rates
for 19 HIPCs

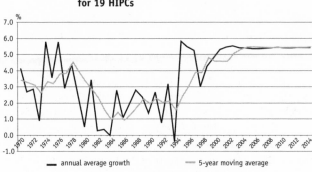

Source: *Debt Sustainability Analyses* (DSAs) for 19 of 22 post-decision point countries as of April 2001
(DSAs for Guinea, Guinea Bissau and Rwanda did not contain the relevant data).

in income over the period 1970-1998 was only 2.7%, and even during a brief
spurt of fast growth in the late 1970s, they only managed an average growth
rate of 4.2% annually. Likewise, the historical export growth rate (1970-1999)
is only 3.9% and the minor export boom of the early to mid 1990s only produced an average growth rate of 5.8%.

Clearly, these estimates are well above anything that these countries have
experienced over even a 5-year period. It is highly unrealistic to presume that
they could sustain such growth rates over 15 years. The (likely) failure to meet
those targets will affect debt-service levels, though the exact effect on debt
ratios cannot readily be gauged.[8] What is certain, however, is that the decline
in debt-to-export ratios envisaged in figure 1 will not materialise.

Lower than expected growth rates will mean lower export quantities that
translate directly into higher debt export ratios. The Bretton Woods institutions (the managers of the Enhanced HIPC Initiative) recognize this. They
show in IDA/IMF 2001 (figure 3) that export growth rates at historical levels
would keep these countries above the sustainability threshold. Lower exports
would also mean a larger external financing gap[9] for these countries and thus
a need for greater resource inflows and, as a result, increased debt flows. Lower
GDP growth rates also translate into significantly greater debt flows, and thus

---

8. Among other things, it would depend on the related effect on savings, the proportion of
net inflows that are debt flows, the degree of concessionality of new debt flows, etc.

9. The difference between foreign exchange earnings and the amount of imports necessary
to prevent a further reduction in domestic output.

Figure 3. **Realized and projected export growth rates for 19 HIPCs**

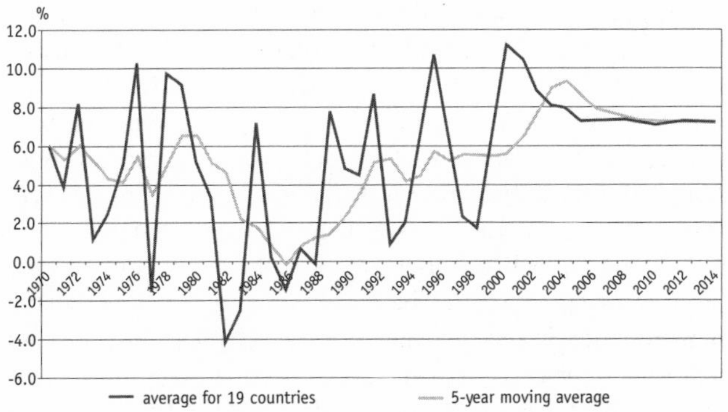

— average for 19 countries   — 5-year moving average

Source: *Debt Sustainability Analyses* (DSAs) for 19 of 22 post-decision point countries as of April 2001 (DSAs for Guinea, Guinea Bissau and Rwanda did not contain the relevant data).

debt ratios, because of both larger internal resource gaps (the difference between domestic savings and investment, and government revenues and expenditure) and a greater need for funding to support the increased poverty reduction challenges that result.

The DSA for these countries also envisage an increase in the concessionality of new borrowing (compared to the average concessionality of current debt stocks) equivalent to a near doubling of the grant element from a simple average of 30% to 58% (IDA/IMF 2001, table 5). While this target may not seem unreasonable at first glance, the fact that most of the new borrowing is expected to come from multilateral financial institutions whose concessional lending (with the exception of the IDA) does not generally meet that criteria, implicitly assumes that there will be an increase in bilateral grant funding to compensate. However, though the grant element of bilateral funding has increased, bilateral funding itself was on a declining trend through most of the 1990s. It would need a significant reversal of that trend to fulfill those expectations. Further, if the need for financing is higher than anticipated, as suggested above, these countries' ability to meet those criteria becomes even less likely, and thus the potential rate of increase in debt ratios will be even higher.

III. REDUCING THE RISK OF FUTURE CRISES

Besides attempting to ensure sufficient debt relief to keep these countries below the sustainability threshold, the Enhanced HIPC Initiative works to reduce their risk of returning to overindebtedness (IDA/IMF 2001). First, these countries are required, through adjustment programs, to provide a record of good fiscal management, to maintain a stable macroeconomic environment, and to implement structural changes in the economy. Second, conditionalities relating to governance (political institutions, the judiciary, corruption etc.) are attached to both the structural adjustment program and the decision point agreements. The expectation is that these changes in the policy environment will increase the country's chances for faster growth, and thus increase its debt carrying capacity and encourage more rapid poverty reduction (IDA/World Bank 2001). In addition, the policy and governance risk generally associated with the uncontrolled accumulation of debt (poor fiscal management, corruption, etc.) can be mitigated.

While it is certainly true that good domestic economic management and governance practices will reduce the policy-related risks associated with the build-up of debt, these are not the only risks related to country type. Table 5 presents the results of a (cross-country) regression of a set of policy and governance related variables (fiscal deficit, inflation and corruption) and a set of structural variables (country size, primary commodity export specialization, and the literacy rate) on the debt-to-export ratios (in 1985 and 1998) of a group of low- and middle-income countries (including most of the post-decision-point countries).[10] The results suggest that structural characteristics were as important in predicting indebtedness as policy variables, if not more so. In fact, among the policy variables, only inflation was significant (though strongly so), but all of the structural variables were significant in at least one of the two equations. This suggests that, though weak policy frameworks tended to increase countries' chances of becoming heavily indebted, small, least developed economies, dependent on the export of primary commodities, were particularly likely to become heavily indebted.

In fact, the evidence would also tend to suggest, though this remains far from proven, that while size and export profile were important determinants of high debt ratios in the mid-1980s, they were less so in 1998. It was the level of underdevelopment (as indicated by the literacy rate) that determined

---

10. The literacy rate is a proxy for the level of human development.

Table 5.   Results of cross-country regression

Explanatory variables	Dependent variable	
	(1) **Debt/export 1985**	**(2)** **Debt/export 1998**
Constant	3.66*	6.00**
	(1.90)	(3.11)
Debt/GNP (1970)	0.85*	0.35
	(1.74)	(0.71)
Index of country size	0.50*	-0.09
	(1.84)	(-0.33)
Specialization index (primary exports)	0.54**	0.28
	(2.78)	(1.35)
Average fiscal deficit (1975-1985)	-0.39	0.34
	(-0.64)	(0.56)
Inflation rate (1975-1985)	1.06**	1.78**
	(2.16)	(3.61)
Literacy index (1970)	-0.21	-1.05**
	(-0.73)	(-3.71)
Corruption index (1980-1989)	-0.57	-0.03
	(-1.62)	(-0.85)
R^2	0.39	0.44
Number of observations	45	44
DW statistic	2.10	1.87

Note: The figures in parentheses are the *t*-values.
  * indicates 10% level of significance.
  ** indicates 5% level of significance.

Table 6.   Debt status by country group

	Severely indebted %	Moderately indebted %	Less indebted %	Country type distribution %
Least developed countries	54	23	14	30
Low-income countries	71	44	17	42
Lower-middle-income countries	23	35	50	37
Upper-middle-income countries	6	21	33	21
All low- and middle-income countries	100	100	100	00

Source: World Bank, *World Development Finance, 2000*.

whether the country still remained heavily indebted in 1998. As table 6 indicates, countries classified by the World Bank as severely indebted in 1998 are disproportionately least developed. This would tend to support the contention in Serieux (2001), that, while a wide range of economies (in terms of development level) were heavily indebted in the mid 1980s, it was the weaker economies, dependent almost exclusively on public credit, that remained heavily indebted into the late 1990s.

What this suggests, generally, is that certain countries are simply more vulnerable to debt-related crises. Small countries have to borrow proportionally more because of less domestic economies of scale, countries that export primary commodities are more likely to face external price shocks and (for agricultural commodities) weather-related shocks, and countries with weaker economic and social infrastructure have greater difficulty recovering from economic calamity. While all of these attributes can be mitigated by appropriate development policies over time, they cannot be solved in short order. Thus, if these countries are to avoid unsustainable debt burdens in the future, the nature and pattern of resource flows and the provisions for mitigating external shocks will need to be reconsidered. None of these considerations are yet part of the HIPC Initiative.

IV. DEBT SUSTAINABILITY BEYOND DEBT RELIEF

What is on offer from the Enhanced HIPC Initiative will prove sufficient for ensuring that HIPCs, as a group, are able to maintain sustainable debt ratios, and avoid or successfully navigate their way through future economic crises, only if future economic performances are superlative, new resource inflows are sufficiently large and concessional, and exogenous shocks are mild and short-lived. While this may come to pass for a few countries, it is surely an untenable presumption for the group.

Even if these countries were able to meet their end of the bargain by implementing sound macroeconomic policies within improved governance environments, that would offer no sure route to the doubling of historical growth rates anticipated in their decision-point documents. Neither would such achievements protect these countries from exogenous shocks nor provide them with an immediate means for removing the structural weaknesses that delay recovery from those shocks. In addition, there is also no clear indication that even the modest funding requirements associated with these high growth expectations, far less the increased magnitudes and concessionality that would be required with more modest growth results, will be forthcoming. Further, the new centrality of poverty reduction engendered by debt relief also means both greater efforts in that direction and concomitant increases in funding requirements. Unless special provision is made for that fact, poverty reduction spending can itself engender a return to unsustainable debt levels.

Clearly, by providing substantial debt reduction and ensuring reduced debt-service burdens well into the future, the Enhanced HIPC Initiative represents a dramatic turn in these countries' debt-related fortunes and an initial step towards permanent exit from over-indebtedness. However, it does not chart a complete path to debt redemption, and guarantees little beyond these countries' completion point. A program that attempts to do so would have to address the considerations enunciated below.

A.   SOME CLEAR ENUNCIATION OF FUTURE FUNDING OPTIONS

One of the advantages of the HIPC experience is that countries have recognized that past borrowing, even at concessional terms, was often too expensive. Even HIPCs are not equal. While some HIPCs (such as Bolivia and Côte d'Ivoire) could possibly afford to borrow at fairly modest concessional terms, others (such as Guinea, Niger and Mozambique) clearly may find even borrowing on average IDA terms (approximately 70% concessionality) more than they can bear over the long term. While many of these countries have addressed this in setting minimum concessionality levels for borrowing, this is not reflected at the institutional level among international financial institutions. Nor for that matter, do countries' specific targets necessarily reflect consistent assessments of countries' debt-carrying capacities. More sluggish, but similarly poor, Zambia and Tanzania have set themselves less stringent concessional borrowing targets than fast-growing Uganda. It would seem that countries will be left to engineer their unilaterally determined concessionality levels by some ad-hoc combination of bilateral grants and multilateral lending.

If future country borrowing is to more closely reflect their debt-carrying capacities, and if they are to be implemented and revised consistently, it will have to be reflected in the lending strategies of international financial institutions as well as country finance ministries. The coherent public management now demanded of HIPCs cannot be a reality if it is not supported by a predictable and appropriate regime for resource flows. This requires both lenders and borrowers to be on the same page. That would be necessary to ensure, for example, that regional bank funds, which would be clearly too expensive for some countries, have an appropriate bilateral grant counterpart (or cheaper

IDA credit) that raises the gross concessionality element as appropriate. That would require all of the relevant creditors to agree to work within a set framework for each country – with an obvious coordinating role for the regional banks. In the absence of such institutionalized arrangements, both borrowers and creditors may find themselves falling short of expectations.

Also related to this is the amount of available funding. If countries do not achieve the exceptionally high GDP and export growth rates anticipated, their funding needs will expand dramatically. Yet, as was previously noted, development assistance has been on a general declining trend since the early 1990s. Unless that is sharply reversed, the potential for anti-cyclical flows to maintain growth and poverty-reduction levels in these countries will be undermined (Culpeper 2001), and the possibility of a return to collective over-indebtedness will increase.

B.   SOME CLEAR ARRANGEMENTS FOR POVERTY REDUCTION
      FUNDING

One can certainly argue that the focus on poverty reduction promoted through the Enhanced HIPC Initiative is good all around. It forces countries to pay more attention to a necessary part of the development process, and provides added resources for doing so. However, the development and implementation of poverty reduction strategies in the context of international poverty-reduction targets, forces countries (implicitly as in the case of Bolivia, and explicitly as in the case of Nicaragua)[11] to pursue poverty reduction targets that are not necessarily dictated by resource availability. If indeed the world is serious about making an attempt to meet global poverty-reduction targets, then these countries should not be put in the position of placing their long-term financial health at risk in the pursuit of faster rates of poverty reduction than financial prudence would dictate.

Poverty-reduction funding that is additional to the debt-relief dividend and at least highly concessional (if not wholly grant-based) needs to be made available to these and other low-income countries at levels that correspond to the financing gap implied by the reasonable application of domestic resources and debt relief *vis à vis* poverty-reduction targets. An additionality approach, for example, based on country income and poverty levels might be one way to proceed.[12] One possible

---

11. See, Andersen (2001) and Castro-Monge (2001), in this issue.

12. Such an approach might imply, for example, that funding provided is a proportion of local spending rather than independent of it. The proportion is to be determined by the country's income and poverty level. This may help mitigate the issue of fungibility (the shifting of funds between uses) that bedevil ODA.

means for providing such funds would be a global Poverty Reduction Fund (or Human Development Fund, if other targets are included) that pools donor resources and allows countries to apply for an extended funding arrangement after meeting reasonable criteria for use, transparency, and accountability.

C.   THE PROVISION OF EMERGENCY ASSISTANCE

As has been pointed out above, the conditionalities attached to HIPC debt relief and related arrangements, do not provide antidotes (at least in the short to medium term) for the structural factors that lead to, and perpetuate, unsustainable debt levels. Yet no provision is made for this, as an adjunct to those programs.

Figure 4.   A comparison of Price Indices

Source: *International Financial Statistics 2000* (IMF, 2000).

Two of the clearly identifiable features of the commodity price cycles, that largely dictate the pattern of these countries' export earnings (and thus a major source of exogenous shocks), are the size and length of these cycles. Figure 4 compares the movement of three commodity group prices (food, agricultural raw materials, and metals) with the average producer price index for industrial countries. Commodity prices have not only fluctuated widely over the last thirty years, their movements have also been highly correlated. In addition, a single cycle (from peak to peak) generally lasts from six to eight years.[13] Given these economies' generally weak endowment of physical, institutional, and

---

13. Note also, that the food price index barely shows an increasing trend over the period.

social infrastructures, it is little wonder that recoveries after negative terms of trade shocks (the down side of the cycle) have generally not been impressive.

The role of appropriate emergency financing for countries facing the effects of a sharp drop in export prices would be to allow these countries to maintain import and public spending levels that allow for continued poverty reduction and growth, without making them too indebted to be able to take advantage of the improvement in prices when it occurs. However, the traditional pattern of balance-of-payments assistance has not been well suited for that task. Stand-by arrangements are more expensive than most other HIPC funding, and also likely to come due before the country experiences a reversal in price trends. Even Poverty Reduction and Growth Facility (PRGF) funding (at approximately 35% grant element) is more expensive than what these countries now recognize as bearable. In addition, recourse to debt restructuring that does not match the cycles can lead to a situation where debt-service payments increase before (or after) the period of better prices. In short, the funding that needs to be cheapest, and most sensitive to country conditions and timing, has generally been most expensive and most rigid.

If these countries are to be able to navigate export price cycles (and other exogenous shocks) in the future, without compromising growth, poverty reduction, and their debt profiles, funding for emergency balance of payments (and fiscal) support will have to be cheaper and more flexible. Lending instruments will have to ensure that repayment of such funds do not negate the opportunities for recovery (or, better yet, a growth spurt). What this means, essentially, is that if debt sustainability is to be seriously pursued for these countries, new lending instruments will have to be developed that better reflect these countries' structural weaknesses, thus enabling them to better navigate the inevitable non-policy-induced crises with minimal growth and poverty-reduction costs.

CONCLUSION

The expectations for the 22 countries that have reached the decision point of the HIPC Initiative is that their debt-relief amounts will be lowered to levels below the debt sustainability threshold of 150% of exports (or 250% of government revenue) and be kept below that level into the foreseeable future. In addition, substantial new resources will be provided for poverty reduction in those countries – providing them with greater wherewithal for meeting internationally agreed targets for poverty reduction.

The evidence suggests, however, that debt sustainability will be maintained in those countries only if they surpass even the best economic performances of the past. Further, no provision is made for the systemic risks faced by these countries. If they face major exogenous shocks again, then a collective return to over-indebtedness is a more than passing probability. Also, the resources for debt relief that will result from the HIPC Initiative will be less than the actual amounts of debt relief, and a decreasing amount over time. Not unexpectedly, country case study evidence already indicates that the funding needs for the poverty reduction envisaged in countries' PRSPs are well beyond the resources that can be provided by current debt relief. In short, a funding gap for poverty reduction continues to exist.

This paper argues, therefore, that, as a long-term solution to the HIPC debt crisis, the Enhanced HIPC Initiative is insufficient. In addition to debt relief, a complete solution to the crisis would require:

- long-term lending that reflects countries' debt carrying capacities;
- overall bilateral and multilateral lending arrangements that anticipate the likelihood that the optimism reflected in countries' DSA (at the decision and completion points) cannot be treated as a bottom line, and that failure to meet these expectations is likely to be more the rule than the exception, even in the absence of policy failures or exogenous shocks;
- the provision of poverty-reduction funding that reflects both the inadequacies of the HIPC debt dividend and the added burden imposed on these countries by internationally agreed targets that are not constrained by country resource endowments;
- the development of better instruments for balance of payments and fiscal support in the event of exogenous shocks. Instruments that are more cognizant of country needs, their debt-carrying capacities, and the length of related price cycles.

In the absence of these additional considerations, we may soon be facing a similar state of collective over-indebtedness and the related developmental costs for the world in general, and the poor of these countries in particular.

REFERENCES

Andersen, L. E. and O. Nina, "The HIPC Initiative in Bolivia," *Canadian Journal of Development Studies*, 22, 2, 2001, p. 343-376.

Andrews, D., A. R. Boote, S. S. Rizavi and S. Sing, *Debt Relief for Low-Income Countries: The Enhanced HIPC Initiative*, Washington, D.C., IMF, 1999.

Boote, A. R. and K. Thugge, *Debt Relief for Low-Income Countries: The HIPC Initiative*, Washington, DC, IMF, 1999.

Castro-Monge, L.-M., "Nicaragua and the HIPC Initiative: The Tortuous Journey to Debt Relief," *Canadian Journal of Development Studies*, 22, 2, 2001, p. 417-454.

Coulibaly, M., A. Diarra and S. Keita, « Étude sur l'endettement des pays les plus pauvres: le cas du Mali », *Revue canadienne d'études du développement*, 22, 2 2001, p. 455-492.

Culpeper, R., *Capital Volatility and Long-term Development Financing*, Ottawa, North-South Institute, 2001.

Degefe, B., "Ethiopia's External Debt: Impact and the Way Forward," *Canadian Journal of Development Studies*, 22, 2, 2001, p. 377-416.

DAC/OECD, *Shaping the 21st Century: The Contribution of Development Cooperation*, Paris, Organisation for Economic Cooperation and Development, 1996.

_____, *Shaping the 21st Century: The Contribution of Development Assistance*, Paris, Organization for Economic Cooperation and Development, 1996.

Government of Nicaragua, *A Strengthened Poverty Reduction Strategy*, Republic of Nicaragua, 2000.

IDA and IMF, *The Challenge of Maintaining Long-Term External Debt Sustainability*, Washington, DC, World Bank, 2001.

Mijumbi, P., "Uganda's External Debt and the HIPC Initiative," *Canadian Journal of Development Studies*, 22, 2, June 2001.

OECD, IMF, World Bank and United Nations, *Progress Towards the International Development Goals*, Paris, Organization for Economic Cooperation and Development, 2000.

Serieux, J., *Reducing the Debt of the Poorest: Challenges and Opportunities*, Ottawa, North-South Institute, 2000.

_____, "Debt of the Poorest Countries: Anatomy of a Crisis Kept on Hold," *Canadian Journal of Development Studies*, 22, 2, 2001.

United Nations, *United Nations Millennium Declaration* (55/2), New York, United Nations, 2000.

World Bank, *Can Africa Regain the 21st Century?* Washington, DC, World Bank, 2000.

_____, *Heavily Indebted Poor Countries (HIPC): Progress Report*, Washington D.C., World Bank, 2001.

About the Contributors
A propos des auteurs

Lykke E. Andersen holds a PhD in economics from the University of Aarhus, Denmark. She is currently Chief Economist for the Sustainable Development Department at the Institute for Socio-Economic Research in La Paz, Bolivia.

Degefe Befekadu holds a PhD in economics from the School of Economics, Humbolt, Germany since 1980. He works for the UN Economic Commission for Africa. Prior to joining the UNECA, he taught economics at Addis Ababa University.

Ligia María Castro-Monge has a Master degree in economics from the University of Chicago. Since 1996, she has been working as an Associate Director for the Latin American Center for Competitiveness and Sustainable Development (INCAE) in Nicaragua and Costa Rica. Her fields of expertise are Monetary Policy, Public Finance, Banking Supervision and Regulation.

Massa Coulibaly est docteur en économie mathématique et économétrie de l'Université Paris 2, France. Présentement, il enseigne à l'Université du Mali et dirige le Groupe de recherche en économie appliquée et théorique. Il a mené des études sur la compétitivité et la productivité dans les entreprises industrielles du Mali, ainsi que sur la dette et l'aide au Mali.

Amadou Diarra est titulaire d'un diplôme supérieur d'économie de l'académie d'économie de Berlin (ex RDA), et d'un doctorat en économie de l'Université de Bonn (RFA). Il est économiste à la Direction Générale de la Dette Publique au Mali depuis Octobre 1998.

Sikoro Keita est docteur en économie de l'Université Laval, Québec, Canada. Après avoir enseigné au Collège militaire royal du Canada de 1995 a 1998, il travaille depuis comme économiste principal a l'USAID/Mali où il a produit plusieurs publications courtes sur l'économie malienne.

Peter Mijumbi is a Visiting Senior Research Fellow at the Economic Policy Research Centre in Uganda. His major research areas are in household and public budget analysis, poverty, health and health economics.

Osvaldo Nina has a Master degree in economics from the Catholic University in Rio de Janeiro, Brazil. He is currently Director of the Institute for Socio-Economic Research and Professor at the Department of Economics at the Catholic University of Bolivia in La Paz, Bolivia.

About the Guest Editors

John Serieux completed this volume as a senior researcher and specialist in international finance for the North-South Institute, an independent research institute based in Ottawa, Canada. He is currently a lecturer in economics at the University of North Carolina at Chapel Hill and continues to do research in the area of developing country debt as well as other areas of international finance and development economics.

Yiagadeesen Samy is a doctoral candidate in Economics at the University of Ottawa. Mr. Samy's broader research interests include international trade and development economics, and his doctoral dissertation is in the area of Trade and Labor Standards. He provided research assistance for the Debt Relief Project.

A propos des Rédacteurs invités

John Serieux a terminé cet ouvrage alors qu'il était chercheur principal et spécialiste des finances internationales à l'Institut Nord-Sud, un institut de recherche indépendant d'Ottawa (Canada). Il est aujourd'hui chargé de cours en économie à l'University of North Carolina de Chapel Hill (États-Unis) et poursuit un travail de recherche sur la dette des pays en développement et dans d'autres domaines des finances internationales et de l'économie du développement.

Yiagadeesen Samy est etudiant dans le programe de doctoral en Science economique de l' Universite d' Ottawa. Ses champs de recherche incluent le commerce international et le developpement economique. Sa these de doctoral porte sur le commerce international et les normes du travail. Il a ete assistant a la recherche pour le projet d'allegement de la dette.